Haunted Landscapes

UNIVERSITY OF

PLACE, MEMORY, AFFECT

Series editors: Neil Campbell, Professor of American Studies at the University of Derby and Christine Berberich, School of Social, Historical and Literary Studies at the University of Portsmouth.

The *Place, Memory, Affect* series seeks to extend and deepen debates around the intersections of place, memory, and affect in innovative and challenging ways. The series will forge an agenda for new approaches to the edgy relations of people and place within the transnational global cultures of the twenty-first century and beyond.

Haunted Landscapes

Super-Nature and the Environment

Edited by Ruth Heholt
and Niamh Downing

ROWMAN &
LITTLEFIELD
————INTERNATIONAL

London • New York

Published by Rowman & Littlefield International Ltd
Unit A, Whitacre Mews, 26-34 Stannary Street, London SE11 4AB
www.rowmaninternational.com

Rowman & Littlefield International Ltd. is an affiliate of Rowman & Littlefield
4501 Forbes Boulevard, Suite 200, Lanham, Maryland 20706, USA
With additional offices in Boulder, New York, Toronto (Canada), and Plymouth (UK)
www.rowman.com

British Library Cataloguing in Publication Data

A catalogue record for this book is available from the British Library
ISBN: HB 978-1-78348-881-0
       PB 978-1-78348-882-7

Library of Congress Cataloging-in-Publication Data Available

ISBN: 978-1-78348-881-0 (cloth : alk. paper)
ISBN: 978-1-78348-882-7 (pbk. : alk. paper)
ISBN: 978-1-78348-883-4 (electronic)

♾™ The paper used in this publication meets the minimum requirements of American
National Standard for Information Sciences—Permanence of Paper for Printed Library
Materials, ANSI/NISO Z39.48-1992.

Printed in the United States of America

Contents

Introduction

Unstable Landscapes: Affect, Representation and a Multiplicity of Hauntings

Ruth Heholt

In 1898 Vernon Lee (Violet Paget) wrote about haunted landscapes in a piece called 'Faustus and Helena: Notes on the Supernatural in Art'. In the essay she says:

> the ghost ... is the damp, the darkness, the silence, the solitude; a ghost is the sound of our steps through a ruined cloister, where the ivy-berries and convolvulus growing in the fissures sway up and down among the sculptured foliage of the windows, it is the scent of mouldering plaster and mouldering bones from beneath the broken pavement; a ghost is the bright moonlight against which the cypresses stand out like black hearse-plumes, in which the blasted grey olives and gnarled fig-trees stretch their branches over the broken walls like fantastic, knotted beckoning fingers ... Each and all of these things, and a hundred others besides, according to our nature, is a ghost, a vague feeling we can scarcely describe, a something pleasing and terrible which invades our whole consciousness. (2006, 310)

Here the ghost is the landscape; there is no separation between ghost and place. Lee believes that these places invade consciousness, affecting our very being. She calls this ghost-of-place Genius Loci and states:

> although what I call the Genius Loci can never be personified, we may yet feel him nearer and more potent , in some individual monument of feature of the landscape. He is immanent very often, and subduing our hearts most deeply, at a given turn of a road; or a path cut in terraces in a hillside, with view of great distant mountains; ... most of all, perhaps, in the meeting-place of streams, or the mouth of a river ... . The genius of places lurks there; or, more strictly, *he is it*. (1898, 6, original emphasis)

For Lee there can be no landscape without haunting. The spirit of the place *is* the place and we have a bodily response to it; it affects us in the moment. Yet any spirit of place is also indelibly linked to the past. Places are always marked by what has gone before, by the people who populated and shaped the environment in many different ways, by the weather of millennia, by the habitations and actions of the non-human. Layers of memory and action are embedded in the landscape alongside the layering of the earth's history in stone. *Haunted Landscapes* explores these spaces; from the beautiful to the terrible and sometimes the mundane, the intersections of space, place, the human, the spectral, the supernatural and the haunted are at the centre of the discussion in the essays collected here.

In 2014 Falmouth University with the Association for the Study of Literature and Environment (ASLE-UKI) held a symposium entitled 'Haunted Landscapes'. Whilst it does not follow proceedings, this collection explores some of the ideas that were discussed and generated at this lively and stimulating event. One of the most marked aspects of the day was the sheer variety of approaches, theoretical positions and scope of topics. Debate was wide ranging and this collection aims to retain this breadth. If we follow Lee's view of landscape, whereby the spirit of the place *is* the landscape, there will be an almost infinite number of haunted places, all inflected by spirits in different ways. *Haunted Landscapes* celebrates this multiplicity in the diversity of its objects of study; some canonical texts, some lesser known but equally important novels, poems, films. Its approaches, which encompass landscape studies, affect theory, psycho-geography, eco-criticism, history, memory studies, literary studies, film studies, folklore, trauma studies and postcolonial theory, reflect the wide range of ways one can talk about haunted spaces. On the first page of *The Routledge Companion to Landscape Studies*, Thompson, Howard and Waterton propose that 'landscape is something which is mental as well as physical, subjective as well as objective' (2013, 1) and this volume takes this as a central premise, in relation to the idea of landscape as well as the concept of haunting. There are different types of landscapes and diverse experiences of haunting. We have deliberately kept this collection of essays about haunted landscapes varied and wide in the subjects it addresses as well as the theoretical approaches it uses. As haunted landscapes themselves are diverse, so too are the texts that explore these extraordinary places. The comment that we want to make with this volume is that this range of texts and the perhaps contradictory approaches are *all* important and useful in specific instances and under particular circumstances.

The fact that this book is about haunting *and* landscape has been particularly fruitful in bringing together strands of theory from the spectral or supernatural, and from the more material plane of place, space and landscape. This juxtaposition of the spectral and the material, the mental and the concrete, was a central concern of Lee's thesis too. She states that 'the Genius Loci, like all worthy divinities, is of the substance of our heart and mind, a spiritual reality. And as for visible embodiment, why that is the place itself, or the country; and the features and speech are the lie of the land, pitch of the streets, sound of bells or of weirs' (1898, 5). At the heart of Lee's work as well as this collection is the fertile interplay between two concepts, absence and presence; the seemingly ephemeral plane of the spectral or supernatural, juxtaposed with the ostensibly material realm of landscape. Later we will examine the more distanced meta-phorical or representative use of tropes of haunting and the presence of various types of ghosts. First, however, we begin (in a somewhat topsy-turvy manner) by looking at the 'affective turn' (Clough and Halley 2007) in relation to the haunting of landscapes.

HAUNTING, AFFECT AND THE NON-REPRESENTATIONAL

Ola Söderström argues that 'non-representational thinking has led geog-raphers to downplay in their approaches the (formerly dominant) role of mental processes, language and vision and to introduce instead, on the stage of their research and publications, new figures such as: the body, emotions, spatial practice, interaction, performance, "things", technology' (2010, 14). This 'non-representational turn' mooted by landscape studies and cultural geography corresponds directly to the 1990s 'affective turn' whereby there is a re-turn to the emotions, the body, the material and experience (Clough and Halley 2007). Yet affect is more than this. It is the body's immersion in the world; beyond consciousness, beyond, sometimes, even recognized emotion. From the point of view of affect theory therefore the landscape is no longer seen as a distant prospect to be looked at, or painted or written about as something removed and external. From the centuries' old view of the landscape as 'scenery', sublime, beautiful or even mundane, ugly and polluted, these newer conceptions, coming largely from cultural geography, no longer conceptualize it as 'over there' at all.[1] Berberich, Campbell and Hudson claim that 'increasingly, [the] acceptance of the "immaterial" has extended beyond the "pictorial" and "representational" view of landscape to also include other modes of phenomenological experience and "bodily practices" through which we encounter, "read", relate and construct space' (2012, 22). The division between the landscape and the body is collapsed and the focus falls onto the *experience* of landscape rather than its depic-tion. For Lee this is also true of the experience of the supernatural and she posits the ghostly as being unable to be represented in literature, music or art. She says:

let us see or hear the ghost, let it become visible or audible to others besides ourselves; paint us that vagueness, mould into shape that darkness, modulate into chords that silence—tell us the character and history of those vague beings ... set to work boldly or cunningly. What do we obtain? A picture, a piece of music, a story; but the ghost is gone. (2006, 310)

The experience of haunting too collapses the division between the ghostly or supernatural and the body. It cannot be 'over there', distanced or properly represented or it will effectively disappear.

Timothy Oakes and Patricia Price in *The Cultural Geography Reader* discuss the move away from seeing landscape as representational.

These cultural geographers instead pursue what is coming to be termed *non-representational* landscapes: in other words, landscapes that exist beyond humans and their dominant interpretive filters (particularly vision). These geographers suggest that landscapes may be understood as quite fluid constructs that are continually in the process of cohering and collapsing as we move through space. Thus rather than constituting fixed, static, material entities whose character is primarily visual, non-representational approaches see landscape as a sort of performance that is enacted much as is music or theatre. (2008, 151, original emphasis)

Landscapes shift and move, 'collapse and cohere', as we traverse them. This makes the static representation of place, catching the essence (or Genius) of the landscape impossible. Lee sees a similar impossibility in the capturing of beauty: 'something—and that the very essence—always escapes, perhaps because real beauty is as much a thing in time—a thing like music, a succession, a series—as in space' (1898, 82). The same is true for haunting—it too is a series, a continuation of feeling and experience that it is hard to catch the essence of. The conception of landscape, as well as haunting, is fluid and experienced by and through the body.

The bodily experience of the landscape is not always a deliberate or intended sensory experience as Clough suggests when she characterizes affectivity as 'a substrate of potential bodily responses, often automatic responses, in excess of consciousness' (2007, 2). From this idea of an experience being 'in excess of consciousness' and in many other ways, non-representational theory and the theory of affect resonate deeply with the texts of haunted landscapes. An uncanny encounter in its nascent 'becoming' will always be beyond consciousness. The recognition of a ghost, the shock of the realization that a place is haunted, is subsequent to the first body-knowledge of the presence of the supernatural. In very many accounts people will feel a haunting before they 'know' it. A haunting is a bodily feeling of *now*, this moment, the feeling or emotion of being haunted. Being haunted is an experience that is inescapable from the body. As Lee says, 'we crave after the supernatural, the ghostly—no longer believed, but still felt' (1898, 312). And it is the feeling that counts even if belief is lacking. Haunting itself is merely or *only* affect; it has no existence without affect. Being haunted is to know that one is haunted or that one is in a haunted place. Being haunted is to feel the hairs on the back of your neck rising; it is something glimpsed but not quite seen from the corner of your eye, a slight misgiving in the pit of your stomach, a delicate rash of goosebumps rising on cooling skin. As Lee asks, 'why do those stories affect us most in which the ghost is heard but not seen? Why do those places affect us most which we merely vaguely know that they are haunted? Why most of all those which look as if they might be haunted?' (1898, 310). Perhaps paradoxically, given the immaterial nature of ghosts, there is no haunting without a material bodily experience of it. And in particular, if that which haunts is unseen, it must be *felt*. I want to suggest therefore that for the concept of haunting the usefulness of non-representational theory and the theory of affect cannot be underestimated. There is, and can be, no haunting without feeling. If one does not emote, or feel a haunting, if one does not experience it, then it is possible to argue that 'haunting' itself cannot, by definition, exist. Can a landscape be haunted without a witness or someone there to recognise the fact that it is haunted? I suggest that a haunting needs an outside, interpretive presence: a haunting is an intervention, an encounter.

If I am correct and haunting requires an intervention, if there must be an encounter, there will be a material presence, of landscape and space and of that-which-haunts, (sometimes manifested as 'ghost'), as well as the one who experiences it. In the introduction to *Popular Ghosts*, María del Pilar Blanco and Esther Peeren suggest that

> we have yet to consolidate the methods used to define the ghost in order to discuss it in spatial terms, as a physical occupation of everyday sites that emphasizes the materiality of the ghost and defines its agency as grounded in a particular locale—in a disturbance of space as much as of time. (2010, xvii)

Ghosts do not merely belong to the past; they are current, present entities that exist, or at least manifest (in whatever manner), *somewhere.* Lee evokes the supernatural figure of the God Pan, the 'weird, shaggy, cloven-hoofed shape' seen by travellers in the woods, but she extends his presence stating that 'Pan is also the wood, with all its sights and noises, the solitude, the gloom, the infinity of rustling leaves, and cracking branches; he is the greenish-yellow light stealing in amid the boughs; he is the foliage, the murmur of unseen waters, the mist hanging over the damp sward' (1898, 297). Pan does not occupy the wood; he *is* the wood; his being is the very materiality of the trees, the light, the sounds, the melancholy atmosphere. The supernatural is not just the beyond or other to the natural; it is native to it.

As Gregg and Seigworth argue,

> Affect is in many ways synonymous with *force* or *forces of encounter*. [Affect] often transpires within and across the subtlest of shuttling intensities: all the miniscule or molecular events of the unnoticed. The ordinary and its extra-. Affect is born in *in-between-ness* and resides as accumulative *beside-ness*. Affect can be understood then as a gradient of bodily capacity. ... Hence affect's always immanent capacity of extending further still: both into and out of the interstices of the inorganic and non-living, the intracellular divulgences of sinew, tissue, and gut economies, and the vaporous evanescences of the incorporeal (events, atmospheres, feeling-tones). At once intimate and impersonal, affect *accumulates* across both relatedness and interruptions in relatedness, becoming a palimpsest of force-encounters traversing the ebbs and swells of intensities that pass between 'bodies' (bodies denied not by an outer skin-envelope or other surface boundary but by their potential to reciprocate or co-participate in the passages of affect). Bindings and unbinding, becomings and un-becomings. (2010, 2, original emphasis)

There are deep resonances with the conceptions of haunting here. A haunting is the 'extra' of the ordinary, the 'super' of the natural. A ghost is a becoming *and* an un-becoming—they exist at the same time as they do not. A ghost is the undoing (the un-becoming) of the human body and its life. Ghosts inevitably reside in the in-between, whilst a haunted space is defined *as* being the in-between. David Matless writes that 'landscape ... carries a relational hybridity, always already natural and cultural, deep and superficial, which makes for something inherently deconstructive' (2003, 231). A haunted landscape deconstructs itself. Boundaries, borders and spaces themselves dissolve in fluid reconfigurations as that which haunts, moves in *and* out, here *and* there, in-between *and* nowhere. The boundaries between ghost, place and those who witness or experience the haunting are deconstructed, only to be re-constructed anew by affect.

In 'Notes on the Supernatural in Art', Lee describes, 'that supernatural which really deserves the name, which is beyond and outside the limits of the possible, the rational, the explicable—that supernatural which is due not to the logical faculties, arguing from wrong premises, but to the imagination wrought upon by certain kinds of physical surroundings' (2006, 296). The natural, the supernatural, the material and the immaterial, the living and the non-living are conflated and remodelled in relation to each other and the affect each has on the other. Boundaries are transgressed and those things that should be separate—the invisible and the visible, the supernatural and the 'real'—are separate no longer. Boundaries and material barriers do not hold back ghosts which can pass through corporeal bodies, through rocks, walls or any other material impediment. Ghosts, that-which-haunts, as well as those who experience the haunting are defined by 'their potential to reciprocate or co-participate in the passages of affect' (Gregg and Seigworth 2010, 2) as the haunted and the haunting each impinge upon one other. A haunting, an encounter with a ghost, is a dialogue of affect. Gregg and Seigworth contend that with the practice of affect theory,

> almost all of the tried-and-true handholds and footholds for so much critical-cultural-philosophical inquiry and for theory—subject/object, representation and meaning, rationality, consciousness, time and space, inside/outside, human/nonhuman, identity, structure, background/foreground and so forth—become decidedly less sure and more nonsequential. (2010, 4)

This is strikingly similar to descriptions of haunting. A haunting is, in some form or other, a return and thus there is an inevitability of the non-sequential. In Lee's evocative story 'Oke of Okehurst' the suggestion is that the present Mrs Alice Oke is a reincarnation of a long-dead ancestor (also called Alice Oke) who murdered her lover. Our narrator, an artist employed to paint the wondrous and other-worldly Mrs Oke, considers that perhaps the idea of a reincarnated woman and the ghostly presence of her murdered lover is not so peculiar. He says 'when you come to think of it, why not? That a weird creature, visibly not of this earth, a reincarnation of a woman who murdered her lover two centuries and a half ago, that such a creature should have the power of attracting about her ... the man who loved her in that previous existence, whose love for her was his death—what is there astonishing in that?' (1898, 111). Nothing is certain, nothing secure and the past melds with the present and the dead with the living. Even when there is a tale of a haunting with a reason or purpose there is a collapse in rationality as well as in time, space and dimensionality. The 'firm' and the graspable are lost. What is left is a feeling, an emotion or a physical unease. This, however, is not separate to, or separable from, place.

Occasionally in ghost stories it is a person who is haunted, with the ghost beside them wherever they may go, but it is not these stories (and they are relatively few and far between) that concern us here.[2] *Haunted Landscapes* is, of course, concerned with haunted places. Roger Luckhurst suggests that 'it is worth recalling that ghosts are held to haunt specific locales, are tied to what late Victorian psychical researchers rather splendidly termed "phantasmogenetic centres". This might suggest that the ghosts of London are different from those of Paris, or those of California (where *Specters of Marx* was first delivered in lecture form)' (541–2, original emphasis). I will return to Derrida and *Specters of Marx*. Here I want to emphasize, following Luckhurst, the idea that ghosts are specific and *placed*. They belong to, and sometimes help to define, locales. And whilst Oakes and Price, talking about the living (the human), state that 'though we are profoundly *emplaced* creatures, we are not *place-bound*' (2008, 253, original emphasis), ghosts and sites of haunting most often *are*. Ghosts, whilst being the very definition of in-betweenness, are caught in-between in the liminal space of here and not-here. Yet 'here' is usually very specific. Oakes and Price suggest that place 'in its most simple expression ... is often equated with locality as in "you are here"' (254), and it is this specificity of locality, this presence of place that *Haunted Landscapes* is concerned with.

Vernon Lee's ghosts too are most often held firmly in place—they exist only within a particular locale. Her ghost stories are filled with luscious, sensuous, exotic and almost erotic descriptions of the landscape. Yet the beauty of these places is enlivened and even created by the presence of the supernatural and she tells us in 'Oke of Okehurst' that 'the very air, with its scent of heady flowers and old perfumed stuffs, seemed redolent of ghosts' (1898, 111). In his essay 'The Ghosts of Place', the environmental sociologist Michael Mayerfeld Bell states that '[g]hosts are ... ubiquitous in the places in which we live, and they give a life to those places. Ghosts are much of what makes a space a place' (1997, 813). For Bell, ghosts can help define a space and give it meaning and 'life'. He continues:

> I have been primarily drawn to the ghosts of place as a way to describe a cen-tral aspect of the social experience of the physical world, the phenomenology of environment. Such experience arises in part from the social relations of memory, and the memory of social relations. But the ghosts of place should not be reduced to mere memories, collective or individual. To do so would be to overlook the spirited and live quality of their presence, and their stubborn rootedness in particular places. (816)

In an understandable, but somewhat peculiar turn of phrase, Bell points to the *liveness* of ghosts. Yet why not? If we continue with our affect theme then any experience of ghosts must be a present and a living one. And an important part of the 'liveness' is the rootedness in place. As Avery F. Gordon in another sociological text suggests, 'The ghost, as I understand it, is not the invisible, or some ineffable excess. The whole essence, if you can use that word, of a ghost is that it has a real presence and demands its due, your attention' (2008, xvi). A haunted landscape must be experienced for it to be haunted at all and therefore we have the cry from that which haunts (albeit perhaps muted, but nonetheless imperative) of 'I am *here*'.

DERRIDA, THEORIES FROM THE MARGINS AND AN ETHICS OF HAUNTING

Thus far I have discussed the 'location of ghosts' of ghosts and haunting and the way that the specificity of place and the resonance of affect impact on their presence as well as their reception. Both ghosts and the concept of haunting, however, have been (and often still are) viewed from different perspectives. The most ubiquitous of these comes from Derrida's oft-cited book, *Specters of Marx* ([1994]2006). Derrida posits a spectre that haunts society, a spectre of the future as much as of the past, of being and of non-being (hauntology). Derrida's discussion is overtly and deeply political. He states: '[h]egemony still organizes the repression and thus the confirmation of a haunting. Haunting belongs to the structure of every hegemony' (2006, 46). Haunting here is a metaphor that points to oppression, repression and terrible social injustices that are occurring at this present moment, in very many societies. For Derrida, to speak of the ghost, of the experience of haunting, one must ethically evoke the spectres of those who have gone before and those who are not yet here. He claims:

> It is necessary to speak *of the* ghost, indeed *to the* ghost and *with* it, from the moment that no ethics, no politics, whether revolutionary or not, seems possible and thinkable and *just* that does not recognize in its principle the respect for those others who are no longer or for those others who are not yet *there*, presently living, whether they are already dead or not yet born. No justice ... seems possible or thinkable without the principle of some *responsibility*, beyond all living present, within that which disjoins the living present, before the ghosts of those who are not yet born or who are already dead, be they victims of wars, political or other kinds of violence, nationalist racist, colonialist, sexist or other kinds of exterminations, victims of oppressions of capitalist imperialism or any of the forms of totalitarianism. (xviii, original emphasis)

For Derrida, it is imperative to address the ghost figure in order to respect and bear responsibility towards those from the past and those from the future who will suffer the most terrible oppressions and violence. This is an *ethics* of haunting and of ghosts. For Derrida, this is another recognition of the cry (even if it belongs to the past, or to that which is not yet come): 'I am *here*.' In this way, the ghost, the haunting, is brought into the present, placed centre stage (where no ghost can comfortably exist) and spoken about, to and with. Julian Wolfreys in *Victorian Hauntings* follows Derrida and argues that perhaps haunting is not to do with the past, but the present: '[A]ccording to Derrida, haunting is not simply a thing of the past or, indeed, something from the past. Instead, the experience of haunting has never been greater' (2002, 1). For both Derrida and Wolfreys these hauntings occur in the landscapes of modernity: the nation-states, hegemonic 'democracies', spaces of totalitarianism and the 'new international'. Haunting makes these landscapes present.

It is this view of haunting and ghosts that postcolonial theory, queer theory and feminism have made such productive use.[3] Haunting as a metaphor, as well as the figure of the ghost, carries powerful resonances. Yet this is not quite accurate. Feminist, postcolonial and queer theorists who employ these tropes do not exactly use haunting as a metaphor, rather it is a way of presenting (in temporal terms too) and bringing to the fore the violences of the past, the terrible oppressions, injustices and traumas. Texts explored in the essays in this volume, the films *The Devil's Backbone* and *Aftermath* and the novels *Beyond Black* and *White Is for Witching*, feature ghosts and use the concept of haunting to explore, and sometimes to lay to rest, the memories of appalling traumas. In a thoughtful essay, 'Postcolonial Haunting: Anxiety, Affect, and the Situated', Michael F. O'Riley discusses the use of the concept of haunting for the postcolonial imagination. He claims:

> [i]n large part, the advent of postcolonial consciousness has emphasized the imperative of returning to occluded colonial history through a reckoning with the specters of the nation's colonial heritage. Postcolonial theory has relied, to a great extent, upon the idea of haunting in order to bring awareness of colonial history to the present. (2007, 1)

Using the concept of haunting makes colonial history more present and visible; hidden histories can return and make their presence felt. O'Riley says that '[c]onventional symbols of historical and psychic dissonance, haunted places have been employed to figure the postcolonial recovery of a past beyond appropriation yet historically emblematic' (4). The concept of haunting has been important in postcolonial reconciliations with past atrocities and traumas and with the violent appropriation and violation of colonised landscapes.

It is not just postcolonial theory or texts that have employed the concepts of haunting and ghosts. Feminist theory and queer theory both utilise the figure of the spectre. In her examination of Victorian ghost stories, Vanessa D. Dickerson positions oppressed Victorian women as 'the ghost in the noontide'. Dickerson argues that women in middle-class Victorian homes were often invisible and taken for granted and she describes them as being ghostly already: 'the Victorian woman was above all the ghost in the noontide, an anomalous spirit on display at the center of Victorian materialism and progress'. The argument is that Victorian women were 'barely-there'—caught in what Dickerson terms 'their own special brand of ghosthood' which pushed them into the margins and the background (1996, 11). As conceptions of ghosts and haunting seem to echo the experience of the marginalized and oppressed it is not surprising that this idea of 'ghosting' is also to be found in the contemporary debates of queer studies. This is Diana Fuss in the introduction to her volume *Inside/Out* speaking about heterosexuality and homosexuality:

> [e]ach is haunted by the other, but ... it is the other who comes to stand in metonymically for the very occurrence of haunting and ghostly visitations. A striking feature of many of the essays collected in this volume is a fascination with the

spectre of abjection, a certain preoccupation with the figure of the homosexual as spectre and phantom, as spirit and revenant, as abject and undead. (1991, 3)

It seems that the ghost itself figures the marginal. And whilst this could be seen more conventionally as a clear demonstration of the 'return of the repressed' conceptualizing the ghost goes further. In her book *The Queer Uncanny*, Paulina Palmer argues:

[t]he figure of the ghost is particularly rich in metaphorical significance, both traditional and post modern. As well as evoking connotations of invisibility and fluctuations in visibility ... it can operate as an image for liminality and border-crossing, as illustrated by its ability to traverse the boundaries between inside and outside, present and past and, even more mysteriously, life and death. (2012, 66)

Palmer examines lesbian and male gay versions of the ghost story, which she argues are 'particularly inventive' and here the figure of the ghost can be seen as positive and liberating. Thus the figure of the ghost can bring into view that which is most usually hidden. The ghost body for those who are marginalised forces notice onto itself and will not be ignored ('I am *here*'). As O'Riley remarks in relation to postcolonial uses of the spectral, '[h]aunting is pervasive in postcolonial thought precisely because of its affective dimension, a dimension that creates a sense of the imminently important, present, and disruptive' (2007, 4).

FROM CRITICISMS TO MULTIPLICITIES

All of these uses of the concepts of haunting and ghosts form a part of what Roger Luckhurst has called 'The Spectral Turn' (2002). He is one of several theorists to critique this more generalized view and use of haunting. The danger, he suggests, is that 'the generalized structure of haunting is symptomatically blind to its generative loci' (528). Hauntings come from somewhere; they are generated by different circumstances, places and histories. Hauntings, ghosts and spectres, he maintains, are specific, historical and located in both space and time. Luckhurst (and others) focus much of their criticism on Derrida and contend that too often he treats these phenomena as representative and general. Luckhurst says: '[t]he spectropoetics or hauntological frameworks encouraged by *Specters of Marx* routinize specificity beneath a general discourse regarding the spooky "secret sharer" of Enlightenment modernity' (541). The argument is that the term 'haunting', used too widely, and in too general a way, can both diffuse the power (perhaps even finally negate the meaning) of the term, and universalise the experience in a manner that is not always useful or positive. O'Riley extends the criticism to the way that postcolonial theory has employed haunting as a conceptual model. He argues that '[t]he compulsion to figure colonial history as a haunting trace does not necessarily lead to a so-called ethical relationship with the Other, nor does it result in an avoidance of some of the theoretical issues related to place, history, and appropriation' (2007, 4). And Blanco and Peeren warn that 'care needs to be taken not to turn the ghost into an abstract, universal figure or catch-all' (2010, xix). For all of these critics the problem stems from a lack of specificity of place, history or individuality.

As we were discussing, hauntings are *placed* and ghosts belong to particular locales. Here though these critics argue that we have what O'Riley terms as haunting in 'a placeless place' (2007, 3, n4). He says:

> [T]he use of haunting in postcolonial theory as a placeless yet always-quotable mode of resistance also suggests a lurking anxiety concerning the ways that situated conflicts and encounters are not always aligned with the often intangible nature of new transnational realities and postcolonial forms of oppression. Viewed this way, we might say that the deployment of haunting in postcolonial theory represents a suspended condition, in-between because it is symptomatic of an era poised between the traces of an increasingly inoperative colonial history and uncertain transnational forms of hierarchy and oppression. (1–2)

O'Riley argues that in this case, haunting can be productive of a state of being 'caught in-between' leading to stasis and imprisonment. He continues: '[r]ather than creating awareness of contemporary conditions of inequality, such a haunting can produce a retrospective gaze that tends to archive instances of colonial injustice, transforming them into colonial sites of memory' (7). This he believes can memorialise people and their experiences of trauma and oppression into a state of static victimization. Further, he suggests that this fixation on the past using the tropes of haunting and ghostliness 'ultimately diverts attention away from contemporary realities that beg our attention' (9). With this conception of haunting, he argues, we lose sight of the present and fix the past. There is a problem here as it is quite obvious that many commentators from the margins see the figure of the ghost and the idea of haunting as useful, productive and empowering. Yet, seen from another side, these concepts can secure a single conception of the past, making it inert, and keep those who are already oppressed in a space of 'otherness', transparency and indeterminacy.

The criticisms of the 'spectral turn' correlate to the criticisms from landscape studies and cultural geography of 'representational theory'. This way of looking at landscape views it from a distance and prioritises the ocular and objective. This, it is argued, is too general, too objective and too distant. As we know, affect theory or non-representational theory brings things literally back down to earth, back to the embodied, lived experience of the landscape. Similarly, the way to move from the universalizing 'spectral turn' is to situate ghosts and haunting, not just in time as Derrida does, but 'in time *and* space' (del Pilar and Peeren 2010, xi, original emphasis). In his own work Luckhurst proposes a strategy for countering 'the generalized conjuring of haunted modernity' by looking instead at the 'grounded manifestation of communities in highly delimited locales' (2002, 536). In Luckhurst's work this involves an examination of London localities. Here what is important is the move back to the specificities of place. For our purposes we need both the specificities of place as well as the specificities of experience. The term 'haunting' echoes a multiplicity of meanings and experiences, from the directly phenomenological, to visions of ghosts, the trace hauntings of trauma or remnants of the past. Hauntings are multiple *and* specific; there are *hauntings*, plural but particular. Therefore, perhaps unsurprisingly, the call in *Haunted Landscapes* is one of, and for, diversity.

As noted, ghosts and the conception of haunting are inherently deconstructive. Haunting disrupts the nature/culture debate that is never far away from discussions around landscape. Haunting breaks down binary distinctions: visible/invisible, present/absent, alive/dead, here/there. Haunting transgresses boundaries as well as binaries. What is the natural and what is the supernatural? Where does one begin and the other end? There are always multiplicities of hauntings and multiplicities of spaces and places. Berberich, Campbell and Hudson claim that landscapes too are plural: 'landscape is not one thing, but always *multiple* and connected relationally to a host of other cultural and political concerns' (2012, 19, original emphasis). Echoing the calls for the pluralizing and diversifying of the definitions and uses of the term 'haunting' they continue, arguing:

> the idea of *landscape* has become increasingly utilized in a much broader, poetic sense, to signify a whole set of meanings and associations—the landscapes of the mind, the landscape of fear, the landscape of loneliness. These uses show the need for a wider definition in the notion of *landscape* to encompass more than just the 'land', the 'surfaces of the earth' and even the 'visible terrain', a term more able to suggest the range of contacts, encounters and experiences one might have with the world, the representations of the world and the feelings, emotions, sensations, affects bound up with that 'exchange' or 'dialogue'. (21–2, original emphasis)

It seems that the most productive way forward is not simply to accept multiplicity, but to actively strive for a pluralizing of definitions, concepts and approaches, whilst remaining attentive to the particularities of landscape and haunting. Echoing this sentiment, Blanco and Peeren claim there is currently

a need 'to understand ghosts and haunting in diverse, rather than theoretically monological ways' (2010, xviii). Plurality, diversity and multiplicity,
an acceptance of differences and the inclusion and juxtaposition of seemingly oppositional theories and approaches characterize the array of essays in
Haunted Landscapes.

MULTIPLICITIES

Representational theory, non-representational theory, the 'spectral turn', the
move away, the 'affective turn', the universalizing tendency all exclusive
ways of perceiving things lead to binaries and schisms, contradictions and
oppositions. Yet why must we choose between 'this' or 'that'? Speaking
about the differences in theoretical perspectives within cultural geography,
Oakes and Price comment that many 'approaches have a great deal in common, and over time the antagonism among various sub-groups has subsided
considerably' (2008, 151). This easing of antagonisms in cultural geography
could be usefully extended to the study of the spectral, the supernatural and
the ghostly. Derrida is useful. The use of the concept of haunting and the
resurrection of a variety of ghosts for theorists and those imagining from the
margins are empowering and productive. Yet the turn to affect, to the lived,
the experienced, the bodily, specific and personal also provides powerful
tools. Owain Jones and Joanne Garde-Hansen cite what they see as 'a creep
towards "presentism"' within non-representational geography and worry
that this presages a neglect of the past (2012, 8). However, if a landscape
of *any* sort is haunted by *any* sort of entity, ghost or memory, the past cannot be neglected. Astrid Erll et al. propose 'different *modes of remembering*
in culture. This approach proceeds from the basic insight that the past is
not given, but must instead continually be re-constructed and re-presented'
(2010, 7, original emphasis). This presents us with a productive way to con-
join affect theory with theories of haunting. The past is not fixed, rooted or
singular itself, and therefore the past represented by, suggested by or evoked
by a haunting is not static either. And it is worth pointing out that a haunted
landscape is *not* a stable one. In the same way that Oakes and Price describe
landscape 'cohering and collapsing as we move through space' (2008, 151),
so must an emplaced haunting be constantly dissipated and then re-made.
A haunting is a very human thing and, as I have been arguing throughout,
cannot exist without someone to experience, witness, remember or recognise
it in some form or another.

   The essays collected in *Haunted Landscapes* explore these encounters.
Coming from all sub-sets of theory, they use the concept of haunting to
heed the echoes left by the terrible traumas of the past; they explore diverse

landscapes from traditional haunted houses to wilderness spaces, imagined places and the haunted landscapes of the psyche and the mind. The approaches range from what could be seen as the unashamedly representative, such as the haunting echoes of Holocaust atrocities, to the psychogeographic exploration of Whitechapel and the more traditional literary and film criticism looking at texts such as *Coraline* and *The Haunting of Hill House*. Fictional ghosts, ghosts of the mind and 'real' ghosts sit side by side. Individual and very personal experiences of hauntings are juxtaposed with communal (if perhaps not universalised) encounters. There is 'collective' memory as well as personal, individual memories in these haunted landscapes. Folklore, legend, urban mythology, narratives of trauma and memory are all present here. The landscapes evinced as 'haunted' are also diverse. There are the urban and the rural, the liminal and the 'other dimensional'. Perhaps inevitably this collection of essays raises more questions than it attempts to answer. As we have been seeing, haunted landscapes themselves have a tendency to deconstruct any familiarities, assumptions or certainties. Even some of our most usual tropes are dissipated, such as that of the idea of the appearance of ghosts or the phenomenon of haunting as being representative of the return of the repressed. 'Haunting' suggests a re-turn or an un-covering of that which has been hidden, yet sometimes this concept of a re-turn becomes redundant within the realm of the always-already-there. A haunted landscape may not be able to exist without someone experiencing it, but it most certainly is not always the case that the haunting came with that person. The specific place itself may be haunted by something 'other'; that which is 'other' to us may be intrinsic to the place; the 'Genius' of specific landscapes may not be familiar or necessarily comfortable for us. Yet whatever haunts the place, be it material (a ghost) or immaterial (memory, nostalgia, emotion) the space between the 'here' and the 'there', the otherworldly and the worldly is itself occupied. And whether light or dark we must always pay heed to that which is calling 'I am *here*'.

STRUCTURE OF THE BOOK

Haunted Landscapes is divided into three parts: 'Landscapes of Trauma', 'Inner and (Sub)Urban Landscapes' and 'Borderlands and Outlands'. The chapters in the first part 'Landscapes of Trauma' demonstrate the contention of the collection as a whole: landscape is indelibly marked and therefore haunted by the past, and the process of mourning while offering some measure of consolation must always remain incomplete. The first two essays deal with the terrible traces and haunted terrain of the Holocaust. In Chapter 1, 'Place as Palimpsest: Paul Celan and Martin Heidegger and the Haunting of

Todtnauberg', Mark Riley investigates a single site, Martin Heidegger's hut in the Black Forest. Riley examines Paul Celan's poem, 'Todtnauberg' which was written in response to a meeting between Heidegger and Celan at the hut in 1967. In the poem, Celan's appreciation of Heidegger's rural mountain life was inflected by his knowledge of Heidegger's involvement in National Socialism. Riley explores fractures and erasures in Heidegger and Celan's 'real' lives as well as the space that haunts them both: the affective terrain of the hut.

Tracing the networks of haunting and spectrality in the cinematic spaces of two films, Matilda Mroz discusses Polish director Wladyslaw Pasikowski's *Aftermath* (2012), and the Spanish-Mexican production, *The Devil's Backbone* (Guillermo del Toro, 2001). This chapter, 'Spectral Cinema: Anamorphosis and the Haunted Landscapes of *Aftermath and The Devil's Backbone*', considers spectral return in terms of the Holocaust and the Spanish Civil War. Using Derrida's writing on haunting in *Spectres of Marx*, Mroz investigates the *look* possessed by the spectral figure. Working with concepts of seeing and not-seeing the chapter explores sites of trauma in relation to remembrance and mourning. Here hauntings are cyclical and whilst *Aftermath* manages to dismiss its ghosts, *The Devil's Backbone* suggests some sort of continuance. Mroz takes both films though as part of the circulation of images of haunting and places them in a culture obsessed by memory and the unearthing and return of past events.

The next essays in this part are concerned with contemporary fiction and move to Britain. Beginning with post-imperial metropolitan landscapes, Ryan Trimm's chapter 'Witching Welcome: Haunting and Post-Imperial Hospitality in Hilary Mantel and Helen Oyeyemi' examines how home spaces still resonate with the ghosts of empire. Trimm examines how in *White Is for Witching* and *Beyond Black*, spirits trouble and fracture time, producing inhospitable spaces for the living. In this essay Trimm argues that the spirits are summoned by place, rather than bound to it. He suggests that the spirits in both novels trouble conceptions of home as the national past haunts the present making habitation anxious and uncomfortable. The present is no longer secure and the ghosts must be exhumed before home can become a hospitable place again.

The final essay of this part, Niamh Downing's ' "Tender Bodies": Embracing the Ecological Uncanny in Jim Crace's *Being Dead*', looks at the notion of super-nature and the ecological uncanny, where the site of trauma is the decaying corpses of a murdered couple who are turning into landscape. Downing contends that *Being Dead* is not a novel that uncovers or exorcises ghosts of the past. Instead the site of trauma is revealed to be the human body itself, which proves to be excessive; less supernatural than super natural, an excess of nature. The putrefying and decaying corpses become uncanny sites of materiality, nature that is haunted.

Part II, 'Inner and (Sub)Urban Landscapes', addresses some of the main themes present in the study of ghosts and haunting: the haunted house, nostalgia and the sub/urban landscape. These essays question power and gender relations, the idealised spaces of the city, the home and the American dream. Examining both literature and film they chart hauntings of inner human, and externally man-made landscapes. In Chapter 5, Karl Bell explores haunted urban spaces. Bell's chapter, 'Phantasmal Cities: The Construction and Function of Haunted Landscapes in Victorian English Cities', draws on urban supernatural folklore and examines the haunted landscapes of Victorian English cities. Arguing that supernatural encounters can be transformative, Bell looks at the experience of communal, collective hauntings and the cityscape. Although inevitably un-mappable, these sites are changed by haunting and ghost lore becomes affective as it is subjectively experienced in the Victorian urban space as supernatural and physical landscapes intertwine.

In Chapter 6, 'The Girl Who Wouldn't Die: Masculinity, Power and Control in *The Haunting of Hill House* and *Hell House*', Kevin Corstorphine discusses the intertextual relationship between Shirley Jackson's *The Haunting of Hill House* and Richard Matheson's *Hell House*. Corstorphine explores the cultural and historical underpinnings of the haunted house in the context of 'bad places' in relation to the idea of the 'Male Gothic' novel's focus on imperilled female victims. He raises questions about how masculinity is portrayed in the novels and argues that they represent valuable examinations of domesticity, nationality, masculinity and their attendant crises and anxieties.

HollyGale Millette's chapter, 'Gothic Chronotopes and Bloodied Cobblestones: The Uncanny Psycho-Geography of London's Whitechapel Ward', maps the spatial geographical area of Whitechapel—site of the infamous late-nineteenth-century murders. Millette examines spaces, the violence done there and the ghosts that are left behind. Using Bhaktin (among other theorists) she argues that Whitechapel as a geographic space has been mythologized and therefore fictionalized. Examining Whitechapel as a gendered haunted place, Millette discusses how, right up until the present day, Whitechapel has been/is being re-imagined. She argues that Whitechapel itself is gendered female and that the violence against women perpetrated in that space has been co-opted and therefore perpetuated and normalized.

In Chapter 8, '(Sub)urban Landscapes and Perception in Neo-Victorian Fiction', Rosario Arias examines the felt experience of landscape in the telluric space of the Margate shell-encrusted grotto, discovered by Joshua Newlove in 1835. Through her phenomenological and sensorial reading, Arias demonstrates that *The Realm of Shells* (2006) operates as a channel for material embodied connections between past and present, Victorian culture and the contemporary reader.

The final part of the book, 'Borderlands and Outlands', extends the discussion to the margins—the Irish and Northern peripheries, the open landscapes of Suffolk and the imagined spaces of Otherness in children's films. Daniel Weston begins this part with his chapter, 'W. G. Sebald's Afterlives: Haunting Contemporary Landscape Writing'. Weston looks at how the influence of Sebald's own work haunts landscape writing that came after. Weston argues that the impact of his work is inescapable and that it haunts subsequent imaginings of the English landscape and particularly that of East Anglia. He wonders whether Sebald's influence has been perhaps too compelling and suggests that his innovative work has been turned into a convention. Perhaps therefore a 'turn away' from these constructed genre boundaries might be more true to the spirit of Sebald's work.

Chapter 10 turns to the borderlands between Scotland and England. Alison and Colin Younger's chapter, 'Reivers, Raiders and Revenants: The Haunted Landscapes of the Anglo-Scots Borders', traces the mythic shadow-lands of this liminal place. Examining supernatural Border ballads and the work of Walter Scott, the Youngers look at what they term the 'debatable lands' of the borders and argue that the folk literature from this region subverts the Anglicised notion that this area is anachronistic and 'other' to itself. Instead, they suggest the uncanny spectrality associated with this 'excluded middle' exudes from the landscape itself.

In Chapter 11, 'Haunting the Grown-Ups: The Borderlands of *ParaNorman* and *Coraline*', Rebecca Lloyd takes us to the fantasy landscapes in two stop animation children's films. Arguing that character and the landscapes they occupy are not separate, Lloyd looks at the desires and wishes of children for home and integration. Yet too often this type of comfort is not to be found either in the home or the outside world and Lloyd examines how the characters of Coraline and Norman negotiate the darkness that surrounds them, finally coming to a place that, if it is not perfect, is at least habitable.

Finally, we turn to Bram Stoker in William Hughes's chapter '"The Triumph of Nature": Borderlands and Sunset Horizons in Bram Stoker's *The Snake's Pass*'. Hughes begins with the description of a sunset given by the novel's English hero Arthur Severn, a first-time traveller in Victorian Ireland. He explores the borders of a sublime landscape that is both close to England and yet resolutely alien in Arthur's perception. Here there are questions of imperial power and ownership of a land that is haunted by myth and legend. Hughes looks at the scholarship on Stoker and how he is defined as Anglo-Irish—with his perceptions coming from London rather than Ireland. Hughes, however, argues that there is a fusion of the two and that in the end *The Snake's Pass* provides a positive outcome whereby the urban and English modern and progressive 'outside' is welcomed whilst the old, haunted landscapes of rural Ireland are not over-run but are made to be productive.

As this introduction has shown, *Haunted Landscapes* is concerned with diversity—of haunting types, landscapes and theoretical approaches. The collection synthesizes ideas from different critical approaches: spectral, affective and spatial, and provides new routes into these subjects. Examining urban and rural landscapes, haunted domestic spaces, landscapes of trauma and borderlands, this collection of essays is designed to cross disciplines and combine seemingly disparate academic approaches under the coherent locus of landscape and haunting. And the ghosts themselves? We will leave the last word of this introduction to Vernon Lee who believed that ghosts are not separate from our environment, but surround us daily: things of the imagination, memory *and* materiality. Ghosts and ghostly things, she says:

> are things of the imagination, born there, sprung from the strange confused heaps, half-rubbish, half-treasure, which lie in our fancy, heaps of half-faded recollections of fragmentary vivid impressions, litter of multi-colored tatters, and faded herbs and flowers, whence arises that odor (we all know it), musty and damp, but penetratingly sweet and intoxicatingly heady, which hangs in the air when a ghost has swept through the unopened door, and the flickering flames of candle and fire start up once more after waning. (1898, 10)

NOTES

1. Although Tim Ingold suggests that perhaps landscape was never perceived as separate or distanced from the self. He argues that 'to perceive, as to imagine, is to participate from within in the self-making of the world' (2012, 14). We are not and cannot be separate from the world or the landscapes we are part of.

2. Sheridan Le Fanu's story 'Green Tea' is one such tale as is M. R. James's 'Oh Whistle and I'll Come to You, My Lad' and Robert Hichens's creepy tale 'How Love Came to Professor Guildea'.

3. See, for example, Fuss (1991), Castle (1995) and Gordon ([1997] 2008).

BIBLIOGRAPHY

Bell, Michael Mayerfeld. 1997. 'The Ghosts of Place.' *Theory and Society*, 26: 813–36.

Benson, E. F. 2012. *Night Terrors: The Ghost Stories of E. F. Benson*. Ware: Wordsworth.

Berberich, Christine, Neil Campbell and Robert Hudson. eds. 2012. *Land and Identity: Theory, Memory, and Practice*. Amsterdam: Rodopi.

Castle, Terry. ed. 1995. *The Apparitional Lesbian: Female Homosexuality and Modern Culture*. New York: Columbia University Press.

Clough, Patricia and Jean Halley. eds. 2007. *The Affective Turn: Theorizing the Social*. Durham: Duke University Press.

del Pilar Blanco, María and Esther Peeren. eds. 2010. *Popular Ghosts: Haunted Spaces of Everyday Culture*. New York: Continuum.

Dickerson, Vanessa, D. 1996. *Victorian Ghosts in the Noontide: Women Writers and the Supernatural*. Columbia, MO: University of Missouri Press.

Derrida, Jacques. (1994) 2006. *Specters of Marx*. New York: Routledge.

Erll, Astrid and Ansgar Nünning. eds. 2010. *A Companion to Cultural Memory Studies*. New York: De Gruyter.

Fuss, Diana. ed. 2008. *Inside/Out: Lesbian Theories, Gay Theories*. New York: Routledge.

Gordon, Avery, F. 1997. *Ghostly Matters: Haunting and the Sociological Imagination*. Minneapolis: University of Minnesota Press.

Gregg, Melissa and Gregory J. Seigworth. eds. 2010. *The Affect Theory Reader*. Durham, NC: Duke University Press.

Ingold, Tim. 2012. 'Introduction.' *Imagining Landscapes: Past, Present and Future*. Ed. Monica Janowski and Tim Ingold, Farnham: Ashgate Publishing 1–18.

Jones, Owain and Joanne Garde-Hanson. eds. 2012. *Geography and Memory: Explorations in Identity, Place and Becoming*. New York: Palgrave Macmillan.

Lee, Vernon. 1898. *Genius Loci: Notes on Places*. Chicago: Leopold Classic Library.

_____. 2006. *Hauntings and Other Fantastic Tales*. Ed. Catherine Maxwell and Patricia Pulham. Peterborough, ON: Broadview Press.

Luckhurst, Roger. 2002. 'The Contemporary London Gothic and the Limits of the "Spectral Turn".' *Textual Practice*, 16 (3): 527–46.

Matless, David. 2003. 'Introduction' to 'Landscape' Section. *Handbook of Cultural Geography*. Ed. Kay Anderson, Mona Domosh, Steve Pile and Nigel Thrift. London: Sage Publications. 227–32.

Palmer, Paulina. 2012. *The Queer Uncanny*. Cardiff: University of Wales Press.

Oakes, Timothy and Patricia Price. 2008. *The Cultural Geography Reader*. New York: Routledge.

O'Riley, Michael F. 2007. 'Postcolonial Haunting: Anxiety, Affect, and the Situated Encounter.' *Postcolonial Text*, 3 (4): 1–5.

Söderström, Ola. 2010. 'Representation.' *Cultural Geography: A Critical Dictionary of Key Concepts*. Ed. David Atkinson, Peter Jackson, David Sibley and Neil Washbourne. London: I. B. Taurus. 11–15.

Thompson, Peter, Ian Howard and Emma Waterton. eds. 2013. *The Routledge Companion to Landscape Studies*. New York: Routledge.

Wolfreys, Julian. 2002. *Victorian Hauntings: Spectrality, the Uncanny and Literature*. New York: Palgrave.

Part I

LANDSCAPES OF TRAUMA

Chapter One

Place as Palimpsest

Paul Celan and Martin Heidegger and the Haunting of Todtnauberg

Mark Riley

There is no landscape whether natural or thought, that is not inscribed, erased and re-inscribed by histories and ghosts. In particular, the German landscape is populated by emotive places and experiencing them is intensified by the complex interweaving of topography and histories with personal and collective memory and forgetting and haunting.

In this chapter I will investigate one particular site: the location of German philosopher Martin Heidegger's hut situated in the mountains of the Black Forest south of Freiburg at Todtnauberg. It has been a contentious building/ location since its construction in the 1920s and has reflected and articulated Heidegger's concerns with landscape in relation to rootedness, dwelling, language and homeland. Heidegger recognized Todtnauberg as a locale 'haunted' by uncertainty and open to possibilities, to a sense of becoming—a site of appearances and disappearances.

However, I will draw attention to the more complex spectral qualities of the site as inscribed by Paul Celan's poem, 'Todtnauberg'. This poem was written in response to a meeting between Heidegger and Celan at the hut at Todtnauberg in July 1967. It presents the site as a palimpsest, haunted by histories and in particular Heidegger's nefarious involvement with National Socialism. In the poem, Celan's appreciation of Heidegger's mountain life was mediated by ghosts and his imaginings of what had happened there before.

Philipe Lacoue-Labarthe argues that 'Todtnauberg' is barely a poem at all. It is not an outline or a map but the remainder or residue of an abortive narrative. The poem presents a site that has not only been actually and symbolically tainted by the fascist past, but also serves as an imperfect setting for events that fractured the poet's own past (Lacoue-Labarthe 1998).

I want to consider Todtnauberg in relation to a distinction that I will make between the ideas of 'landscape' and 'terrain'. I will argue that 'landscape' should be understood as a symbolic setting for an individual's passage through time and is a continuous and coherent whole. 'Terrain' is a more fragmentary experience onto which a coherent sense of self cannot be projected. The concept of 'terrain' suggests a 'de-coherence' that exceeds the geographic setting; it is a place of haunting and ghosts. The place of the poem presents past and present as a 'terrain' that can be described only in abstract fragments rather than a coherent whole. Both locale and poem are traced with the paths of inscriptions and erasures.

This chapter will explore this spectral experience of remnants and shards evident in Celan's poem 'Todtnauberg'. It will consider how these qualities transform Heidegger's familial home into a fractured and residual place: a palimpsest.

On the northern slope of a secluded valley in the Black Forest, a small shingle-clad building is situated. It was the thinking place of German philosopher Martin Heidegger (1889–1976). The site of this hut, and the 'site' of Paul Celan's poem 'Todtnauberg' are inextricably linked by ideas of haunting and de-coherence in relation to place. Heidegger wrote extensively on the significance of 'dwelling' and 'place' in relation to 'Being' and the importance of poetic language to philosophical thought. One of his published collections of essays is titled *Wegmarken*[1] (1998) and is an edited collection that maps a landscape of thinking. The title reflects this desire to orientate oneself in thought through relational strategies that suggest the importance of a proximal experience of the world. This sense of an understanding of intimacy and proximity through language permeated his writing as did the importance and particularity of place. However, to one particular place Heidegger claimed 'an emotional and intellectual intimacy' (Sharr 2007, 3). This was a small wooden hut (the footprint measuring approximately 6 × 7 metres), built for him and situated on the north side of a valley facing south, in the mountains of the Black Forest south of Freiburg and close to the village of Todtnauberg.[2] This building and its surrounding landscape have been interpreted at different times as a retreat for a thinker from the intensities of academic and political concerns, a place of intense routines of living, thinking, writing and work, and a site of significant historical encounters. In his book, *A Phenomenology of Landscape*, Christopher Tilley argues:

> A landscape is a series of named locales, a set of relational places linked by paths, movements and narratives. It is a 'natural' topography perspectivally linked to the existential Being of the body in societal space. It is a cultural code for living, an anonymous 'text' to be read and interpreted, a writing pad for

inscription, a scape of and for human praxis, a mode of dwelling and a mode of experiencing. (1997, 34)

Tilley's proposal that a landscape is a 'text' to be 'read and interpreted' is a useful starting point; however, I want to introduce an additional topographic theme of 'inscription' and 'erasure' at Todtnauberg. I will argue that this event of inscribing, erasing and re-inscribing can be expressed as 'terrain'. Whereas 'landscape' suggests a literal reading, 'terrain' offers a more ambiguous and palimpsestic interpretation of a locale.

Historian Claude Magris argues that 'the Black Forest surrounding (Heidegger's) hut had become a transcendental, universal landscape of philosophy. In the luminous clearing in the wood in which ... there is nothing that can be grasped, but only a horizon within which things appear' (2001, 47). This suggests a haunted topology manifest in the *folding*, *unfolding* and *refolding* of histories in both poem and locale. It indicates, as Celan noted in his 'Meridan Speech of October 1960,[3] an animation of 'tremors and hints' that are both inclusive *to* and exclusive *of* the 'poetic event'. These are the tracings of 'what is', 'what has been' and 'what will be'—the variance of protentions and retentions marking the visibility of invisibility that is both transcribed and partially erased in the plurality of the poem and the 'place' as the 'locale' of the hut.

Figure 1.1.   Heidgger's hut at Todtnauberg from the east.

This building represented not just a thinking place for the philosopher but also a recreational space for his family and invited guests (see figures 1.1–1.4).

In 1922, Martin Heidegger's wife Elfride commissioned a local carpenter, Pius Schweitzer, to build a cabin on land she had purchased on the hillside above Rütte and close to the village of Todtnauberg. This building represented not just a thinking place for the philosopher but also a recreational space for his family and invited guests. In his 1934 essay *Why Do I Stay in the Provinces?* Heidegger wrote:

> On the steep slope of a wide mountain valley in the southern Black Forest at an elevation of 1150 meters, there stands a small ski hut. The floor plan measures six meters by seven. The low hanging roof covers three rooms: the kitchen which is also the living room, a bedroom and a study. Scattered at wide intervals throughout the narrow base of the valley and on the equally steep slope opposite, lie farmhouses with their large over-hanging roofs. Higher up the slope the meadows and pasture lands lead to the woods with its dark fir-tress, old and towering … This is my work world. (Heidegger in Sheehan 2010, 27)

In *Why Do I Stay in the Provinces?* (1934) and later *The Festival Address* (made as part of a celebratory event at Todtnauberg in 1966), Heidegger made a specific claim for the activities of thinking and writing at the hut. He argued that his philosophical work (did) not take place as an aloof, eccentric study but 'belongs right in the midst of peasants work' (Mugerauer 2008, 524). In the *Festival Address*, Heidegger proposed that the thinker's task/craft does not merely belong together with other skills of members of the community, but *all* derive their power and continuity specifically from the landscape where they are grounded and sheltered. In this sense, the hut and its locale are steeped in Heidegger's concerns with authenticity and rootedness and dwelling. Daniel Maier-Katkin argues that 'in addition to his fantasies about German destiny, Heidegger's thought also intersected with Nazi propaganda on the authenticity of rural life, especially at his rustic cottage at Todtnauberg in the Black Forest. He believed that the character of the people there had been shaped over centuries by the hard granite and rugged beauty of the natural environment' (2010, 79). Certainly Heidegger wrote the text *Why Do I Stay in the Provinces?* at a particular historical moment for Germany and at a particular point in his academic career. In 1934, he had resigned the Rectorate at Freiburg University and was seemingly distancing himself from the political machinations of the National Socialist regime. Ultimately, he sought to immerse himself in a rarefied world that brought into proximity thinking and manual work. Clearly there are points in the text where this relationship reflects a spiritual dimension that suggests the hut at Todtnauberg was almost a monastic retreat for the philosopher. Heidegger's repeated over-emphatic identification with a familiar, neighbourly and immediate community—its woods, its hearth and its dialect—was a claim to a monopoly of authenticity.

Todtnauberg was a locale haunted by uncertainty and open to possibilities; to a sense of becoming—a site of appearances and disappearances; a place to hear the call of *Being*. However, we can question the nature of this recognition (its 'visibility') and reflect on what steadfastly remained contentiously invisible and unspoken at Todtnauberg. The limits of this intimate connection are emphasized by Claude Magris. He proposes that Heidegger had 'almost an exclusive, patented trademark as if his sincere attachment to his own soil *allowed no room for the loyalties of other men towards other soils and other lands—to their log cabins, or their blocked-rent tenements, or their skyscrapers*' (Magris 2008, 45, my emphasis). The refusal at play in this overemphasis on attachment and authenticity suggests that within this familial locale there are already hints at elements of uncertainty and anxiety; a lack of recognition; an 'otherness'. For Heidegger, without the experience of loss and disorientation and the potential to wander paths that peter out in the woods, there is no call and, most importantly, there is no possibility of hearing the authentic word of *Being*. Such a landscape haunted by loss and disorientation explains why a Jewish poet such as Celan, lacerated by the Nazis exterminations and its aftermath, was able to set foot on the path to Heidegger's cabin, to climb to that cabin and to attempt a genuine dialogue with the ex-rector of Freiburg University, who in 1934 had put his philosophical ideas at the service of the newly fledged Reich.

Historian Simon Schama notes: 'After the war, Heidegger, whose deep engagement in the ambiguities that lie between language and act marked him out as the link between Nietzsche and modern phenomenology, retreated into the depths of the Black Forest. There for some years, he affected a kind of sylvan[4] hermitage, still implacably alienated from the technological 20th century' (1996, 129). If there is no landscape that is not inscribed by history, then the essential place of a poet's poetic saying is a point of convergence. 'Saying' 'gathers' with the hidden source or origin of that 'saying'—what remains 'unsaid'.

The hut sits on the northern slope of the valley, facing south and overlooking farmland and the hamlet of Rütte. It is one of the several properties situated on this ridge and remains (to this day) in the possession of the Heidegger family and therefore a private residence. From below it is partly obscured by a small stand of trees planted on level ground at its right hand corner and from above by a more substantial copse to the left of the property. The *rundweg*[5] is a concession to the 'Heidegger pilgrim' who makes their way on foot or by car or public transport to this locale in order to attempt to engage Heidegger's 'work world'. Robert Mugerauer asks: 'what goes on in Todtnauberg that is so special?' He answers: 'Perhaps the chance to retrieve and keep lost idioms and to experience that still robust way of life and speaking? Perhaps an openness to strangers, and a possibility of insiders coming

Figure 1.2.   The spring with the star-die on top, Todtnauberg.

to accept outsiders as belonging? The giving of region, its locality, dialect, intertwined natural and communal rhythms: the giving and receiving of the belonging together—that constitute home and homecoming?' (Mugerauer 2008, 526)

The *rundweg* allows the visitor a certain proximity to the hut while attempting to enforce some semblance of privacy (clear signage specifying the family's desire to keep the uninvited visitor at a distance). Importantly, modern transport links have made the hut and *rundweg* more accessible than in Heidegger's lifetime (a regular train from Freiburg takes one to Kirchzarten where a bus heads into the mountains, dropping one at Todtnauberg's Rathaus—a journey of just over an hour). However, historically it was a difficult place to get to from Heidegger's permanent home in the *Rötebuckweg* in the northern suburb of Freiburg-Zähringen. Heidegger's wife Elfride noted in 1923:

> Reaching the cabin at Todtnauberg was an arduous business, particularly in winter. There were various ways of getting to Todtnauberg: by train to Hinterzarten and from there on foot or by ski over Rinken, Feldberg and Stübenwasen; by train via Lörrach up the Wiesen Valley to Todtnau and from there on foot up a steep slope; by train to Kirchzarten and from there by carriage via Oberried and

Notschrei … All these routes were arduous, especially in adverse weather conditions. (E. Heidegger in Heidegger 2008, 89)

Elfride Heidegger's description of the alternative routes to reach the hut from Freiburg places the idea of the path as a means of accessing a location at the forefront of the topography of Todtnauberg. A path is the tracing of a journey into a landscape and marks the trace of passing. The importance of the motif of the 'path' throughout Heidegger's thought remains compelling as it not only acts as a metaphor for the process of thinking but also inscribes itself across the actual topography of Todtnauberg. In addition, Celan's poem both inscribes and erases through the tracing of 'Todtnauberg' as a poetic event. A 'trace' is at once inscribed and erased and the event of transcription is a tracing that both defines and withholds. Writer Robert Macfarlane identifies the word *shul* from Tibetan Buddhism as 'a mark that remains after that which made it has passed by: footprints are *shul*, a path is *shul* and such impressions draw one backwards into awareness of past events' (2012, 28). Histories then emerge in the tracing of a path. Macfarlane also argues that 'paths were figured as *rifts within which time might exist as pure surface, prone to weird morphologies [and] uncanny origins*' (22, my emphasis).

The hut has been a site of numerous encounters both personal and professional. Jewish poet Paul Celan's visited Heidegger at the hut in 1967 and as

Figure 1.3. **Heidegger's hut at Todtnauberg from the south west.**

a result 'commemorated' the meeting with a poem he titled 'Todtnauberg'. Celan's poem suggests his appreciation of Heidegger's mountain life was mediated by his imaginings of what had happened there before. The poem reads:

> Arnica, eyebright, the
> draft from the well with the
> star-die on top,
> In the
> hütte,
> written in the book
> – whose name did it record
> before mine –?
> In this book
> the line about
> a hope; today,
> for a thinker's
> word
> to come,
> in the heart,
> forest sward, unleveled,
> orchis and orchis, singly,
> crudeness, later, while driving,
> clearly,
> he who drives us, the man,
> he who also hears it,
> the half-
> trod log-
> trails on the highmoor,
> humidity,
> much.[6]

Celan asks a question in the poem—'whose name did it record before mine?'—hinting at co-signatory's (arguably with questionable credentials) that would have previously signed their names in the hut guest book and by doing identified their presence there. While visiting Heidegger, Celan was invited to write something in the visitor's book. He wrote: 'In the hut-book, looking at the well-star, with a hope for a coming word in the heart. On 25 July 1967 Paul Celan'.

'Todtnauberg' is both an aesthetic experiment in language and a palimpsestic place haunted by partial erasures. Adam Sharr argues that 'Celan's appreciation of Heidegger's mountain life was seemingly mediated by his imaginings of what had happened there before. He could not join the philosopher in his most intimate landscape without speculating who might have travelled there in different times and what had been discussed, without intense feeling for the role of the past in this meeting' (2006, 84–5).

Celan's question in the poem marks the anguish prompted by the thought of a strange kind of fraternal affiliation with 'the other'—the previous visitors/inscribers (academics and others associated with the Nazi Party who visited the hut in the period of Heidegger's most conspicuous pro-Nazi activities in the 1930s). This affiliation (an association made by Celan as a later but still a co-signatory of the guest book) transgresses the order of forgiveness that overarches the poem.

The question in the poem interrupts any clear designation of one who seeks forgiveness (Heidegger) and one who grants it (Celan) with the complication of Celan's perceived 'guilt' at being a co-signatory of the guest book. Importantly the poem is not the description of a 'literal landscape', what we might call a stenographic notation of the immediate surroundings. It is a fragmentary and elusive text, haunted by temporal and spatial anomalies which, through concealment and effacement, transgress its textural body: a *shul*. In his essay 'Catastrophe', Philip Lacoue-Labarthe states:

> The place of poetry, the place where poetry takes place, every time is *the place without place* of *the intimate gaping*—something that must certainly be thought as the pure spacing which places (do not) suppose and which upholds them with no hold. (1998, 140, my emphasis)

This is a 'differential unification'—it remains 'spiritual' precisely in that spirit unifies 'polemically' and thus contains within itself the power of transition and transformation. The poem implies the notion of a 'landscape' that has been actually and symbolically tainted by the fascist past. It also served as an imperfect setting for events that fractured Celan's past. Recollections of this past have to be placed in a terrain that can be described only in abstract fragments rather than a coherent whole. Baer argues that '*Celan presents us not with a coherent experience but with its remnants, its shards*' (2000, 231, my emphasis).

Here there is a shift from a coherent, topographic spacing to something much more complex, fragmentary and lacking coherence: a 'terrain'. Baer proposes a clear distinction between 'landscape' and 'terrain'. He argues that 'landscape' is a continuous and coherent whole whereas 'terrain' is a more fragmentary and disjointed experience. The concept of 'terrain' thus suggests a 'de-coherence' that exceeds the geographic setting of the encounter between poet and thinker. It harbours the encrypted unsaid of Heidegger's involvements and subsequent silence about Germany's fascist regime; 'in the words of the poem, this painful and finally irreconcilable past lies buried just below the wet forest soil on which Celan and Heidegger took their walk' (Baer 2000, 228).[7]

The indeterminacy of 'terrain' interrupts the topographic integrity of a landscape steeped in the temporal ordering and continuity. Baer argues that the romantic 'topos' of a particular place has been invalidated as a means of coherently framing life experiences and home. More importantly, he suggests that such devices are always and already tainted by the ideological uses of that tradition to link a specific group or nation to a given geographic location (Baer 2000, 219). Landscape is already haunted by what remains unspoken— what is 'ungrounded', permeable and fractured.

It is the language of Celan's poem that suggests an *Unheimlich Heimat* (an 'unhomely home'). For Heidegger, the idea of *The Fatherland* (a 'homeland') 'stands under the heaviest prohibition' (Philips 2005, 173)—by this he means that it is 'prohibited' from being uncovered too easily. Its 'proper' state is elusive and is not to be 'found' in the way that something merely present-at-hand (an everyday object: a tool) is found. This suggests an intrinsic difficulty of 'locating' 'home' within the realm of the 'thingly': the everyday. In this, Heidegger's 'homeland' is closer to the missing homeland of Franz Rosenzweig's *The Star of Redemption* where 'to the eternal people, home never is home in the sense of land … in the most profound sense possible, this people has a land of its own only in that it has a land it yearns for—a holy land' (174).[8]

James Philips argues that although the question of 'homeland' could not be enunciated in the 1930s, this does not mean it went unanswered. The National Socialists were 'unable to locate a *living national mythology* and in their attempts to do so "identified a fatherland that lay elsewhere"'. The name of this '*Unheimlich Heimat*' (literally 'un-homelike home') was Greece. The relationship that Philips identifies between mythology, home and location is interesting here. Greece as an 'unhomely' home for the Germans was something that Heidegger returned to in the numerous texts of the late 1930s and early 1940s. He 'set forth' Greek thought as that which must be *overcome*. Through the overcoming of Greek thought through its interrogation the 'forgetfulness of *Being*' could be retrieved. In this sense, 'Greece was to be made to give way to its Un-thought' (Philips 2005, 169).

The notion of the 'Un-thought' is suggestive of something not yet visible, that which is concealed. The event of *concealment* and *unconcealment* was fundamental for Heidegger and from this we can conclude that visibility and invisibility are also intrinsic to *Being*. Further, understanding 'homeland' as a concept of something 'not yet visible' can also be addressed in terms of illumination, not in the sense of that *which is* illuminated but that *which* illuminates. In this sense, 'homeland' is not that which *is* visible, but is that which makes that which is visible, visible. If Todtnauberg is a 'terrain', it is a place haunted by other temporal events: some visible and others hidden and elusive. In Celan's poem, the very notion of a 'landscape' has been corrupted by Germany's recent history. The poetic encounter with these historical events is not only fragmentary but drifts between coherence and de-coherence. For Celan, Todtnauberg's topography was a palimpsestic encryption of what continued to remain unspoken about Heidegger's past. At the boundaries of visibility and invisibility, inscription and erasure; the landscape was still haunted by what lay buried under its surface where he and Heidegger walked on that day in 1967.

Emmanuel Faye in his book *Heidegger; the Introduction of Nazism into Philosophy* argues that Celan's visit to the *Hütte* was not in anticipation of reconciliation but of redemption. He suggests that in leading Heidegger on a walk to the 'quagmire of the Black Forest', where supposedly, 'the Nazis had set up their camps' (2009, 306), Celan wanted to show Heidegger that the earth of the Black Forest did not consist solely of granite (that determining 'substructure' as indicated in Heidegger's Schlageter address of 1933), but was fluid and indeterminate. The very landscape that day reflected the outcome of the conversation between thinker and poet. The path on which they walked became so sodden that they were forced to retreat to the hut. This poses the question as to whether the 'purity' and simplicity of Heidegger's retreat in the Black Forest was (and arguably remains) tainted by the political past. Baer argues that Celan's juxtaposition of noun and adjective ('forest meadows unleveled')[9] leaves grammatically and semantically undecided whether these fascist traces would 'disappear' when the forest meadows are levelled or whether the fascist past resists complete erasure. He notes:

> Heidegger's failure to address his past involvement in fascism is revealed by drawing on a word's propensity to assume regionally specific connotations. Because a speaker from one part of Germany may hear an equivalent of 'fascine' where others hear nothing but 'meadow',[10] Celan effectively employs dialect—the link of location and a sense of particularised speech—against itself. (Baer 2000, 229)

Veronique Foti in her text, *Heidegger and the Poets; Poiesis/Sophia/Techne*, argues that Celan's poem evokes Heidegger's 'retreat in a work-enabling rural simplicity and solitude as he experienced it: the plain homestead, fountain and star, mountain flowers, the book, the moor. Celan, indeed, allows the landscape to come into discontinuous presencing in a manner which echoes Heidegger's own relationship to it' (2005, 80). A term that might indicate the complexities of such a lingual encounter in Celan's later poems that is both poetic in background and psychological in utterance would be in the form of a lack of fluency—a 'disfluency'. Language is both pressured into silence and pressed by silence. It is rife with traces and fragments that interrupt and disrupt it. In his text *Aesthetic Theory*, Adorno acknowledges the pressure inherent in Celan's poetry, claiming

> Celan's poems articulate *unspeakable horror* by being silent, thus turning their truth content into a negative quality. They emulate a language *below* the help-less prattle of human beings—even below the level of organic life as such. It is a language of *dead matter*; of stones and stars [...] Celan writes poetry without an aura. (1998, 444, my emphasis)

Emmanuel Faye elaborates on Heidegger's 'silence' as not one of the guilt of association, but of incomprehension. He suggests that 'according to Heidegger, no one died in a death camp, because none of those who were exterminated there bore within their essence the possibility of death' (2009, 305).

Here Faye draws on an interpretation of one of Heidegger's *Bremen Lectures* (1949) titled 'The Danger' (*Die Gefuhr*). For Faye, this is no longer a revisionist view of the Holocaust, but a negation. None died in the death camps because none were able to die. Those liquidated could not be saved by *Being*—they were not 'mortal' and therefore not 'human'. They could not 'die' because they could not even 'live'. Heidegger apparently attacks the very 'being' of those exterminated. In showing that they were always already 'nothing', it is clear to see in Faye's interpretation how Heidegger could construe that 'nothing' happened to 'nothing'. The poem does not attempt to express the 'illness of the poet' but rather the 'madness of the thinker'.

Claudio Magris proposes that for Heidegger, stressing his own links to the Black Forest 'led him to accept only the wood outside his own door as authentic, only those peasants whom he knew by name, only that gesture of raising an axe above a chopping block ... other peasants, woods or words ... struck him as abstract and unreal, as if they existed only in dry statistics and were inventions of propaganda' (2001, 45).

In *Paul Celan and Martin Heidegger; an Unresolved Conversation, 1951–70*, James K. Lyon argues that we should not be too quick to assume that the poem was written as either a judgement in the form of 'resent-ment' or as 'a disappointment'. He suggests that there is no recorded evidence from the period to suggest such an interpretation is necessarily appropriate. In a letter written by Celan to Werner Weber (editor of the literary section of *Neve Zürcher Zeitung*), Celan describes the poem as an attempt to 'register' (*festhalten*) or to 'put on record', in a detached impersonal fashion. He registers sights and events related to his encounter and conversation with Heidegger (2006, 181). Lyon quotes from Celan's letter to his estranged wife written on 2 August 1967: 'On the day after my reading I was in Heidegger's cabin in the Black Forest with Herr Neumann. ... Then in the car we had a very serious conversation in words that were unmistakable on my part. Afterwards Herr Naumann, who was a witness, told me that for him this conversation had an epoch-making aspect to it' (165). Celan added later to Naumann that 'I hope Heidegger will take his pen and write a few pages echoing (the conversation) that will be a warning in view of resurgent Nazism' (167). Lyon further suggests that its form would be in line with Celan's *Meridian Speech* and this would indicate an 'anti-metaphorical' perspective. It is also evident that Celan is not addressing Heidegger explicitly in the poem—it is clearly not intended to be a dialogue with the philosopher (addressees are common to Celan's other writings, e.g., speaking to an identifiable person either living or dead). However, Lyon argues that Celan's tone changed on his return to Paris after the meeting at the hut. This tone becomes more judgemental of Heidegger. In a letter sent to Franz Wurm, dated 25 August 1967, he referred to the *Hütte* as 'Denkhütte' (literally, his 'thinkers hut') at Todtnauberg. Lyon suggests that Celan's wordplay is not intended as a compliment but a 'jarring paradox with an implicit criticism' (175). The association of a 'hut' with a certain class of people and 'thinking' with another might suggest that Heidegger was being pretentious. Lyon goes further to suggest that Celan's comment is a more oblique reference to the modest dwelling circumstances of the 'volk' in Nazi ideology. In a later letter dated 24 January 1968, Celan asks whether he should publish the poem or wait for an answer from 'the one from the mountain' (Celan cited in 175). Here Lyon suggests this phrase has a double meaning—Celan referencing a term used by Hitler's Reich Chancellery Group of associates during the Nazi era, who referred to themselves as 'those from the mountain' alluding to their privileged position that allowed them to visit Hitler at 'The Eagles Nest' on the mountain above Berchtesgarten. Lyon argues that rather than explore its 'multiple, sometimes contradictory meanings interpreters often reduce rather than expand the poem's possibilities' (178). This leads to *reductionist* readings that follow a template imposed on the poem latterly. The 'anti-Nazi' template was arguably applied by Celan himself in order to direct the appropriate reading of the poem and in so doing 'close off' possibilities that did not conform to that reading. All these associations were made in the aftermath of the poem's inscription and are based on a singular interpretation where meanings are fixed at the expense of other possible interpretations. Lyon suggests that Celan may have contributed to these later interpretations but that there is little evidence to suggest that they were necessarily foregrounded in the writing of the poem.

The 'above' of the hut could and would only be interpreted by Heidegger as a place of vision. For him it was a place of insight, presenting him with a panoramic view suggesting that a physical location might reflect the opportunity for and realization of clarity of thought. Rüdiger Safrinski argues that at 'Todtnauberg, on his hill in the Black Forest, Heidegger felt close to his Greek dream; from there he had descended into the political lowlands' (1999, 278). However, to understand the metaphor of the locale of the hut as more than geographically an 'above', we must also address this in relation to a sense of 'below'—as Safrinski describes it, a descent into another locale troubled by uncertainty, disrupted vision and perspectival thought. Arguably, Heidegger's life was structured in this twofold way. The clarity of vision associated with Todtnauberg was set against the political complexities of academic life at the university in Freiburg and arguably by default his town house in Rötebuckweg in the northern suburb of Freiburg at Zähringen. According to Adam Sharr, this two story house apparently did not hold any specific importance for Heidegger in the way

Figure 1.4.   Heidegger's hut and the spring from the east.

that the hut did. He notes that it was his wife Elfride who was responsible for the layout of the property (in order that it reflect Heidegger's professorial status).[11] At Todtnauberg, Heidegger was happiest as a solitary writer, single-minded in his concentration on a vision of the future and removed from the machinations of family and academic life. Even in the aftermath, of war and the collapse of the Third Reich, Heidegger seemingly refuted the idea that Germany was 'lost' and it was the landscape of hut that sustained this refusal in the post-war period until his death in 1976. As Hugo Ott argues:

> Even in 1946, Heidegger may have been imbued with the conviction that the Germans had *not* gone under ... seeing things as he did in the long term, and placing his trust in the clarifying light of distant perspectives, like the distant panorama of the Swiss Alps that was constantly before his eyes at the mountain hut on the Todtnauberg. (1994, 351)

In this chapter I have argued that the 'terrain' of the hut remains discontinuous and fragmentary. Celan's poem articulates an array of possible pathways (*Holzwege*), temporal and otherwise, which trace out a 'terrain' across the landscape occupied by Heidegger's hut. Otto Pöggeler suggests that 'in his publications, the philosopher made the hut into a sign of identity with the homeland, a rootedness in the land that maintains itself *even* in the present world civilisation' (1997, 105).[12] This interpretation of the hut at Todtnauberg and Celan's poem animate a much more complex and rich palimpsestic 'terrain'. Even today the unassuming wooden building persists as the site of meditations on its multiple histories and interpretations. It is at once both worldly and other-worldly.

I have argued that de-coherence of Todtnauberg exceeds its purely geographic setting. Place and poem are terrains haunted by spectral traces and can only be described in abstract fragments rather than as coherent wholes. This spectral experience of remnants and shards transforms Heidegger's familial home into a fractured and residual place where partial erasure ensures that visibility and invisibility and vocal and unvoiced coincide. Todtnauberg the location and 'Todtnauberg' the poem continue to be at once palimpsestic and dis-fluent. 'Terrain', then, is an 'affective' event. 'Affect' is an interpretation of the particularities of a landscape that resist the orthodoxies of topographic investigation and animates the ordinary to reveal the extraordinary.[13] The locale of Heidegger's hut is such an affective 'terrain'. It continues to be the site of complex discourses traversing the boundaries of visibility and invisibility, landscape and terrain, being 'rooted' and 'rootlessness'. It is a site that continues to be open to the possibilities of re-imagining and re-mythologizing.

NOTES

1. *Wegmarken* translates as 'path marks'.
2. In the prologue to Adam Sharr's book *Heidegger's Hut*, Andrew Benjamin states that 'the hut, rather than involving a merely literal commitment to the countryside or the provinces involves a commitment to a particular relationship between philosophy and place' (2006, xix).
3. 'The Meridian Speech' is published in *Collected Prose* (1986, 37–57).
4. 'Sylvan' refers to an association with the woods, specifically those who inhabit the wood are made from tree materials or comprise the forest themselves. The term can also refer to a person who resides in the woods or a spirit of the wood.
5. The *rundweg* (which translates into English as *circular path*) is a sign-posted route that begins on the outskirts of Todtnauberg village and follows the rim of the valley where the hut is situated. It takes the walker to the perimeter of the site where the hut is located and then follows a route of approximately 4 km around the valley, punctuated with information boards about Heidegger's time at Todtnauberg.
6. This is Pierre Joris's translation found in the collection *Lightduress* (2005), 62–5.
7. In the poem, Celan refers to 'the half-trod log trails on the highmoor, humidity much', suggesting a walk curtailed by dampness.
8. Philips cites a number of examples in Heidegger's writings during the 1930s and 1940s where the subject of 'fatherland' is addressed, including the 1934–1935 lecture course, *Hölderlin's Hymnen 'Germanien' und 'Der Rhein'*, 1937–1938 lecture, *Grunfragen der Philosophie* and the 1942 lecture course, *Hölderlin's Hymn 'The Ister'*. For more specific writing on 'Germany's historic mission', see *An Introduction to Metaphysics* (lecture given in 1935) and published in German in 1953 and English in 1959.
9. 'Unleveled' here is understood as meaning 'not level' or 'uneven terrain'. Later in the poem Celan refers to the 'half-trod log trails' on which he and Heidegger walked. The common construction for such a path would have used brushwood bundles known as 'fascine'. These are used to strengthen an earth structure or to make a path across uneven terrain.
10. 'Fascine' has an etymological link to the ancient Roman word 'fasces' or 'fascio littorio'. This consists of a bundle of rods tied around an axe and suggests 'strength through unity'—a single rod can be easily broken while a bundle is more difficult to break. The link between 'fascine' and the term 'fascism' is clear and something Celan wishes to draw attention to in his observations of the landscape at Todtnauberg.
11. Sharr draws comparisons in construction between hut and town house. The Rötebuckweg property reflected a vernacular architecture more in keeping with a rural farmhouse than an urban town house. This may be due to the period when it was constructed in the late 1920s. At that time, the northern outskirts of Freiburg was still undeveloped and largely agricultural. Today it is a substantial suburb (see pages 43–4 and 88–9 in *Heidegger's Hut*). It is also worth noting that Heidegger's wife, Elfride, was involved in the development of both locations. She funded the purchase of the land and commissioned the building of the hut and was responsible for the layout and décor of the house in Zähringen.

12. In *The Paths of Heidegger's Life and Thought* (1997), Pöggeler further argues that whenever Celan himself speaks of a hut, it is a hut that belongs to another world: 'The poem *Hüttenfenster* (*Hut Windows*) in the same volume speaks of those who were persecuted and exterminated, of East European Jewry out of which Celan emerged' (105). In *Sites of the Uncanny* (2007), Eric Kligerman argues that Celan converted Todtnauberg's landscape into the terrain that Heidegger himself refused to approach: the catastrophic *topos* of the extermination camps. He transformed Heidegger's familiar home into a fractured and uncanny post-memorial space (76).

13. In her book *Ordinary Affects*, Kathleen Stewart argues that 'Ordinary affects, then[,] are an animate circuit that conducts force and maps connections, routes and disjunctures' (2007, 3).

BIBLIOGRAPHY

Adorno, Theodor and R. Hullot-Kentor. ed. 1998. *Aesthetic Theory*. Minneapolis, MN: University of Minnesota Press.

Baer, Ulrich. 2000. *Remnants of Song: Trauma and the Experience of Modernity in Charles Baudelaire and Paul Celan*. Stanford, CA: Stanford University Press.

Celan, Paul. 1986. *Collected Prose*. Trans. R. Waldrop. Manchester: Carcanet Press.

_____. 2005. *Lightduress*. Trans. P. Joris. Los Angeles, CA: Green Integer Books.

Faye, Emmanuel. 2009. *Heidegger: The Introduction of Nazism into Philosophy*. Yale, CT: Yale University Press.

Foti, Veronique. 2005. *M. Heidegger and the Poets: Poiesis/Sophia/Techne*. New York: Humanity Books.

Heidegger, Martin. 1971. *Poetry, Language, Thought*. Trans. A. Hofstadter. New York: Harper & Row.

_____. 1987. *An Introduction to Metaphysics*. Trans. R. Manheim. New Haven, CN: Yale University Press.

_____. 2002. *Off the Beaten Track*. Ed. and Trans. J. Young and K. Haynes. Cambridge: Cambridge University Press.

_____. 2008. *Letters to His Wife (Selected and Edited by Gertrude Heidegger)*. Ed. R. D. V. Glasgow. Cambridge, UK: Polity Press.

_____. and W. McNeill. ed. 1998. *Pathmarks*. Cambridge: Cambridge University Press.

Kligerman, Eric. 2007. *Sites of the Uncanny: Paul Celan, Specularity and the Visual Arts*. New York, NY, and Berlin: De Gruyter.

Lacoue-Labarthe, Philippe. 1998. *Poetry as Experience*. Trans. Andrea Tarnowski. Stanford CA: Stanford University Press 35–6.

Lyon, James K. 2006. *Paul Celan and Martin Heidegger; An Unresolved Conversation, 1951–70*. Baltimore, MA: John Hopkins University Press.

Macfarlane, Robert. 2012. *Old Ways: A Journey on Foot*. London, UK: Hamish Hamilton.

Magris, Claudio. 2001. *Danube*. London, UK: Harvill Press.

Maier-Katkin, Daniel. 2010. *Stranger from Abroad: Hannah Arendt, Martin Heidegger, Friendship and Forgiveness*. New York: W. W. Norton.

Mugerauer, Robert. 2008. *Heidegger and Homecoming: The Leitmotif in the Later Writings*. Toronto, Canada: University of Toronto Press.

Ott, Hugo. 1994. *Martin Heidegger: A Political Life*. Trans. A. Blunden. London, UK: Fontana.

Philips, James. 2005. *Heidegger's Volk: Between National Socialism and Poetry*. Stanford CA: University of Stanford Press.

Pöggeler, Otto. 1997. *The Paths of Heidegger's Life and Thought*. Trans. J. Bailiff. New Jersey: Humanities Press International.

Safrinski, R. 1999. *Martin Heidegger: Between Good and Evil*. Trans. E. Osers. Cambridge, MA: Harvard University Press.

Shama, Simon. 1996. *Landscape and Memory*. London, UK: Vintage.

Sharr, Adam. 2006. *Heidegger's Hut*. Cambridge, MA: MIT Press.

_____. 2007. *Heidegger for Architects*. London, UK: Routledge.

Sheehan, Thomas. ed. 2010. *Heidegger: The Man and the Thinker*. New Brunswick, NJ: Transaction.

Stewart, Kathleen. 2007. *Ordinary Affects*. Durham and London: Duke University Press.

Tilley, Christopher. 1997. *A Phenomenology of Landscape*. Oxford, UK: Berg.

Chapter Two

Spectral Cinema

Anamorphosis and the Haunted Landscapes of Aftermath *and* The Devil's Backbone

Matilda Mroz

This chapter traces the networks of haunting and spectrality in the cinematic spaces of two films, Polish director Władysław Pasikowski's *Aftermath* (2012) and the Spanish-Mexican production *The Devil's Backbone* (Guillermo del Toro 2001). Both films envision the re-emergence of a repressed past as a spectral return. In *Aftermath*, the spaces of a Polish village are haunted by traces of a violent episode, suppressed in the collective memory of the village, in which Catholic villagers burned alive their Jewish neighbours. The film's narrative is partially based on events that occurred in the village of Jedwabne in 1941, an incident that has been debated at length in Poland since it came to public awareness approximately in 2000.[1] In *The Devil's Backbone*, set during the Spanish Civil War, the ghost of a young boy stalks an isolated Spanish orphanage. Like the Jewish villagers of *Aftermath*, he has been secretly murdered and his body is un-mourned, hidden in the cistern in which he was drowned. Both films can be seen in the context of the 'memory boom' or 'memory events' that have preoccupied these (and other) countries in recent decades (Labanyi 2007, 95; Etkind et al. 2012, 10). In the Spanish context, *The Devil's Backbone*, as Keith McDonald and Roger Clark write, demonstrates 'the persistence of ghostly hauntological traces within the national psyche' concerning the legacy of the Civil War and the Franco dictatorship (2014, 136). In Poland, *Aftermath* is one of a series of works of visual culture that has responded to the growing need to address the country's Jewish past in ways that differ from the official narratives established under Communism (see also Lehrer and Waligórska 2013).

In *Spectres of Marx*, Jacques Derrida describes the project of speaking to ghosts, what he terms a 'being-with' the spectral, as bound up with a '*politics of memory, of inheritance, and of generations*' (2006, xviii). In its concern with delineating the formal and thematic aspects of what we might call a spectral cinema, this chapter will not focus explicitly on the films' political contexts, yet it is worth signalling the question of inheritance and transgenerational memory that Derrida's statement points to. Both *Aftermath* and *The Devil's Backbone* constitute attempts to grapple with, and re-shape, a politics of memory that has been inherited by generations that did not directly experience the traumatic events—the Civil War, World War II—at the films' core. In this sense, the films might be seen as engagements with 'post-memory', which, as Marianne Hirsch has argued, defines the modes of remembering 'of those who grow up dominated by narratives that preceded their birth' (1997, 22), or what Alexander Etkind et al. have termed 'remembering things that have not happened to us' (2012, 12), which are played out in the imaginative realm of poetics and art.

Both films, furthermore, are in part *about* transgenerational haunting and troubled inheritances. In *Aftermath*, two brothers discover that the land that they inherited from their father was taken from the village Jews following the massacre. The events that take place in *The Devil's Backbone* are filtered through the perspective of orphaned children, who seemingly have nothing to inherit from their parents apart from photographs, and who exist in a conflict created by their elders. Both films use the trope of haunting, as Jo Labanyi notes, in a way that 'elides direct representation of the past in favour of the representation of its aftereffects' in order to stress 'the legacy of the past to the present' (2007, 113). It is also at the point where Derrida is concerned with legacy and inheritance through the figure of the ghost that his writing intersects with the obsessions of the Gothic genre (Castricano 2001, 21), which del Toro draws on heavily in *The Devil's Backbone*.

In bringing *The Devil's Backbone* into dialogue with *Aftermath* my aim is not, however, to draw general conclusions about national or global cultural memory practices, but rather to sift through some of the aesthetic and conceptual configurations of spectrality in cinema. The cinematic invocation of the figure of the ghost is, I argue, only one of a series of images that form a network of spectral looking. This network extends between images that are not themselves necessarily 'ghostly', but which nevertheless *haunt*. In order to clarify the troubling nature of such haunting images, the chapter suggests that the nature of spectral looking can productively be read in conjunction with the concept of anamorphosis, which describes a point in an otherwise ordinary image that appears distorted unless seen from a particular angle, and particularly the theorization of anamorphosis for cinema by Slavoj Žižek and Vivian Sobchack. Despite their cultural and generic differences, the films under discussion productively crystallize the experience of being haunted as one fundamentally concerned with seeing, not-yet seeing and *being seen by*, something paradoxically material and immaterial, obtuse and significant. In both films, events have left indexical traces of themselves behind—imprints, footprints, photographs. As del Toro has stated in his commentary for *The Devil's Backbone* DVD, spaces can record and replay events again and again: 'this is a ghostly occurrence', he says, and 'it is playing just for you'.

SPECTRAL LOOKING AND ANAMORPHOSIS

Derrida's writing on haunting, as articulated in *Spectres of Marx* and other texts, has, as McDonald and Clark point out, 'gained considerable currency in the last few years as a theoretical tool in the reading of post-millennial culture' (2014, 114). Particularly striking for the analysis of works of visual culture is the theoretical delineation of connections between the spectre and the notion of visibility. In Avery Gordon's work, for example, haunting can be thought of as occurring 'when what's been in your blind spot comes into view ... spectres or ghosts appear when the trouble they represent and symptomize is no longer being contained or repressed or blocked from view' (2008, xvi). While such a statement emphasizes the becoming-visible of the spectral, Derrida's writing itself goes further in positing a network of spectral looking. In *Spectres of Marx*, the spectral is figured as a presence that *looks at* its addressees, before and beyond their awareness of this look. As Derrida writes, the spectre is 'this thing that looks at us, that concerns us' (2006, 5), but also more specifically a thing that looks at us, even when we don't see it:

> This Thing meanwhile looks at us and sees us not see it even when it is there ... this spectral *someone other looks at us*, we feel ourselves being looked at by it, outside of any synchrony, even before and beyond any look on our part. (6)

When the spectral appears in what was previously our 'blind spot', there is a discomfiting sense that it may be a witness of our initial blindness to it.

This configuration of visuality and blindness, the play of seeing and not seeing, can productively be thought in dialogue with the concept of anamorphosis. In relation to Hans Holbein's painting 'The Ambassadors', Jacques Lacan describes how an apparent stain that appears when the painting is looked at straight on becomes, when viewed obliquely, a death's head that irrupts onto the visual field, which makes visible 'the subject as annihilated' (1973, 88). Žižek adopts the concept of anamorphosis for the cinema in a way that can perhaps best be demonstrated by his analysis of a scene from Alfred Hitchcock's *Foreign Correspondent* (1940) in which the hero, searching for the kidnappers of a diplomat, finds himself in an idyllic Dutch countryside (Žižek 1991, 88). He becomes suddenly aware that one of the windmills is rotating in a different direction from all the others (after watching it with some consternation, he comes to the conclusion that the windmill is 'signal-ling' to a plane flying nearby). Žižek describes how

> a perfectly 'natural' and 'familiar' situation is denatured, becomes 'uncanny', loaded with horror and threatening possibilities, as soon as we add to it a small supplementary feature, a detail that 'does not belong', that sticks out, is 'out of place', does not make any sense within the frame of the idyllic scene. (88)

What has previously been perceived as ordinary, he continues, suddenly acquires an air of 'strangeness', where 'everything seems to contain some hidden meaning' (88). The 'horror' is not be 'placed *outside, next to*, the idyllic interior, but well *within* it, more precisely, *under* it, as its "repressed" underside' (89, original emphasis). It is this, Žižek continues, that may func-tion as the point of anamorphosis in a film; like the seemingly meaningless stain in 'The Ambassadors', the windmill renders the rest of the image 'sus-picious': 'The ground of the established, familiar signification opens up; we find ourselves in a realm of total ambiguity' (91). The point of anamorphosis undermines our position as neutral or objective observers, as though 'we' are already 'inscribed in the observed scene—in a way, it is the point from which the picture itself looks back at us' (91). As Adrian Kear has argued, citing Ned Lukacher, anamorphosis can be thought of as 'Lacan's figure for the way in which we "feel" seeing [...] as an invisible materiality', that is, as a sense of being looked at even when we do not see who looks at us, which evokes Derrida's construction of asymmetrical spectral looking' (1999, 181).

For Žižek and Lacan the point of anamorphosis, that which, phallus-like, 'sticks out' from the scene, is part of a broader understanding of the gaze in the libidinal economy and the psychoanalytic process. For the purposes of this chapter, however, I will risk theoretical irreverence to remain with the sense of conceiving anamorphosis for the way in which it informs the close reading of visual images that somehow 'look back' at their viewers. Sobchack's writing on anamorphosis in *Carnal Thoughts* also brackets much of this phallocentricity and is thus able to bring other aspects into relief that are more useful for thinking about the spectral. In this text, Sobchack draws on Holbein's stain to explore how the inanimate things in the films of Krzysztof Kieslowski seem to 'assert a signifying power and mysterious autonomy that emerge through the hyperbolic excess of ontic presence cre-ated by both the camera's close-up framing of them and its hyperempirical detailing of their material presentness' (2004, 91–2). Sobchack also relates this sense that the objects have an 'oddly autonomous and intimidating claim on our attention' to Lacan's 'epiphanic visual encounter' with a sardine can floating in the ocean, which seemed to look back at him, despite, of course, not possessing the sensory capacity to see him looking at it (92). In her gloss on this section of Lacan's text, Sobchack emphasizes that when an object seems to 'look back' at us, momentarily startling and perhaps intimidating us, it may encourage us to interpret it (as the windmill signals), but its ultimate significance and presence is fundamentally elusive; such objects and images may refuse 'human comprehension and reduction' (93). The stain, like the ghost, exceeds us, is 'before or beyond' us (Derrida 2006, 6). Sobchack, however, also critiques what she calls Lacan's 'limited—and negative—sense of subjective displacement and annihilation' (2004, 97). She argues that the sense of being thrown into a non-anthropocentric world that we cannot easily understand may also be liberating and expansive, prompting us to think in renewed ethical and political ways about what is outside of our vision.

Derrida, Lacan, Žižek and Sobchack might make for somewhat unlikely companions, and, as I have indicated, they have numerous differences. It might be reasonably objected, for example, that there is a distinct difference between a spectre that appears for, looks at and interacts with the characters, such as Santi in *The Devil's Backbone* or the spectre of Hamlet's father in Derrida's text, and images that cannot literally 'see' (a stain, a sardine can, a windmill) yet seem to somehow be addressing us. In this chapter, however, I want to create a crossroads where these concepts might converge, or might be made to look, as it were, at each other. In order to do so, the concept of anamorphosis must admittedly be asked to transgress some of its original theoretical boundaries, becoming as liminal as a spectre. I hope, however, that the conjunctions carried out here may better inform a close reading of the entanglements between different images that haunt the viewing process.

AFTERMATH'S BLIND SPOTS

Pasikowski's *Aftermath* was the first fiction feature film to draw heavily on the events at Jedwabne. It was also, however, marketed as a thriller, and despite its conjuring of a historical context, presents itself like a dark fairytale, taking place in an unnamed village and uncertain time (though a poster glimpsed in the opening scenes suggests it is 2001), complete with hauntings, secret burials, crumbling ruins and a mysterious wizened woman who dwells in the forest. The fact that the film's events and sub-plots do not 'add up', make logical sense or become fully intelligible seems a testament to its status as an explicit fabulation.

The opening minutes of *Aftermath* chart the return of Franek Kalina from Chicago to the village of his birth in Poland, to reunite with his brother, Józef. As soon as Franek treads the ground of the rural landscape, the film suggests that a presence is haunting the space. As Franek walks down a road next to the forest, he senses something in the trees, and moves amongst them to investigate. The scene cuts between frontal views of Franek, hand-held camera shots from within the trees which suggest a stalking and voyeuristic presence watching him and close-up shots of the back of Franek's head, which also suggest a presence hovering above him. Meanwhile, we can hear trees creaking unnaturally, snapping twigs and what seems to be whisperings or loud breathing, accompanied by a score of extended high-pitched notes. These visual and aural techniques draw on a long tradition of horror and thriller films to suggest that something, which appears to be weighty enough to draw breath and snap twigs, but which is also invisible, is watching Franek. This potentially spectral thing is both material and immaterial, what Derrida has called 'a certain phenomenal and carnal form of the spirit ... some "thing" that remains difficult to name' (2006, 5). Throughout the film, Franek and Józef are watched, intimidated and attacked as they attempt to discover what happened to the village's missing Jews, in ways that we might assume are connected to diegetic human agents. The opening images, however, introduce an unexplained haunting presence that lingers throughout the film, encouraging us to question: what haunts this seemingly innocent landscape?

If, as Gordon writes, haunting involves the becoming-visible of what was previously in your blind spot, then Józef plays an active part in making the repressed memory of Jewish presence present. It is notable that he himself cannot explain why he develops this 'unusual' interest in Jewish memory; in a different context, Etkind has described 'a black energy' that leaks out of traumatic archives to infect those who take on the responsibility of attempting to understand them (2009, 182). Józef initially seems seized by something similar. Prior to the film's beginning, he discovers that one of the roads in the village was paved with Jewish gravestones by the Germans during World War II, and subsequently allowed to remain there. Further, the flagstones around the village church also partly comprised old Jewish headstones. Trampled underfoot, they are no longer properly 'seen' by the residents. Józef begins to collect these grave markers and places them in his field, an action with great symbolic resonance: he creates a de facto Jewish cemetery, as well as planting the sacred slabs in the earth as though 'cultivating' memory. In doing so, however, he invokes the ire of the village. Franek is initially condemnatory of his efforts and expresses anti-Semitic views on several occasions, but eventually (and somewhat reluctantly) changes his perspective, and begins to *see differently*.

To explicate this perspectival change, it is necessary to return to the first rural scene. There is something else that stands out in this sequence, or, perhaps more accurately, initially fails to properly stand out to Franek. When he alights at the rural bus stop, a long shot shows that the side of the shelter has been covered with anti-Semitic graffiti. In white paint, the Star of David has been depicted hanging from a gallows, with the words 'Żydy won' ('Jews piss off') written above it. Neither Franek, nor the camera, pays any special attention to it; it is only towards the end of the film that Franek becomes visibly aware of its presence. Similarly to the scene in *Foreign Correspondent* described by Žižek, then, we are initially placed within a seemingly idyllic rural landscape. Picturesque visions of fields and forests have been framed by the train and bus windows during Franek's journey, a mobile framing for a medium of movement rather than the static frame of Holbein's painting. However, even before the events of the film unfold and we may realize what anti-Semitic graffiti 'means' in this context, we have here, figured in Franek's blind spot, something within the space that demands an address. The innocuous landscape suddenly seems infected by something threatening, and indeed will quite literally turn out to signal the ' "repressed" underside' (Žižek 1991, 89) of this village in the form of the buried Jewish villagers. The graffiti is thus a cinematic structuring of a blind spot within a field of vision, like the point of anamorphosis. Unlike in Hitchcock's film, however, it is the viewer, rather than the protagonist, who is likely to first notice the sign. It is we who are already being addressed and tested in this scene.

As the film continues, Franek becomes the driving force behind revealing the truth: it is his investigation in the land registry which reveals that the Poles now occupy former Jewish land and homes. It is Franek who interviews the village's eldest residents concerning their memories of the Jews, and he who suggests that they dig in the foundations of the old Kalina homestead. When they find the bones of the Jewish villagers, it is Franek who insists that they must make the public find, while Józef would prefer to re-bury the bones and forget all about it. By the end of the film, then, Franek has significantly shifted his position. It is such a movement in perspective that we can see as figurally correlating to the movement in physical position needed in front of 'The Ambassadors' in order to obtain the full anamorphic effect (though, as I will argue, literal spatial movements are also vital). This, then, is the significance of Franek's re-encountering of the graffiti near the film's end, when the secret of the murders has been revealed. His shift in perspective allows him to see the image, and, indeed, he attempts to destroy the graffiti with a few swift kicks.[2]

The network of spectral looking is extended when two further images seem to erupt from their diegetic context. These moments occur close together, when the Kalinas's field, and Józef's makeshift graveyard, is set alight. Despite the brothers' pleading, the fire department refuses to tend to it. As the brothers physically fight with the firemen, there is a cut to a mid-shot of the Jewish gravestones on fire. The dark night lends an abstract black background and the soundtrack a melancholic atmosphere as the camera moves to pick out the details of the gravestones engulfed in flames, then cuts to the middle section of another burning grave marker and finally cuts to a group of gravestones surrounded by fire, before tracking slowly closer to them. These shots are not anchored to a diegetic perspective—the following shot is of the brothers in a police car at dawn. Instead, the tombstones are picked out for the benefit of the viewer and seem to look back at us. The burning tombstones have, to use Sobchack's terms, both a material and signifying power (2004, 91). The images point to the German destruction of the Jews during the Holocaust in general, and the Polish crimes against Jews committed in this semi-fictional village in particular, as well as the devastation of Jewish memory and associated material objects such as gravestones. Inserted in the sequence in which the brothers are taken to the police station is another striking image: a burning barn, which has become iconic of the horrific events at Jedwabne. The image of the barn is also disconnected from diegetic perspectives, for while the brothers are within a moving vehicle, the shot itself is static, and held for several seconds. Emerging outwards from their diegetic context, then, these images on fire seem to address viewers directly, as we are invited to see not just a rural fire but an entire context of destruction.

SPECTRAL SPACE: PATHS AND DETOURS

In *Spectres of Marx*, Derrida places much emphasis upon the fact that 'the time is out of joint' in *Hamlet*, and instead a 'dislocated' time of the spectral is operating (2006, 23). The spatiality of Derrida's terms is striking. He writes:

> [T]he perversion of that which, out of joint, does not work well, does not walk straight, or goes askew ... can easily be seen to oppose itself as does the oblique, twisted, wrong and crooked to the good direction of that which goes, right, straight, to the spirit of that which orients or founds the law [*le droit*]—and sets off directly, without detour, toward the right address. (23)

Hamlet 'curses the fate that would have caused him to be born to set right a time that walks crooked' (23). In *Aftermath*, the Kalina brothers similarly find themselves attempting to set things right, and their grappling with the law is correspondingly convoluted. The film is careful to inform us that the land reforms following World War II retrospectively legalized the unofficial Polish takeover of Jewish property in the village, thus paving the way for an official forgetting of the initial crime of these property acquisitions through the murder of their inhabitants. Meanwhile, roads and yards were paved with the exemplars of Jewish memory. It is not coincidental that Józef initially gets in trouble with the law for destroying a road, while throughout the film, Franek is followed on the road and then forced off it by faceless thugs in a car. The villagers dominate these straight roads and legal institutions.

And yet, these two spaces (the 'old' road that Józef has dug up and the 'new' road that the villagers use) have significant differences. It is, in fact, generally the straight road (and the law) that we can associate with the repression of the 'truth', while the brothers are continually drawn off-road, to the space of the spectral. In the first four minutes of the film, we see a series of roads and tracks, from the airport runway to the highway, travelled on by Franek in an initial state of ignorance of what awaits him in the village. As I described earlier, his first action when he arrives in the rural landscape is to leave the road and penetrate the winding forest paths. The 'old' road that Józef has destroyed, which reveals its secret only when it is no longer usable as such, is initially accessed with some difficulty through a dense thicket. Once Józef has removed the gravestones from it, the road is imprinted with the indexical outlines of their former presence. The camera frequently tracks Franek through various dark passageways and corridors, which are often littered with obstacles; for example, he bumps awkwardly through an improbably dark and labyrinthine bar in search of his brother, as well as through an old tannery in the forest, where he discovers evidence of Nazi crimes against Poles, rather than Polish crimes against Jews. These obstructed passageways point symbolically to obfuscated pasts, as well as being literally the paths one needs to take in order to find the 'truth', including the detours that don't directly lead to it (e.g., the tannery).

Two particularly significant spaces in the film, the ruins of the old farmhouse and the ramshackle cemetery, share similar spatial characteristics. The characters enter Józef's cemetery through the forest, and its deconstructed arrangement is contrasted with the grid-like and well-tended Catholic cemetery where the brothers pay their respects to the graves of their parents. The old farmhouse, and site of the mass grave, can be accessed only through a densely forested and flooded area. Both sites are thus areas of potential memory that have become overgrown. Once again, this has material and figural dimensions: the spaces are literally difficult to access, and one must take oblique routes and paths to get there, while they are also nearly impassable in memory, for few will speak of them or the events they condense within themselves.

THE DEVIL'S BACKBONE: SPECTRAL DEVELOPMENTS

One can trace a similar network of spectral images and snaking spaces in *The Devil's Backbone*. Unlike *Aftermath*, however, the film features an 'actual' ghost (insofar as a spectre can be actual) and a much more explicit commentary on haunting. The paradoxes of preservation play a major role in this commentary, from the preservation of memory through photography, to the conservation of corpses in fluid. The film's spectre, the ghost of the orphan Santi, epitomizes what Derrida has called a 'paradoxical incorporation', both material and immaterial at once (2006, 5). He leaves indexical watery footprints and a trace of blood in the air where he has been; he is seen through reflections in window panes and shadows on walls, yet is also substantial enough to drag his murderer, the groundskeeper of the orphanage Jacinto, to his death in the cistern.

In discussing *The Devil's Backbone*, it seems wise to begin at the film's own beginning, which condenses so many of the narratorial, affective and theoretical points that the film will thenceforth unravel, and is thus worth describing at length. The film opens onto a space that appears to be the exterior of a building, while the camera moves smoothly forward into the depths of a doorway. A disembodied voice hovers over these images, asking,

> [W]hat is a ghost? A tragedy condemned to repeat itself time and again? An instant of pain, perhaps. Something dead which still seems to be alive. An emotion suspended in time. Like a blurred photograph. Like an insect trapped in amber.

Parallel to Derrida's conception of the ghost that sees us before we see it, this voice is already a spectral emanation, although we do not yet know it; it is only at the film's end that it 'reveals' itself to be the voice of Dr Casares, who dies in the course of the film.

Alongside the voice, the film unfolds a series of seemingly disconnected images. The hold of a plane, which replaces the opening images of the doorway, is seen opening and releasing a bomb, while offering a glimpse of a dark landscape from above. We then see a small boy lying on the ground, bleeding, while another covers his mouth in shock. A fluid transition dissolves this image into one of a bubbling amber liquid, through which we can soon see the dead body of the young boy sinking, and the second boy squatting above the pool in tears. Through further dissolves and superimpositions, which render the images immaterial and ephemeral, the image again modulates into amber liquid, but of a somehow more bright and viscous quality. In this liquid, we can distinguish the blurred images of child-like limbs, faces and strange, ridged spines. After the credits have rolled over this sequence, through a slow dissolve the amber liquid seems to seep into the subsequent establishing shot of the desert landscape, overflowing boundaries between one space and the next. These opening shots are initially unanchored to a narrative and haunt its development as the film progresses. We are encouraged to retrospectively assign meaning and significance to the images; the bomb, unexploded, is visible in the school's courtyard, and the anonymous bleeding child becomes Santi. The amber liquid that surrounds the bleeding boy is eventually given a specific location, the cistern within the orphanage, while the floating shapes in amber liquid become identifiable as the foetuses with a deformation of the spine known as the 'devil's backbone'. Like the stain of 'The Ambassadors', then, the images address us before we can properly interpret them.

The opening images also condense the film's concerns with various forms of preservational paradoxes, in which lives are captured or embalmed, and deaths persist into the present. The deformed foetuses are preserved in what Casares will call 'limbo water', a kind of perversion of a life-developing womb. In the opening sequence, these still objects seem to be animated through the digital imaging; they swirl in their sepia-coloured soup. The fluid editing and colour palette, encouraged by the spoken words referencing 'insects trapped in amber', links these miniature bodies to Santi's, and his suspension in the yellowish water of the cistern. This water seems to preserve him almost as completely as the jars preserve the small bodies. Santi floats in his own limbo water, in the spectral between-ness of animation and stillness, life and death.

The voice-over's association between the ghostly and the photographic particularly encourages us to think of preservation via the photographic index. Santi's ghost appears throughout the film as preserved at the very moment of his submersion in the cistern; a thin stream of blood undulates upwards from his head, as though he is still encased in water. The air around him appears viscous, and his white, mottled skin also suggests that we are seeing him underwater. The cistern water can be seen as a kind of developing fluid, as one might have, in the days before digitalization, submerged photographic paper in a chemical bath in order to reveal the image preserved within it. Santi, then, does indeed appear as a kind of 'blurred photograph', as the voice-over suggests, suspended in indeterminate matter, bringing to mind Mulvey's writing on photography's indexicality: 'the index, fixed as it is in the photograph, is a record of a fraction of time. When rays of light record an object's presence they also inscribe that moment of time, henceforth suspended' (2006, 56).

The association between embalming, ghostliness, preserving and the photographic index has been discussed at length following the work of, particularly, Andre Bazin and Roland Barthes. Bazin famously wrote that photography 'embalms time ... preserve[s] the object, enshrouded as it were in an instant, as the bodies of insects are preserved intact, out of the distant past, in amber' (2005, 14). For Mulvey Bazin's writing 'indicates the way in which [...] the photograph as index almost literally "haunts" the blurred boundary between life and death. He uses words and terms that evoke the ghostly' (2006, 64). As Mulvey notes, Bazin's writing moves continuously between the material (photography as indexical) and the immaterial (photographs as the return of the dead) (64–5). Although Barthes barely mentions Bazin in his meditation on photography, *Camera Lucida*, the latter's writing 'haunt[s] the margins' (Rabaté 1997, 9) of Barthes's work and his exploration of the photograph as the 'image that produces Death while trying to preserve life' (Barthes 2000, 92). When looking at a photograph of an assassin about to be executed, the time, for Barthes, is out of joint: 'I read at the same time: This will be and this has been' (96). In linking photography to haunting, Labanyi writes that photographs can function 'as *revenants* resuscitating the past in the present' (2007, 101). The recurrence of photographs as objects within the film also have, for Labanyi, a political significance: their dismissal by Jacinto in his search for gold signifies the way in which fascist capitalist modernity 'requires the destruction of the past' (102). It is, however, the photographs that have the last word: when Jacinto sinks into the cistern, the photographs that he was holding float to the surface: 'the photographic image is thus shown to function as an afterlife of the past, literally resurfacing in the present' (102).

GOTHIC GHOSTLINESS

As del Toro explains in the DVD director's commentary for *The Devil's Backbone*, Gothic literature, and particularly Horace Walpole's 2014 novel *The Castle of Otranto*, was a major influence on the film. Because the Gothic is concerned with how a repressed past intrudes into the present, it is well suited to exploring the effects of a traumatic history, where the 'repressed or abjected material returns in a terrifying guise and demands recognition' (Brinks 2004, 292). According to Ellen Brinks, the Gothic's interest in the supernatural and extreme psychological states is invoked by del Toro 'to interrogate what Spain psychologically and ideologically represses about the Civil War and its ongoing legacy' (293). Del Toro thus uses the Gothic in a manner that recalls *Aftermath*'s examination of the past snagging on the present.

We are encouraged by del Toro to read his film's configuration of liminal spatiality in particular as a key feature of his borrowing from the Gothic genre, where the film's exploration of 'secret' or forbidden spaces lies in parallel with the uncovering of a terrible existence behind what appears to be 'normal' everyday life. Beyond this attention to the Gothic, however, one can note a similarity to the spatial construction of *Aftermath* that leads back to the winding paths of Derrida's text. Similarly to *Aftermath*, the film's opening scenes (following the introductory montage described above) feature the main protagonist journeying along a straight road, in this case, through a vast arid landscape, and also arriving in a location that must be explored to reveal its secret. In both films, the straight roads initially followed will cede to labyrinthine paths. In *The Devil's Backbone*, as in *Aftermath*, the place of the spectral, the cavernous room with the cistern which is forbidden to the boys, diverges from the building's straight corridors. Intriguingly, the spectral spaces of both films are decidedly watery: flooded, swampy, rainy and 'seemingly unfathomable' (McDonald and Clark 2014, 138). In these spaces, the solidity of matter (earth, stone, concrete) begins to give way; a spatial fluidity is indicated which mirrors the boundary transgressions of the spectral.

Nestled within these liminal spaces are a set of objects that might be read as Sobchack's 'irrationally' autonomous images, which stir our interpretative desires while remaining largely 'obdurate and opaque' (2004, 93). Most obvious is the afore-mentioned bomb in the middle of the courtyard. Del Toro specifically links this bomb to the knight's helmet that falls in the middle of the courtyard in the opening of the *Castle of Otranto*, and which remains as a reminder of a terrible crime that took place in the past. For Brinks, similarly, the giant helmet is a 'supernatural manifestation of the "sins of the fathers coming to rest upon the sons"' (2004, 292). Although it has apparently been defused, the bomb seems alarmingly sentient; it whispers and ticks ('it knows we're here', Jaime says) and, when Carlos asks it where Santi is, one of its streamers breaks off and flies in the ghost's direction, 'pointing' to his location. Like Hitchcock's windmill, the bomb's presence seems to open up 'the abyss of the search for a meaning—nothing is what it seems to be, everything is to be interpreted, everything is supposed to possess some supplementary meaning' (Žižek 1991, 91). The bomb is loaded with metaphorical significance; as McDonald and Clark write, it 'carries a symbolic payload of trauma as a signifier of the memory of war that can never fully be "defused" or repressed' (2014, 141) (similarly, we never actually see the fire that burns the barn and tombstones in *Aftermath* in the process of being put out). The bomb's interpretive value seems to spiral into ever vaster networks of potential, though unestablished, signification; it is, as del Toro states, both a menace and a guard for the boys, symbolizing impending doom in the future as well as the crimes of the past. The bomb, like the photograph, is temporally out of joint.

As Brinks has written, recurrent 'quasi-hallucinogenic, non-narrative images' in *The Devil's Backbone*, such as the bomb, the cistern and the slugs, haunt the film and the viewer (2004, 293). These images are woven together to create what Gordon (drawing on Walter Benjamin) has termed a network of 'ghostly signals … flashing half-signs ordinarily overlooked until one day when they become animated' (2008, 204). The slugs in particular, as ubiquitous and shapeless as a stain, lend themselves to an interpretation concerned with anamorphosis. Shortly after Carlos's arrival at the orphanage, the film cuts from a dialogue scene between Carmen and Casares to a close-up shot of a slug, which Carlos is in the process of picking up and admiring as he stands close to the bomb. With great satisfaction, he puts it into the box he is carrying. Something distracts him: the ghost of Santi, standing in the door-way. The slug thus initially appears amongst two more obviously symbolic or spectral images, the bomb and the ghost, woven into a spectral network that viewers will not yet fully comprehend. The molluscs will appear again around the cistern when Carlos attempts to speak to the ghost, but it may only gradually occur to us that they feed off the slowly decomposing corpse of Santi. When another boy, holding the slug, asks 'what do they eat?', Santi's ghostly whisper is heard in response. Far from being the play-thing and col-lectible item that it seemed, the slug is thus suddenly seen as the harbinger of death, making us aware, to use Sobchack's words on Holbein's stain, 'of our depersonalisation on a field of visuality and meaning that immediately and infinitely exceeds us, but also makes us, through its sudden and dark excess, acutely aware of human *finitude* and *death*' (2004, 94).

THE END(S) OF HAUNTING

Haunting, while emerging from the past, is orientated towards the future, towards what Derrida has called a 'justice concerning those who *are not there*' (2006, xviii). For Gordon, it is this concern for future justice that demarcates haunting from trauma. While haunting, she argues, 'registers the harm inflicted or the loss sustained by a social violence done in the past or in the present' it is distinguishable from trauma in that it produces a 'something-to-be-done' (2008, xvi). The ghost represents a future possibility and 'it has designs on us such that we must reckon with it graciously, attempting to offer it a hospitable memory *out of a concern for justice*' (64). Similarly, Labanyi argues that in the genre of the ghost story, with its emphasis on transgenera-tional legacies, what one tends to inherit is an 'injustice requiring reparation' (2007, 113).

   By way of conclusion, one might then question what kinds of futures are posited by *Aftermath* and *The Devil's Backbone*: what has been cultivated from the gravestones planted in the earth?; what has been developed in the limbo water of the cistern? The Kalina brothers' travels along winding paths and detours, which eventually lead them to the truth buried at the heart of their ancestral home, also allow Franek to attempt to make some kind of reparation, for in the last images of the film, we can see that Józef's make-shift cemetery has been cleaned up and made 'official' as mourners say Kaddish over the graves. Shining buses bring visitors to the site as the straight roads of the village are re-appropriated. This result has, however, required a sacrifice—Józef, who wanted to back out of revealing his father's crime, is literally crucified on the barn door by unknown agents. The end of the film, however, suggests that the haunting has been terminated: in *Aftermath*, then, the ghosts of the past are invoked in order to be sent away again. As Colin Davis has written, once the 'disturbance' caused by a haunting has been rectified, 'once our symbolic debt has been duly paid, the domains of the living and the dead can be kept decently separate again' (2007, 2).

In *The Devil's Backbone*, the orphans also emerge from the dark labyrinthine corridors of the orphanage onto the straight road through the desert. Santi is avenged by the death of Jacinto. The haunting, however, is far from terminated, for a new ghost takes Santi's place. Casares, who has died during the fighting with Jacinto's band, is seen standing at the doorway of the orphanage as the children walk away. In what might be seen (or heard) as a kind of aural anamorphosis, the monologue from the film's opening is replayed, but the images have changed; we see, for example, Santi hovering above the cistern, the photographs from the safe floating on top of the water, and the children leaving the orphanage. The film offers us a kind of conclusion to its opening gambit 'what is a ghost?' as Casares concludes that 'a ghost. Is what I am.' However, despite this suggestion of finality, the film projects an uncertain future: the boys strike out into the unknown, while the haunting seems to be cyclical. The film doesn't quite 'conclude' in the way that *Aftermath* somewhat self-satisfactorily does.

When Derrida calls on us to attend to the spectres of deceased others, this is not necessarily so that they can deliver a specific message, but rather that this attendance 'may open us up to the experience of … an essential unknowing which underlies and may undermine what we think we know' (Davis 2007, 11). The Derridean encounter with the spectral, like the encounter with Holbein's stain or Lacan's sardine, can 'rupture the surface cohesion of the quotidian world' (Sobchack 2004, 87). This undermining or rupture should, however, be seen as a continual process. For Davis and Derrida, our ethical obligation to the deceased entails a refusal to 'terminate the process of grieving' (Davis 2007, 148). It seems clear that *Aftermath* envisions an end to haunting, while *The Devil's Backbone* does not, *diegetically*. Yet, in the broader context of a visual culture that is obsessed with memory and the unearthing of previously occluded pasts and narratives, both works take their place in a spectral network of cultural products in which haunted, and haunting, images interminably circulate.

NOTES

1. This awareness was primarily precipitated by the publication of Professor Jan Gross's research on Jedwabne in Poland in 2000 as *Sasiedzi: Historia zagłady żydowskiego miasteczka*, Sejny: Fundacja Pogranicze, and in an English-language version in 2001 as *Neighbours: The Destruction of the Jewish Community in Jedwabne, Poland*. Princeton: Princeton University Press.

2. The Kalina brothers have previously been targeted by anti-Semitic graffiti, though they are not themselves Jewish; it may be that Franek sees the hanged Star of David as specifically addressing him, although it has pre-existed his arrival.

BIBLIOGRAPHY

Aftermath/Poklosie. 2012. Dir. Wladyslaw Pasikowski. Poland: Apple Film Productions.

Barthes, Roland. 2000. *Camera Lucida*. London: Vintage Books.

Bazin, Andre. 2005. *What Is Cinema?* Vol. 1. Berkeley, Los Angeles and London: University of California Press.

Brinks, Ellen. 2004. ' "Nobody's Children": Gothic Representation and Traumatic History in the Devil's Backbone.' *JAC*, 24: 291–312.

Castricano, Jodey. 2001. *Cryptomimesis: The Gothic and Jacques Derrida's Ghost Writing*. Montreal and Kingston: McGill-Queen's University Press.

Davis, Colin. 2007. *Haunted Subjects: Deconstruction, Psychoanalysis and the Return of the Dead*. Basingstoke: Palgrave Macmillan.

Derrida, Jacques. 2006. *Spectres of Marx: The State of the Debt, the Work of Mourning and the New International*. New York and London: Routledge.

The Devil's Backbone/El Espinazo del Diablo. 2001. Dir. Guillermo del Toro. Spain/ Mexico: El Deseo, Tequila Gang.

Etkind, Alexander. 2009. 'PostSoviet Hauntology: Cultural Memory of the Soviet Terror.' *Constellations*, 16(1): 182–200.

Etkind, Alexander, Rory Finnin, Uilleam Blacker, Julie Fedor, Simon Lewis, Maria Mälksoo and Matilda Mroz. 2012. *Remembering Katyn*. Cambridge, UK: Polity Press.

Foreign Correspondent. 1940. Dir. Alfred Hitchcock. USA: Walter Wanger Productions.

Gordon, Avery. 2008. *Ghostly Matters: Haunting and the Sociological Imagination*. Minneapolis and London: University of Minnesota Press.

Hirsch, Marianne. 1997. *Family Frames: Photography, Narrative and Postmemory*. Cambridge, MA: Harvard University Press.

Kear, Adrian. 1999. 'Diana between Two Deaths: Spectral Ethics and the Time of Mourning.' *Mourning Diana: Nation, Culture and the Performance of Grief*. Ed. Adrian Kear and Deborah Lynn Steinberg. New York: Routledge. 169–86.

Labanyi, Jo. 2007. 'Memory and Modernity in Democratic Spain: The Difficulty of Coming to Terms with the Spanish Civil War.' *Poetics Today*, 28 (1): 89–116.

Lacan, Jacques. 1973. *The Four Fundamental Concepts of Psycho-Analysis*. London and New York: Karnac.

Lehrer, Erica and Magdalena Waligórska. 2013. 'Cur(at)ing History: New Genre Art Interventions and the Polish-Jewish Past.' *East European Politics and Societies and Cultures*, 27: 510–44.

McDonald, Keith and Roger Clark. 2014. *Guillermo del Toro: Film as Alchemic Art*. New York and London: Bloomsbury.

Mulvey, Laura. 2006. *Death 24x a Second: Stillness and the Moving Image.* London: Reaktion Books.

Rabaté, Jean-Michel. 1997. 'Introduction.' *Writing the Image after Roland Barthes.* Ed. Jean-Michel Rabaté. Philadelphia: University of Pennsylvania Press. 1–16.

Sobchack, Vivian. 2004. *Carnal Thoughts: Embodiment and Moving Image Culture.* Berkeley, Los Angeles and London: University of California Press.

Walpole, Horace. 2014. *The Castle of Otranto.* 3rd Revised Edition. Oxford: Oxford University Press.

Žižek, Slavoj. 1991. *Looking Awry: An Introduction to Jacques Lacan through Popular Culture.* Cambridge and London: MIT Press.

Chapter Three

Witching Welcome

Haunting and Post-Imperial Landscape in Hilary Mantel and Helen Oyeyemi

Ryan Trimm

British fiction's post-war experience of place is framed by a post-imperial hangover. As demographics shifted, as collisions of the 'over there' and the 'here' became increasingly visible, a host of novels explored these issues through interrelated tropes: migrant communities, a remapped suburbia, hospitality, echoes of Empire, a reframed country house novel. Both in town and country, Britain appears haunted by spectres of Empire, by the way internal spaces are beset by traces of the past marked by violence and legacies of the imperial elsewhere. This absent present materializes as a spectre, a ghostly image haunting the present. However, such spirits are not the traditional ghouls who linger as legacies of a painful past that once transpired at a particular place. In such a model, some places have a meaningful past, one still marking the lay of the land as a never-fully departed presence; these places then stand out (as an aestheticized landscape or heritage site) and are contrasted with sites unmarked. Rather, these post-imperial spectres suppose no such distinctions, for all spaces are haunted, even those seemingly unmarked by the upheavals of the past. This essay examines Hilary Mantel's 2005 novel *Beyond Black* and Helen Oyeyemi's 2009 *White Is for Witching*, novels foregrounding ghosts whose impact on the present surprises and disrupts, hauntings signaling a post-imperial problem of place. In these novels, spectres are not so much bound to particular isolated places but are rather summoned by sites networked by history and migration.

Topography reflects the aesthetic—and political—desires of those who gaze upon it: Benedict Anderson finds specific landscape features help construct a national imagined community, offering 'a sociological landscape of a fixity that fuses the world inside the novel with the world outside', a realm composed of similar spaces: villages, hospitals, prisons, churches, schools (1991, 30). This catalogue of distinctive yet comparable spaces characterize the nation, providing an itinerary of shared places standing as a collective backdrop linking citizens together. Pheng Cheah transforms this argument by emphasizing the spiritual side of national identity: as he traces through figures like J. G. Fichte, identification with nationness offers a transcendence of our too evident mortality. Nationness offers an identity persisting after death and preceding birth, a non-divine temporal transcendence helping locate and situate our too brief lives. This living on grants is something spectral to the nation, a spirit sustained beyond the mortal frames that carry it. This spiritual dimension animates the material manifestations of the nation: 'The territorial state and its institutions are an external mechanism of national culture that should be subsumed by the nation, infused with its vital spirit, and made to serve its work' (Cheah 2003, 130). Through this infusion, even the land and the built environment themselves become expressive of national character and vehicles through which the national spirit manifests. Landscape is thus as much ideational as topographical; as Christine Berberich, Neil Campbell, and Robert Hudson suggest, landscape is 'inherently *dialogical*, "shuttling" between material and immaterial, perception and presence, human and non-human, as spatial heterogeneity, mixing, crossing-over, contradicting; always processive—and always unfinished' (2012b, 20). Similarly, Kirby Farrell suggests 'landscape is a form of psychic topography' (118). Landscape's ambivalent existence renders it uncertain, a chthonic thing conjuring an immaterial identity or an ideational appeal invoking a plot of earth. This double existence renders it a spectral presence: a sensation suggesting something beyond what meets the eye. This forcible intersection of actual and that which is affectual or conceptualized renders topography an 'affective landscape' (Berberich, Campbell & Hudson 2012a, 9). As such, landscape moves from 'a noun to a verb' and becomes not 'an object to be seen or a text to be read, but as a process by which social and subjective identities are formed' (Mitchell 2002, 1). Or, in Edward Casey's terminology, landscape must be seen as 'an *event*, a happening not only in space but in time and history as well' (2009, xxv). In sum, as Casey maintains, landscape exemplifies the fact 'places not only are, they happen' (2000, 330). As such, particular places take on a narrative resonance and come to signify events or peoples no longer present.

Here the spectral quality of landscape, one bringing the past into the present, manifests in terms of this uncertain quality of landscape blending the material and the immaterial. As such, landscape destabilizes time. Indeed, Julian Wolfreys foregrounds temporal disturbance as what is ultimately unsettling about spectres: they cite a previous moment, an allusion colliding past and present into uncertain relations, 'undermin[ing] the articulation of the present moment, especially in the resonance of the present tense of the citation, which is clearly the return of another "present", though never the present as such. All presence, all presentation, of the present is internally disturbed' (2002a, n.p.). Ghosts disrupt presence, for they trouble time—and space—appearing where they are seemingly absent, forging connections between non-contiguous times and sites. Indeed, '[t]he spectral is ... a matter of recognizing what is disorderly within an apparently straightforward temporal framework' (2002b, 5).[1]

This emphasis on the disruption of purportedly unified national time and space became increasingly resonant as Britain increasingly moved towards multiculturalism, landscape revealing shifting boundary lines of nationness. Conservative figures such as Margaret Thatcher, as Philip Dodd remarks, often trade on recounting Britishness distinctiveness through a contrast of places:

> Britain was a special place, beset now as of old, by enemies within and without, but possessed of a destiny that could never be thwarted. ... Mrs Thatcher's Britishness depended rather on a sustained process of *purification* and *exclusion*. In her British story, enemies were here, there and everywhere. Britishness was singular, not plural and it was enough to be one of 'them' by not being 'one of us'. (1995, 26–7, original emphasis)

The here stressed a singular Britishness, the elsewhere anything evocative of difference, a realm (potentially) threatening British purity. This contrast also developed a temporal tension: the past with its lost racial and cultural purity, the present begrudgingly acknowledged as multicultural. However, as Rashi Naidoo points out,

> The 'white past/multicultural present' binary in the historical understanding of Britain is a fallacy that wipes from public consciousness the fact of a long-standing non-white presence on the islands dating from Roman times, the view of a Britain fundamentally and irrevocably shaped by its relations with other countries, as well as obscuring an understanding of Britishness itself as a historically unstable and contested national identity. (2005, 42)

This misconstrual still has much purchase and forms a subtext for many cultural representations of Englishness: the essence of the nation in its mostly white identity can be located in the past while only in the present can a diverse Britain be found. Consequently, the 2000 Parekh Commission on the Future of Multi-Ethnic Britain identified 'reimagining Britain's past story and present identity' as a primary goal for the nation (105). Landscape then presents an opportunity for re-conjuring that past, for finding historical resonances even in sites apparently unmarked.

Accordingly, both Mantel's *Beyond Black* and Oyeyemi's *White Is for Witching* reframe the national past and ideas of *genius loci* 'spirit of the place' through their presentation of haunted landscapes. This spectrality evokes not only continuity but also death and change, alterations both past and present, shifts in the nation such as demographic transformations through immigration. Both novels conjure place and home as beset with lingering resonances of the national past literally haunting the present, one making habitation an anxious thing. Mantel's novel follows Alison Hart, a medium with a troubled past, as she pursues her profession, begins a business and personal friendship with her new assistant and undertakes to purchase a new house, all against the backdrop of outer London suburbs of the years around and following Princess Diana's death. The novel takes spirits and ghosts quite literally, though often in a comic vein—the spectres Alison encounters are real and usually disappointingly prosaic in their concerns, even in their greed and quest for revenge. Oyeyemi's novel centres on Miranda Silver, a young woman living in a Dover bed-and-breakfast owned by her family. As she applies for and begins study at Cambridge, she experiences mental breakdown and an ongoing battle with eating issues, most especially pica, the ingestion of non-food items such as chalk or plastic. In the novel's fairy-tale-inflected mode, it is the spirit of the house who afflicts Miranda, a spectre who compoundly manifests as Miranda's mother, grandmother and great-grandmother. These novels interrogate how the purported hospitality of the historic environment collides with lingering imperial and national spectres, betraying the past as a varied and inescapable ghost haunting people rather than places, and manifesting the imperial after-image as less than a welcoming presence.

SPECTRAL SUBURBIA IN *BEYOND BLACK*

Mantel's novel begins with an epigraph attributed to Queen Elizabeth II: 'There are powers at work in this country about which we have no knowledge.' However, rather than malign and clandestine human forces (whether Rupert Murdoch's journalists, Scotland Yard or the NSA), the novel uncovers a realm of spirits investing the nation. *Beyond Black* encounters spectres by focalizing around its main character Alison Hart. Alison calls herself a 'sensitive': 'a person [who i]s attuned to spirit' (35). Rather than an occult or Gothic encounter, the engagement with spirits is droll: her familiar spirit, Morris, is rudely impish and base; Alison is beset with banal concerns such as how psychics register VAT or work with a non-sensitive assistant; the dead are worried about quotidian issues such as acquiring stairlifts and kitchen units. In sum, the novel offers a pervasive deflation of death and the spiritual as elevated realms. *Beyond Black*'s dark turn involves not hellish figures (though Old Nick appears as a 'family man' dispensing diplomas for Human Resources [444]) but rather grim memories of violence and molestation from Alison's past.

Significantly, the novel is set not in a historic city or country house but in the suburban and exurban landscape ringing the London orbital. *Beyond Black* opens on the M25, a world decidedly not picturesque: 'the motorway, its wastes looping London. ... Colour has run out from the land. Only form is left' (1–2). This realm is one of waste and wasteground, refuse and relentless uniformity. This suburban sameness forms the backdrop for most of the novel, a world apparently stripped of anything historical that might generate lingering spirits or an environment resonant enough to compose a 'historic environment'. These orbital towns are places where 'nobody has roots here; and maybe they don't want to acknowledge roots' (17); consequently, residents do not know the names of their own grandparents, a not 'uncommon' experience as 'family memory [is] so short, in these towns where nobody comes from, these south-eastern towns with their floating populations and their car parks where the centre should be' (16–17). Mantel notes in a short postscript (in the novel's Harper Perennial edition) she herself witnessed at a psychic show as an audience member who did not know the names of her grandparents, an experience 'that drove the book. The thing that frightens me most is confiscation of history. If you don't own the past, and can't speak up for it, your past can be stolen and falsified, it can be changed behind you. I am interested in the way people remember, and just as interested— since that night—in the way they won't remember' (Mantel 2005, 13). Accordingly, the novel's towns lack true organization or distinctiveness, becoming indistinguishable from one another, a similarity rendering them forgettable, a problem with memory extending to residents not even knowing their own ancestors who strive to make contact. This blighted landscape appears cursed not by spectres of the past, some ancient malediction or spirit, but thorough-going conformity and forgetfulness, a placelessness seemingly spurring the refuse littering its anonymity. Such sites offer Alison not *lieux des memoires* but spots where you felt 'seventeen again, and had chances in life' (29). In apparently lacking a history (not even a full life history), in not properly possessing a narrative, these towns signal regression, an erasure of events populating a life and narrative. The past is forgotten, disconnected from the present, a divorce necessitating a medium that can summon the spirit of the bygone.

Obviously, this apparent pastlessness supports the novel's comic thrust: how could there be a ghost story in suburbia, in housing developments whose entire point is their newness and lack of past?[2] Indeed, when Alison's success means she can purchase a home for herself, her criteria is strictly modern: she wants 'Somewhere new. A house that nobody's lived in before' (199); in fact, Alison 'hates history' (41). Such flight to newness stems from attempts to outrun her own ghosts: pursued by 'low spirits', impish and malicious characters from her past who haunt her, Alison relishes moving to the new housing development's open fields, where the suburban infrastructural grid must be imagined for it to even be drawn on the map (221). Such placelessness is inhospitable to the fiends plaguing her. In short, she chooses what is seemingly the most unhistoric and unspiritual of spots. However, suburbia, rather than being a new place, one permitting escape from the past, in fact becomes yet another site where such histories catch up.

Alison's escape does not last long. The newly built development is quickly subjected to rumors of far-fetched hauntings: tales of past underground atomic tests spurring knotweed, white worms, rabbit deaths, black slime and radiation, all of which are alleged to beset the neighborhood, spectres bedeviling house prices (251–2, 311, 319). These suburban legends, though, betray the destruction wrought for the construction of the development, a rending of earth destroying flora and fauna alike. Visiting the site on a weekend, looking at poised bulldozers, Alison finds:

> Violence hung in the air, like the smell of explosive. Birds had flown. Foxes had abandoned their lairs. The bones of mice and voles were mulched into mud, and she sensed the minute snapping of frail necks and the grinding into paste of muscle and fur. Through the soles of her shoes she felt gashed worms, turning, twisting. ... She looked up, to the grassland that remained. (218)

Even the fresh suburban landscape seemingly completely divorced from the past is not immune to the hauntings of time, intimations of tragic moments lingering and besetting the present, past failures and violence lurking underground, awaiting their moment to erupt and break up the smooth surface of the present, just as the development witnesses its new asphalt systematically fractured and roiled up (341). Suburban sameness is not an escape from the past; the ring communities might have lost their memories but they are not without history, are not disconnected from a violent past. In being connected to this destruction, they are 'indifferent place[s]; no better nor worse than most others' (218).

With no place free from past legacies, spirits seem everywhere. This spectral ubiquity entails the dead outnumber the living, for there are 'thirty-three airside, for every one [living] earthside', a numerical discrepancy spurring Colette's wry thought she is 'backing the dead' (180). This teeming of the passed materializes in Alison's massive form, the dead packed within her (80). Such numbers mean Alison is constantly beset by hordes of airsiders, masses who leave traces of themselves behind (153) and compromise all manner of recording devices she utilizes (video and audio tape, even pen and paper).[3] The medium is continually confronted by the presence of those passed: 'A loud humming began inside Al's head; it was the brush of skin as a thousand dead people twiddled their thumbs' (363). She wants Colette's

company in part because spirits of the dead insist on occupying the unoc-
cupied passenger seat when Alison drives by herself (91). This inescapability
of the past links Alison's new house with the past she wished to escape: the
novel's turning point transpires after her new prefabricated garden shed is
delivered, one possessed even at the hardware store: 'Bugger, she thought, a
haunted shed' (276); moreover, her Old Smoky is not the only haunted structure at the store (278). This shed becomes the site where Alison's fiendish
spirits from the past reconvene to enact violence, producing a forced suicide
and more conventional hauntings. Moreover, the shed's spectre, Mart, is
posed uneasily between ghost and live homeless man, and haunts the shed as
a spirit even before he kills himself.[4] In essence, he himself is a prefabricated
ghost. The pervasiveness of those passed, a presence extending even to the
brand-new, to that without history, signifies all environments have a history,
are bound to a past scored with violence and misery.

Despite their ubiquity, the dead are certainly not all the same, for cultural
and ethnic differences persist. Alison maintains ethnicity stands as a barrier
for her mediumship: 'It wasn't just the language barrier ... but these people,
those races, who think they have more than one life. Which means, of course,
more than one family' (150). Such multiplicity means Alison is unable to
locate their time and place of origin, would not be able to smoothly connect
interlocutive spirit and clients jostling to receive messages from those passed
over. However, this apparent racial bar, this stress on unified origins, is
undone by forceful hauntings from the imperial past; these spectral intrusions
give the lie to the idea of singular and strictly domestic pasts. Even the ghosts
communicating with Alison's punters hail from elsewhere, for the suburban
towns are places where 'nobody has roots here; and maybe they don't want
to acknowledge roots, or recall their grimy places of origin and their illiter-
ate foremothers up north' (17).[5] These elsewheres, both British and imperial,
are the spectres besetting the bedroom communities. Most particularly, given
Alison's childhood in Aldershot, a youth marked by violence from soldiers,
the legacy of Empire is never far away. The fiends are marked by tattoos they
received in Egypt and the Far East (165, 385); they target those who are *sans
papier* for confidence schemes and violence (386, 392); Alison is afflicted
by an unbidden memory of an Irish paramilitary who was tortured to death
(182, 185, 189); she is the medium for an Iraqi grandmother (403). Even
the Admiral Drive housing development Alison moves into is a subdivision
where all house types are named after British naval heroes (and constructed
by the Galleon company [216]). Though Alison might have difficulty linking herself with such legacies, they nonetheless haunt her and their voices
manifest themselves upon her unbidden. The apparently bland, unremarkable
and unhistoric suburban landscape betrays the ongoing legacies of violence
haunting the present, an imperial historicity besetting green suburbia.

Given the manner spirits beset suburbia and the way they trail Alison
even to freshly fabricated habitations, *Beyond Black* re-envisions haunting
not solely as traces of the past lingering around milieu scored by history but
rather as that past trailing the living, continually intruding upon their lives
despite attempts to inhabit a world of anodyne newness. If the historic environment was to have charted a world where all have equal claim to the pasts
of the neighborhoods in which they dwell, haunting in *Beyond Black* reveals
this impulse to be naïve: the pasts haunting an environment include the historical contexts for all who reside. Moreover, ignorance of these pasts, claims
of disconnection and even physical flight provide no relief: ghosts come for
those who do not know their past, for those who claim to be divided by race
or culture from violent eruptions and for those who flee their family origins.
Alison, rather than the environment, becomes the focal point of these haunting: the dead swarm around and in her (347, 363), a past distracting through
the endless 'chatting inside her' (391). She experiences these departed voices
as an 'infliction' (258), a forcible imposition of spirits breaking in upon her
'like a burglar' (372), an 'entourage' trailing her like 'baggage' (155). It is
Alison who is haunted by the past rather than spirits and historical residue
accruing around particular environments. This teeming past is not just the
eruption of completed lives and history into Alison's present but also stems
from conflicted stories and memories of Alison's origins, a confused upbringing, complete with name change (112), providing the medium with 'previous identities' and 'past lives' (112, 338). This past is one the medium must
confront, an assault back into the past itself: 'I'll have to go back by myself,
back to Aldershot ... back to the swampish waters of the womb, and maybe
back before that: back to where there is no Alison, only a space where Alison
will be' (417). Her struggle with the past positions her history as separate
from her, a division of past and present manifesting as a fragmented self for
Alison's regressing movement jumps back before she was born, envisioning
herself from outside and from antecedent moments. Rather than place serving
as a historic palimpsest, the different pasts in relation with the present, it is
Alison herself who is haunted by the past, the environment serving merely as
screen upon which these fragments might be projected. Rather than offering
a communal neighborhood all present denizens might share, the environment
manifests the fissures of the present.

THE HAUNTED HABITATION OF
WHITE IS FOR WITCHING

White Is for Witching gives voice to the historic environment through the
Silver House, a structure whose speech reveals it to be a menacing ghost.

Oyeyemi suggests this link between the spectral and the built environment is fitting, for 'habitation is in itself a form of haunting' (2012). Dwelling sites an entity with a spiritual dimension in an edifice or territory imagined as purely material, a formulation entailing the very notion of historic environment suggests a ghost story: the narrative of the past conjured through the material landscape or built environment. The house itself views habitation as a problem, one leading to its own malevolence—or, better, its violent, misdirected protectionism: 'Why do people go to these places, these places that are not for them?' (8). Place and populace are organically linked for the house: the English should not go abroad; those born overseas should not come to England. Consequently, the Silver House takes it upon itself to enforce these lines of division, acting to drive away foreigners and those it perceives as strangers. Not surprisingly, the house appears from the outside almost as a defensive fortification, a 'castle' (15): it towers above the road (15), with 'windows [that] didn't look as if they could be opened' (14) and a protective hedge serving as battlement (15). The structure appears anything but welcoming, functioning rather as a citadel in Dover, the 'key' to England, warding off those who would enter the country. In sum, the house has taken upon itself a task of preserving some projected and imagined past, a historic environment turned monstrously against those in the present who would take shelter there.

The house offers a more benign face, at least initially, for those whom it feels belong to it. For the Silvers, their house presents itself as their own background environment, their *umwelt*: 'I am here, reading with you. I am reading this over your shoulder. I make your home home, I'm the Braille on your newspaper that only your fingers can read—I tell you where you are. Don't turn to look at me. I am only tangible when you don't look' (68). This sense of security is not something developing instantaneously but must accrue over time, as one becomes habituated in the home. The house's status as background depends on this accumulation of time, the sedimentation of years rendering an environment or structure a home, something one can no longer fully see anymore. However, the house proves to be less than hospitable for any foreign-born guest or resident. Even with Miranda's father, the French-born Luc Dufresne, the house retains a sense of mischievous distance: 'because he is not mine I don't care about him. I do, however, take great delight in the power of a push, a false burst of light at the bottom of a cliff, just one little encouragement to the end. Sometimes it seems too easy to toy with him' (13). The house attempts to push Luc toward suicide shortly after Lily's death, but does so half-heartedly, without a stake in Luc's life, for he is outside that to which the house feels a sense of belonging.

The house, though, worries Lily's (Luc's wife and the heir to the structure) death means Luc 'got even more control of the house. Lily's dying meant he didn't have to ask anyone about anything' (18). This power upsets the house, as Luc is devoted to the arts of hospitality, of welcoming guests and outsiders: cooking, writing restaurant reviews and cookbooks, and—of most concern for the Silver House—converting the house into a bed-and-breakfast (14). The house's distress with Luc stems from his welcoming strangers: 'It's Luc that keeps letting people in. To keep himself company ... because he knows he is not welcome (if he doesn't know this he is very stupid). They shouldn't be allowed in though, those others, so eventually I make them leave' (110). The house 29 Barton Road reacts to Luc not only because he is foreign and not of the Silver line, but even more because he insistently welcomes outsiders the house feels are unacceptable: the Kurdish housekeeping family, the Nigerian Sade, various guests whose nationality (American) or skin colour (black) mean they are outsiders in the home, and finally Ore, a girl born to a Nigerian immigrant. The house might tolerate Luc but these other guests must be driven out by all manner of tricks: entrapping them in hidden levels, confining them to their rooms, making ominous noises, playing tricks with 'all season apples' (217), a magical and poisonous fruit akin to the bewitched apples offered to Snow White.

Rather than the occupants claiming a historic environment, the Silver House insists on control over those who enter it, as well as those whom the house holds to be its own: the Silvers, most particularly Miranda. However, these claims by the house depend on a tyrannical expunging of previous histories and identities, for 29 Barton Road threatens to erase previous memories elsewhere: though Miranda's family had begun in London, living there until her great-grandmother Anna Good's death, after a few years, Miranda tells herself 'they had never lived in London, they had always lived in her GrandAnna's house' (121). The house is particularly controlling with Miranda, calling her 'my Miranda' (178) and becoming mortally offended when she confesses her love for Ore: 'We saw who she meant. The squashed nose, the pillow lips. ... The skin. The skin' (179). The house cannot and will not accept the racial difference figured in Miranda's girlfriend, using a language of pollution and impurity reminiscent of Enoch Powell: 'Disgusting ... When clear water moves unseen a taint creeps into it. ... It becomes foul, undrinkable. ... I would save Miranda even if I had to break her' (180). Indeed, the house proclaims in the novel's first section that the girl 'has *wronged* me/ I will not allow her to live' (4). Here the environment endeavors to dictate a sense of self, a controlling past threatening to imprison the present.

For the house, this controlling drive derives from Anna Good, Miranda's GrandAnna, who serves as origin for the house's spirit: Anna is 'a mother of mine, you gave me a kind of life, mine, the kind of alive that I am' (22). From this 'birth', Anna, the 'Goodlady', becomes the personification of the house's haunting and protectively xenophobic spirit; however, she only arrived in

1938 after her marriage to Andrew Silver. Her original connection to the house is by no means native: '*The house is Andrew's*, she told herself; *I have no part in it*' (21). However, her outlook had long been patriotic, focusing on traditional symbols and purity. Anna embodies British national identity: during a school programme, 'she'd been picked to wear a bronze-coloured helmet and a white gown and a blue sash and sit at the top of a chariot. ... She was Britannia. ... Britannia had to have pluck' (107). Anna Good incarnates Britishness, a martial sense of national identity complete with helmet, shield and home front spirit. Because of this past, she has little patience with those questioning or complicating purported national virtues: 'Anna never thought she would have a granddaughter who didn't know what Britannia meant; Lily said that patriotism was embarrassing and dangerous. *Who gave you your mind?* ... How had Britannia become embarrassing and dangerous? It was the incomers. They had twisted it so that everything they were not part of was bad' (107). Anna is unapologetic in her traditional and straightforward patriotism, regarding any complexity or shading with suspicion, as the work of strangers who, to her mind, only weaken and undermine the nation. Anna and her attitudes embody what the house comes to associate itself with. Her attitudes, particularly her stance towards outsiders (109), becomes the 'duty' of 29 Barton Road. Anna—and through her, the Silver House—incarnates a retrograde jingoism, one finding any divergence from a pure national identity and simple celebration of national qualities and history a traitorous betrayal.

Despite this emphasis on purity, Anna is herself afraid to wear white (107) and must wear a cream-coloured dress (108). Likewise, the house's English background is not entirely pure, for Andrew Silver's own background is compromised: 'From an American merchant family, but they had him schooled over here and he's almost English. ... It's just him in that big house on Barton Road' (108). Andrew, the house's origin for Anna Good and the subsequent Silvers, is not even English but an approximation achieved through migration and schooling. His last name hints at other backgrounds, at an ethnicity further complicating the English roots of the house. Thus, the progenitor of the entire line and the original owner of the Silver House links the house itself with a foreign background. Furthermore, he meets his end overseas, dying during the war in Africa. Andrew is not bound to the house at either end of his life, a disconnection rendering his bond to the house less than natality or blood. Such detachment—and the fact his English offspring only acquire the home through one not English—deracinates the structure, reveals the house to not be an organic historic environment, for it is dependent on outside events and the influx of new peoples. The purportedly English home is only English through the intervention of outsiders.

Andrew's death, though, gives the house its xenophobic task of protection, for Anna's violent grief assigns the Silver House its mission: 'I hate them. ... Blackies, Germans, killers, dirty ... dirty killers. He should have stayed here with me. Shouldn't have let him leave' (109). This reaction, an extreme response to racial and national otherness, becomes for the house an injunction. Hearing Anna condemn outsiders, hearing disgust levelled at the external world, the house uses this affective rejection of the outside to bond with Anna, finding in her exclamation an antecedent identity for her and for the house itself: 'She spoke from that part of her that was older than her. The part of her that will always tie me to her, to her daughter Jennifer, to Jennifer's stubborn daughter Lily, to Lily's even more stubborn daughter Miranda. I can only be as good as they are. We are on the inside, and we have to stay together, and we absolutely cannot have anyone else' (109). The house appeals to some atavistic, pre-existing identity, one retroactively located after confronting what is perceived to be national and racial otherness. The house, a structure rooted to a locale, appeals to some familial or racial union connecting place and people, a chthonic identity, one binding 29 Barton Road and the Silver women together, connecting them over time, establishing a sense of an inside cloistered within itself in reaction to the violence and racial otherness of the outside. This link is revealed when Miranda tells Ore '[w]e are the goodlady. ... The house and I' (202). The Goodlady stands as a familial compound ghost or soucouyant, comprising Anna Good, Miranda and the house. The spectre of loss establishes the historic environment of the Silver house, a structure to which the women of the clan are rooted. The past, rather than welling up within identity, fractures this sense of self and folds it in on itself. The house is haunted, not so much by a history that broke in on it, but rather by a failure to ever get outside of itself, a faltering causing the family to collapse in on itself.

The Silvers manifest this folding in upon themselves through the hint of incest between Eliot and Miranda: they joke and are self-conscious about this issue (41); Eliot stalks Miranda at Cambridge and sleeps in her bed after she disappears. The Silver women likewise betray an inability to fully open themselves to the outside world through eating disorders such as pica (20, 70, 175) and feeding off one's own blood like a 'heraldic pelican' (22, 67). Both are revealed to be a failure to properly incorporate outside elements that might sustain one's body by ingesting the external elements permitting life to continue. Similarly, the house curls in upon itself, generating hidden layers, rooms and spaces allowing it to open up without opening out. Most obviously, the house contains a trapdoor with a hidden room (17). The house also is able to be 'bigger than you know! There are extra floors, with lots of people on them' (53). These hidden levels, and occupants, are those revealed when the house wishes to play tricks to frighten away outsiders (Sade, Ore, the Kurdish girls Suryaz and Deme). These folds and hidden layers allow it to provide different levels of hospitality and hostility to those residing there, offering one face to the Silvers and quite another to those born outside England who take residence. Miranda is disheartened when the Kurdish family leaves, for she is deflated in realizing that instead of having a large happy homestead, she has now lost 'someone different and distant, someone who had lived in a different house from her when she'd thought they were all living in the same house' (53). These extra levels began when the house reforms itself to comfort and protect Anna after she hears of her husband's death: 'I curved myself into a deep cup, a safe container for her. I did not let her take any harm to herself. ... I was like a child with its mouth obstinately closed, refusing speech, refusing air' (109). Likewise, one of Miranda's dream sequences takes her inside the bomb shelter, a snug safe harbor in which she finds the women of the Silver clan: 'It's safe in here. ... Us Silver girls together' (119). The house's ability to expand itself substitutes for opening itself to the outside world, an internal expansion of space compensating for its self-enclosure. Confronted with the uncertainty of the outside world, the house reacts by reshaping its own environment, providing a seemingly safe shelter. In not fully allowing that outside in, the house undertakes to other itself, creating a strange alterity and doubling through the levels and selves within its walls. However, as these hidden folds are generated in response to the outside, are a means of protection from anything exterior, this response is a type of auto-immune system of the house, one leading it to turn on those (Luc, Eliot, Jennifer, Miranda) who are already resident there. The house's hospitality shades into hostility even for its hosts. Consequently, in *White Is for Witching*, the place of the past within the present is less some positive historic environment and more a haunting, a past rooted and folded in on itself, a binding to the spectral aura of the past pervading a specific spot, one capable of following the person so possessed.

CONJURING THE PAST

Theodor Adorno maintains that 'perhaps the most profound force of resistance stored in the cultural landscape is the expression of history that is compelling, aesthetically, because it is etched by the real suffering of the past. ... The cultural landscape, which resembles a ruin even when the house still stands, embodies a wailful lament that has since fallen mute' (1997, 64–5). If, as Jacques Derrida instructs us, spectres are the spirit of that 'which could come back' (1994, 39), then this landscape articulates this silenced cry as hauntings persisting even in the most seemingly unmarked abodes and environments. As a result, exploring place as the occasion for haunting provides a more extensive encounter with vestiges of the past persisting through place. As both *Beyond Black* and *White Is for Witching* indicate, haunting becomes something impacting people, not place. That is, the past locates inhabitants, disclosing networks that align them with places far beyond the traditional haunted house. Now suburbia, planned communities, and bed-and-breakfast establishments all prove to have a spectral aspect, a stereoscopic sense of time and place. However, as Michel de Certeau observes, 'there is no place that is not haunted by many different spirits hidden there in silence, spirits one can "invoke" or not. Haunted places are the only ones people can live in' (1984, 108). Negotiating with these ghosts then entails grappling with this only partially materialized past. Moreover, an inclusive vision of past and place does not mean dealing with the same pasts (or similar relations to those pasts), nor with a unitary environment. Instead, such legacies are broken up, dispersed as multiple encounters and siftings, a lengthy and uncertain process offering not neat communion but rather messy points of dialogue. By fore-grounding a divided sense of the past and by suggesting spirits are directed at people, the past is not presented as some benign bequest acquired through citizenship, or living in a particular locale, or belonging to a particular group. Rather, encountering and dealing with the past is offered as a process, a par-ticular form of grappling distinctive to each of us, just as the characters in these novels must navigate different relations with the ghosts besetting such environments. The past stands not as a distinctive and separated realm but as a numinous spirit, one signaling not only events whose legacy lingers on but also spectres that might be conjured anew and recast for a more hospitable future.

NOTES

1. Roger Luckhurst insists the uncertainty and ambivalence attending ghosts after Jacques Derrida's work on the spectral not come at the cost of their traditional asso-ciations: that ghosts 'appear precisely as *symptoms*, points of rupture that insist their singular tale be retold and their wrongs acknowledged' (2002, 542).

2. Catherine Spooner makes a similar point, suggesting 'the inhospitability of the outer suburbs to local stories and legends paralyses both their living and dead inhabit-ants' (2010, 82).

3. The tapes Alison makes offer the best illustration of spirit traces, for ghosts intrude on the recording to leave a mélange of different voices: 'The machine plays back tapes that aren't even in it, we get material coming through from the year before last. All the tapes are speaking on top of each other, it's like a compost heap' (320).

4. Mart appears as a compound ghost, a collage of discrepant impulses and tenden-cies: 'You could spend your life trying to fit Mart together. ... There's no cause and effect to him. He feels as if he might be the clue to something or other, made up as he is out of bits and pieces of the past and the fag end of other people's phrases. He's like a picture where you don't know which way up it goes. He's like a walking jigsaw, but you've lost the box lid to him' (344).

5. As Catherine Spooner remarks, this suburban scene where ancestral ghosts chase their upwardly mobile descendants is 'the haunting of the recently middle class by their lower-class upbringing' (2010, 84).

BIBLIOGRAPHY

Adorno, Theodor. 1997. *Aesthetic Theory*. Trans. Robert Hullot-Kentor. Minneapolis: University of Minnesota Press.
Anderson, Benedict. 1991. *Imagined Communities*. Rev. ed. New York: Routledge.
Berberich, Christine, Neil Campbell and Robert Hudson. 2012a. 'Introduction: Affective Landscapes.' *Affective Landscapes in Literature, Art and Everyday Life*. Ed. Christine Berberich, Neil Campbell and Robert Hudson. Burlington, VT: Ashgate. 1–17.
_____. Neil Campbell and Robert Hudson. 2012b. 'Introduction: Framing and Reframing Land and Identity.' *Land & Identity: Theory, Memory, and Practice*. Ed. Christine Berberich, Neil Campbell and Robert Hudson. New York: Rodopi. 17–42.
Casey, Edward S. 2000. *Remembering: A Phenomenological Study*. 2nd ed. Indianapolis: Indiana University Press.
_____. 2009. *Getting Back into Place: Toward a Renewed Understanding of the Place-World*. 2nd ed. Bloomington, IN: Indiana University Press.
Cheah, Pheng. 2003. *Spectral Nationality: Passages of Freedom from Kant to Postcolonial Literatures of Liberation*. New York: Columbia University Press.
Commission on the Future of Multi-Ethnic Britain (Chair: Bhikhu Parekh). 2000. *The Future of Multi-Ethnic Britain*. London: Profile Books.
de Certeau, Michel. 1984. *The Practice of Everyday Life*. Trans. Steven Rendall. Los Angeles: University of California Press.
Derrida, Jacques. 1994. *Specters of Marx: The State of the Debt, the Work of Mourning, and the New International*. Trans. Peggy Kamuf. New York: Routledge.
Dodd, Philip. 1995. *The Battle over Britain*. London: Demos.
Farrell, Kirby. 2012. 'Eschatological Landscape.' *Land & Identity: Theory, Memory, and Practice*. Ed. Christine Berberich, Neil Campbell and Robert Hudson. New York: Rodopi. 117–39.
Luckhurst, Roger. 2002. 'The Contemporary London Gothic and the Limits of the "Spectral Turn".' *Textual Practice*, 16 (3): 527–46.
Mantel, Hilary. 2005. *Beyond Black*. London: Harper.
Mason, Rhiannon. 2004. 'Conflict and Complement: An Exploration of the Discourses Informing the Concept of the Social Inclusive Museum in Contemporary Britain.' *International Journal of Heritage Studies*, 10 (1): 49–73.
Mitchell, W. J. T. 2002. 'Introduction.' *Landscape and Power*. Ed. W. J. T. Mitchell. Chicago: University of Chicago Press. 1–4.
Naidoo, Rashi. 2005. 'Never Mind the Buzzwords.' *The Politics of Heritage*. Ed. Rashi Naidoo and Jo Littler. New York: Routledge. 36–48.
Oyeyemi, Helen. 2009. *White Is for Witching*. New York: Random House.

Oyeyemi, Helen.. 2012. 'Helen Oyeyemi on Haunted House Novels.' Accessed 3 March 2014. http://cle.ens-lyon.fr/anglais/helen-oyeyemi-on-haunted-house-novels-157115.kjsp?RH=CLE_ANG110100.

Spooner, Catherine. 2010. ' "[T]hat Eventless Realm": Hilary Mantel's *Beyond Black* and the Ghosts of the M25.' *London Gothic: Place, Space and the Gothic Imagination*. Ed. Lawrence Witchard and Anne Phillips. New York: Continuum. 80–90.

Wolfreys, Julian. 2002a. 'Citation's Haunt: Specters of Derrida.' *Mosaic*, 35 (1): 21–34.

Wolfreys, Julian.. 2002b. *Victorian Hauntings: Spectrality, Gothic, the Uncanny and Literature*. New York: Palgrave.

Chapter Four

'Tender Bodies'

Embracing the Ecological Uncanny in Jim Crace's Being Dead

Niamh Downing

What sort of insects do you rejoice in, where *you* come from?' the Gnat inquired.

'I don't rejoice in insects at all,' Alice explained, 'because I'm rather afraid of them—at least the large kinds. But I can tell you the names of some of them.'

'Of course they answer to their names?' the Gnat remarked carelessly.

'I never knew them do it.'

'What's the use of their having names,' the Gnat said, 'if they won't answer to them?'

'No us to *them*,' said Alice; 'but it's useful to the people that name them, I suppose. If not, why do things have names at all?'

—Lewis Carroll, *Through the Looking Glass*, 1872.

Jim Crace's *Being Dead* is rightly characterized as a *memento mori* by its critics. It charts the decay over six days of the corpses of a middle-aged married couple, both zoologists, murdered on the shoreline at Baritone Bay, where they first met thirty years before. Yet, the most disquieting aspect of this novel is less its reminder that death comes to us all, than its persistent recourse to *memento vitae*, to painting a vivid image of the intimate intermingling of living organisms and dead flesh. For, despite their untimely and brutal end at Baritone Bay, Joseph and Celice are very much alive, animated by the crabs, flies, other insects and occasional gull that in death their deliquescing bodies sustain. 'These are the everending days of being dead' (Crace 1999, 210) the novel's final lines aver, echoing its title. 'Being dead' of course is an oxymoron in terms of the logic of human bodies as discrete experiencing selves, and this is where the reader undergoes an affective crisis, one which this essay will argue, is grounded in the ecological uncanny. Rebecca Giggs locates 'the recursive logic of the ecological uncanny' in *The Road*, where 'the characters experience themselves as foreign bodies in the system' unable to extricate themselves from the alienating 'commingling of the anthropogenic and the natural' (2011, 209). A comparable unhomeliness is provoked in the reader of *Being Dead*, as, while in narrative terms we need our protagonists to exist and live on, the corollary to this is the dissolution of human being-ness into another form of living assemblage, a breaching of boundaries that is all at once marked by horror and desire.

This change from one form of being to another, or from being to becoming, is as Jussi Parikka suggests in his discussion of ethological ethics in *Insect Media*, no longer 'a question of a body representing drives [or] forces ... but of intermingling with the world'. The reanimation of Joseph and Celice by other species recalls that all animals, human or otherwise, are 'continuously coupled with [their] environment, stretched through counterpoints such as the plant and the rain, the spider and the fly'. Such a Spinozan-Deleuzian ethology attempts to embrace, or 'move toward the horizon of the unliveable and the inhuman forces and nonhuman material intensities and rhythms in contrast to the phenomenological enterprise of what can be experienced as human beings' (Parikka 2010, 74). The reader of the couple's metamorphoses is as likely to recoil from, as embrace these 'tender bodies' (Crace 1999, 12) and their new plane of experience, however. The horror at the idea of non-human animals, mainly arthropods, devouring and taking up temporary residence in the bodies of Joseph and Celice can be understood in terms of the uncanny, where the body itself as home (*heimlich*) or secure locus of being-in-the-world is rendered increasingly unfamiliar (*unheimlich*). For though Joseph and Celice are still recognizably human, and we as readers are therefore compelled to recognize ourselves in them, their bodies are interpenetrated with foreign bodies (flies, microorganisms), and undergo a transformation that makes them radically different. The reader is further confronted by the uncanniness of life-in-death, for alongside the depiction of time's effects on the decaying bodies of Joseph and Celice, the characters are conversely fleshed out by the analeptic trajectory of two additional narrative threads.

Echoing the intermingling of the zoologists' bodies with the world, these three strands of Crace's storytelling intersect to provide a *memento vitae* and radically open ecology, which nevertheless reminds the reader of the limits of a discrete human life, and the inevitable arrival of 'Fish', Crace's figure for death. 'Fish' is an invention of Mondazy, one of Crace's fictional authors: 'Sometimes, his superstitious readers and adherents used to say, Mondazy's Fish would show itself only as silvering across the corpse, or by its smell. Death was hardly visible. Yet it was already in the room.' (1999, 106). Death is immanent in life, 'already in the room' or home that is the human body, but its limits are surpassed by the coupling of human and animal. For Joseph and Celice this process begins with their physical encounter with 'Fish', which 'gasping', 'wriggled on its fins across the dunes to touch their skin' (108).

The novel opens with the couple making a nostalgic 'visit to the singing salt dunes', where with 'their heads caved in', they become 'unlikely victims of unlikely passions': 'Who would have thought that unattractive people of that age and learning would encounter sex and murder in the open air' (Crace 1999, 1). The murder is followed by the first narrative thread, Crace's *'quivering'* or remembrance, which moves through the hours preceding their deaths, delivering the couple back to the comfort of their bed at 6:10 am. The omniscient narrator explains: 'A day lived forward has retrieved itself by fleeing from the future to the past. The dead are resurrected and they lie in bed at backward-running dawn' (204). This narrative revivification of Joseph and Celice is interspersed with the story of their decomposition and discovery, which charts the six days of 'grace' during which they lie 'cushioned by the sunlight and the grass', his hand touching her shin 'held in place by nothing firmer than his fingertip', untouched, except by scavengers, microorganisms, 'the weather and the earth' (12–13). A final thread of the novel takes us back thirty years to the time when Joseph and Celice met as young zoology students on a field trip to Baritone Bay. Celice is haunted by the death of another student, Festa, who died trapped in a fire at the study house, at the same time that the young couple were making love in the dunes. They return to Baritone Bay then 'to lay a ghost' (1), but they can only do so through repeating the circumstances of the trauma that haunts the site and their memories. For, Joseph means 'to lay more than a ghost': 'He meant to reinflate their past, if only she'd agree. A *quivering*' (54). It is the resurrection of their early passion that he hopes for, not a ghostly return, a physical *'quivering'* as a result of sex rather than death. This story arc acts as a double of the first narrative thread that runs backward through the hours before their murder, insofar as it repeats not only their sexual encounter on the dunes, but also death, this time their own. They pay a 'heavy price for their nostalgia' then, for what they do not realize (although it is apparent to the reader) is that they are caught up in what Freud refers to as an 'unintended recurrence of the same situation' (1953–1974 [1919], 237): as they reenact the past they instigate an uncanny repetition. Moreover, they fail to anticipate that 'being middle-aged and cautious is no defence against Mondazy's Fish. Its bite does not discriminate. None of its deaths is premature' (Crace 1999, 62).

Being Dead is not a novel that is particularly concerned with uncovering or exorcising ghosts of the past, however. When the couple return to the site of the fire, the study house, 30 years later on the day of their murder, they find that 'this was not a haunted place, as it turned out', the study house had simply become 'fertile ground for rock shrubs and carbon-loving plants' (Crace 1999, 152):

> There was no evidence of any building on that side of the house. The scrubby backshore plants, the hollow-stemmed flute bushes and the thorns had colonized the long rectangle of the glass veranda and were growing deeply. …What did she expect? Some bones? A snake? A woman, sitting up in bed? The red glow of tobacco? The odours of a barbecue? A scream? The sudden ending of her guilt as if the study house had pardons to give out? The smell was only vegetation and the sound was only leaves and stalks. (153)

Celice expects a haunting of some kind accompanied by the usual ghostly accoutrements, but all she finds is nature in all its abundance, nurtured by the carbon released in the fire 30 years previously, a colonization that has stripped away the signs of former human activity. What is repressed and returns in *Being Dead* is less supernatural then, than super natural, an excess of nature, and the corresponding knowledge of our already being—as Crace describes his murdered zoologists—'sullied' organic matter (1999, 109). Instead of a haunted beach house, the site of trauma is revealed to be the human body itself, and the threat to what it houses—the human subject. The most ecologically uncanny thing then is this body itself, the 'me-myself' that is 'embodied by this organism', which, Richard Zaner reminds us, is *'susceptible to what can happen to material things in general'* (1981, 52).

Sarah Bezan characterizes the interpenetration of the human and more-than-human world in *Being Dead* as 'necro-ecology', or 'an ecology of decomposition' (2015, 192), although she rejects the possibility of the uncanny as part of this exploration of 'being dead'. Drawing on Deleuze's vitalism, Bezan suggests that *Being Dead* refutes the concept of finitude as the teleological backdrop against which we understand subjectivity and agency. The novel does so through lingering on the biochemical processes and the activity of various arthropods that animate the decomposing corpses, coupled with a narrative composition that reverses the chronology of events in order to bring the zoologists back to life. For Bezan, this series of 'dynamic inter-species connections and relations' enacts a Deleuzian 'philosophy of vitalism', which 'dismantles the division that separates the human and non-human animal and, with it, challenges the life-death distinction that runs parallel to it' (194). In extending the possibility of agency beyond a 'framework of finitude', Bezan follows thinkers such as Claire Colebrook and Rosa Braidotti, who have sought to release death and the subject from the 'negative structure of loss' that marks much European philosophy and critical theory (Heidegger, Lacan,

Derrida, Agamben) and she argues, Modernist literature. Bezan suggests that although the 'framework of finitude' has enabled philosophy to address 'notions of grievability, ethical responsibility, and suffering' it also presents some difficulties.

> First, finitude depends on the notion that the *subject is subjected* to external (if not also malevolent) forces, which implies that life itself is ultimately weak, vulnerable, and easily assailable. Even further, finitude maintains a sharp division of the living from the dead as it interprets death as the definitive end of being. Thus embedded in a negative structure of loss, mourning, difference, and vulnerability, the subjected subject of the framework of finitude views life as finite, with death as the final terminus. (192)

Joseph and Celice are indeed subjected to external and malevolent forces, namely, the blows from their granite-wielding assailant, yet their dead bodies continue to nourish and propagate life, to participate in a mesh of affective relations for at least six days after their murder. Compelling though this argument is in its affirmation of a kind of agency and being that can continue to function beyond the finitude that obtains to a discrete human life, the novel nevertheless vacillates between the idea that life (human and otherwise) is both vulnerable as well as generative. This ambivalence also emerges in Crace's rejection of the idea that the spiritual or scientific can provide solace in the face of death on one hand, while on the other, he offers a narrative structure that operates as a form of consolation, mourning, or 'a *quivering* of sorts' (1999, 4). The novel's resistance to mourning is evident from the beginning in the invented epigraph poem 'The Biologist's Valediction to His Wife', which is somewhere between the nonsense verse of Edward Lear or Lewis Carroll and John Donne's entreaty to the beloved against mourning. Where Donne's 'Valediction against Mourning' argues that there is no need to mourn a temporary parting, as the lovers are united in a 'refined' spiritual realm (Donne), Crace's poet is clear that all mourning is meaningless. Though he will 'Grieve', doing so will neither lengthen 'Life' nor stop the inevitable 'Putrefaction' which is all that the dead have to look forward to (n.p).

Despite this decree against mourning, the novel's reverse storytelling reclaims the lovers 'from death' in a form of narrative consolation: 'The doctors of zoology were out of time, perhaps, but they can be rescued from the dunes by memory, receding, and tucked up in their waking beds again, still tenants of the room' (5). Teasing the reader with this ambiguity, Crace's omniscient narrator tells us:

> Do not be fooled. There was no beauty for them in the dunes, no painterly tranquility in death framed by the sky, the ocean and the land, that pious trinity,

in which their two bodies, supine, prone, were posed as lifeless waxworks of themselves, sweetly unperturbed and ruffled only by the wind. ...They were dishonoured by the sudden vileness of their deaths. ...Their characters had bled out on the grass. The universe could not care less. (11)

If the universe is indifferent to the couple (indeed human life in general) the writer appears not to be so dismissive. Although the 'dunes' offer 'no painterly tranquility', the narrative does, even if this is in the decomposing bodies with their kaleidoscope of colour and pattern. Where 'their characters had bled out on the grass', Crace undertakes to recreate them through his intersecting narratives, thus 'reclaiming them from death': 'To start their journey as they disembark, but then to take them back where they have travelled from, is to produce a vision of eternity' (5). He creates a six-day 'period of grace' for them that defies death and even the gruesomeness of their murder, while embracing their newfound ecologically extended lives as corpses.

Though optimistic in its depiction of decomposition, *Being Dead* offers a less clear-cut assertion of vitalism than Bezan puts forward. For, it is these very points of tension that drive the narrative experience, ambiguities which vitalism might prefer to surmount in its affirmative embrace of holism. Uncanniness, abjection, haunting, repetition are all understood as part of the 'negative' structure of finitude, which Bezan argues, following Colebrook, 'arises from the notion that death haunts or infects life' (2015, 193). In removing the possibility of haunting, however, something that we might understand as ecological is potentially lost in the argument that weighs on the side of vitalism and life. Rather than reading the novel as resisting 'the view that the corpse is uncanny, abject waste, or a ghastly threshold of self and other' (196), I would suggest instead that it lingers in abjection and uncanniness, in order to generate a series of conflicting affective responses that propel the reader into what Timothy Morton might describe as ecological thought.

UNCANNY EFFECTS/AFFECTS

In his introduction to *The Uncanny*, Nicholas Royle sets out the characteristics, objects and effects of the uncanny. Never quite tangible, but always felt, the uncanny can manifest in the body as 'experience', a 'feeling', a 'sense' or an 'apprehension'. The uncanny is 'a disturbance ... of proper names', 'a crisis of the natural', 'a matter of something gruesome or terrible', 'a feeling of something beautiful but at the same time frightening', 'something that should have remained secret and hidden', it is also 'never far from something comic'

(2003, 1–2). All these elements are present in *Being Dead*, from the invented taxonomies that are almost but not quite right, to the improper display of the beautifully depicted internal organs as 'pixelated', 'abstract' 'pointillist' and the tragi-comedy of bungled lovemaking and robbery gone wrong (Crace 1999, 6).

Most of all though, the novel enacts Royle's explanation of the uncanny as 'a crisis of the proper', insofar as the uncanny disturbs what is proper (*propius*) to the self, or belonging to the self—one's own (2003, 1). As a 'feeling that happens only to oneself, within oneself', but with a 'meaning or significance may have to do, most of all, with what is not oneself', the uncanny is intrinsically tied to affect; to what a body can do; what affects it can undergo when brought into contact with an-other body which is not itself. As Melissa Gregg and Gregory Seigworth suggest, 'affect is found in those intensities that pass body to body (human, nonhuman, part-body, and otherwise), in those resonances that circulate about, between, and sometimes stick to bodies and worlds, and in the very passages or variations between these intensities and resonances themselves' (2010, 1). Joseph and Celice undergo affects from other organisms, intensities that pass from one organism to another, creating an ecological assemblage that is radically uncanny, but this only occurs as they become other than themselves. During their six days of grace, Joseph and Celice are 'cast forward' in a state of 'open-ended in-between-ness', which Gregg and Seigworth associate with affect.

> Affect is integral to a body's perpetual becoming (always becoming otherwise, however, subtly, than what it already is), pulled beyond its seeming surface-boundedness by way of its relation to, indeed its composition through, forces of encounter. With affect, a body is as much outside itself as in itself—webbed in its relations—until ultimately such firm distinctions cease to matter. (2010, 3)

Thus, affect, like the uncanny, causes 'a body' to be 'as much outside itself as in itself'. For Royle, the uncanny can be 'construed as a foreign body within oneself, even the experience of oneself *as* a foreign body' (2). The insects and other arthropods in the novel are foreign bodies that invade Celice and Joseph almost immediately after their deaths, but it is the reader, not the characters, whose affective response includes feelings of the uncanny. When presented with bodies that provide a mirror to ourselves, yet are becoming other-than-human through the process of decay we not only react to the narrative horror of the foreign species encroaching on the human, we also experience ourselves as foreign bodies in a wider ecosystem.

Jacques Lacan's translation of the uncanny similarly hinges on the transgression of boundaries proper to the self by something external. Given that the accurate French translation of uncanny—*l'inquiétante étrangeté* (worrying or disturbing strangeness)—is somewhat inadequate, Lacan developed the neologism, *extimité*. Although *extimité* appears infrequently in Lacan's writings, contemporaries such as Jacques-Alain Miller have since glossed the term: 'Extimacy is not the contrary of intimacy. Extimacy says that the intimate is Other—like a foreign body, a parasite' (1994, 76). *Extimité* or extimacy is therefore an encounter between what is most intimate to the self, and something external. This is usually, as Mladen Dolar suggests, a disturbing or unsettling experience, and importantly it is located somewhere—in the body: *Extimité* 'points neither to the interior nor to the exterior, but is located there where the most intimate interiority coincides with the exterior and becomes threatening, provoking horror and anxiety. The *extimité* is simultaneously the intimate kernel and foreign body; in a word it is *unheimlich*' (1991, 6). Nothing is more a 'home' or habitation to the self than the human body, and nothing is more unhomely than something that transgresses its bounds. The Lacanian term extimacy recalls Freud's etymological excavation in 'The Uncanny' where 'intimate' is one of the definitions of *Heimlich* ([1919] 1953–1974, 225). For Freud such intimacy is linked to the body, specifically its sexual organs, which for him are its most hidden aspects and should remain secret; the pathology or trauma emerges when what should properly be concealed is instead revealed. In *Being Dead* this kind of revealing of the intimate parts of the body is present: Joseph's stiffened penis, the description of internal organs slowly revealed over six days of post-mortem experience, both to the elements and the reader. Yet, intimacy here also works as an unsettling reminder of human entanglement with other bodies: plants, animals, microorganisms that make up what Crace refers to as 'landscape'. And this, for Morton, is where the intimacy or extimacy of the uncanny emerges as a potential tool for ecological thought.

Desire for intimacy with (and in the case of our zoologists, knowledge of) the natural world is part of the rhetoric of much of what we call environmentalism. Crudely put, such a relationship of immersion depends on their being, on the one hand, a human subject/body that can know/experience and, on the other hand, an object, nature, which is infinitely available to bear the weight of this knowing or experiencing. However, as Morton pithily suggests, 'to have subjects and objects, one must have abjects to vomit or excrete' (2010, 274). Intimacy with nature is always troubled by that disturbing feeling associated with the uncanny. This is because such intimacy—as the zoologist's lives, occupations and decaying bodies suggest—can easily become much too close for comfort: 'extra Nature, more than you bargained for' as Morton puts it (2012, 45). The forensic descriptions of Joseph's and Celice's decaying bodies are brilliantly compelling, while simultaneously disturbing: 'Viewed from closer up, there were colours and motifs on Joseph and Celice that Fish could never leave. A dazzling filigree of pine-brown surface veins. The blossoming of blisters, their flaring red corollas and yellow ovaries like rock roses' (108). Morton describes a similar effect at work in Coleridge's *Rime*, which in being 'relentlessly super-natural and uncanny' is potentially 'better for the ecological thought than "realistic" [nature] writing' (108). 'Supernatural' or 'super natural' (108) does not simply refer here to the presence of haunting or the dead; rather 'nature' is always and already uncanny, strange and excessive, especially when we get up close and intimate.

As suggested earlier, the uncanny is always located somewhere, home, whether that is a place or a body. Morton notes that Freud connected the uncanny with place, particular places such as forests and cities, which produce the uncanny effect due to the repetition of the experience of wandering around somewhere familiar yet strange. Ecology is also linked to the home-liness/unhomeliness of the uncanny through its derivation from the Greek word for 'household' or home—*oikos* (Morton 2015, 45). The home of the self might be in proper terms the human body, but to participate in ecological thinking its *oikos* must be extended outwards towards other beings, animals, insects, plants, and for Morton, non-living entities:

> When we think the ecological thought, we encounter all kinds of beings that are not strictly 'natural.' This isn't surprising either, since what we call 'nature' is a 'denatured,' unnatural, uncanny sequence of mutations and catastrophic events: just read Darwin. The ecological view … is a vast, sprawling mesh of interconnections without a definite center or edge. It is radical intimacy, coexistence with other beings, sentient and otherwise. (2012, 8)

As with the real and invented species, humans, insects, microorganisms and plant life that coexist on the shifting dunes of *Being Dead*, the ecological is for Morton a necessarily peculiar 'spectral realm in which all kinds of strange, uncanny entities flit about, hard to distinguish from one another in a thin or rigid way: vampires, ghosts, fingers, pieces of brain, phantom limbs, flowers, tropes, self-concepts, earlobes, appendices, swim bladders, minds, eyes, meadows, tardigrades, viruses' (2015, 44).

It is part of their intimate foreignness, their extimacy that makes 'ecological beings at whatever scale are uncanny; that is, they are what they are, yet not exactly what they are, whichever way you look':

> They exemplify what Derrida calls the arrivant, and arrival—he is thinking of the future—that cannot be predicted in advance, yet is not just anything at all, or nothing. Welcoming this arrivant is the ultimate gesture of hospitality. My term for the arrivant is strange stranger. A badger, a flock of starlings, a bee swarm or an antelope are all strange strangers—they are strange even to themselves and

their strangeness is irreducible such that the more we know (about) them, the more strange they become. (Morton 2015, 46)

The arrivant cannot be predicted; it arrives on the threshold, a figure from the future that calls into question the familiar, 'the very border that delineated a legitimate home' (Derrida 1993, 34). Derrida's arrival/arrivant is a rethinking of Heidegger's finitude, whereby death is that which both limits and consti-tutes *Dasein* or being; it is one thing of which we can be certain, but even as the host of our own bodies, we cannot predict its arrival. For Derrida, the arrivant disturbs the proper ('the legitimate home') in the same way as the uncanny. It is not possible to distinguish between the revenant or ghost that returns from the past to haunt and the arrivant that turns up so unexpectedly from the future and haunts the present insofar as its arrival is inevitable as well as simultaneously impossible to anticipate. Just as for our protagonists, who feel haunted by the traumatic death of Festa, it is not the return of the past that truly haunts them, instead it is the arrival of death, 'Mondazy's Fish', an arrivant that makes possible the impossibility of their 'being dead', and pres-ages their entrance into the ecological uncanny, or world of strange strangers.

Morton riffs on Derrida's figure to produce his 'strange stranger', an uncanny entity that arrives from nowhere and which we neglect to welcome at our peril, or to the peril of ecological thought. They are characterized by their uncanniness, and also like the arrivant, by their irreducibility:

> Strange strangers are uncanny, familiar and strange simultaneously. Their famil-iarity is strange, their strangeness familiar. They cannot be thought as part of a series (such as species or genus) without violence. Yet their uniqueness is not such that they are independent. They are composites of other strange strangers. Every life-form is familiar, since we are related to it. We share its DNA, its cell structure, the subroutines in the software of its brain. (2010, 277)

Crace's *Being Dead* resonates with Morton's brand of eco-philosophy. Nature is not benign, or does not care; life and non-life is curiously intermingled, composite; embracing the abject is the best we subjects can hope for. Joseph's and Celice's bodies are teeming with life, made up from a variety of strange strangers, insects and microorganisms whose DNA they share. Day one of the couple's six days of grace shifts from 'swag flies' and crabs feasting on the corpses to another narrative thread where Celice gives a lecture to would-be zoologists on the immanence of death in life. Students inspect the 'monofiles under the microscope', single celled organisms that reproduce continually, all 'their DNA identical. No deaths. No corpses. Evermore' (40). Staving off mortality under the microscope, it seems that the closest you can get to eter-nity is an assemblage of single cells.

THE UNCANNY ECOLOGIES OF *BEING DEAD*

Like the settings of Crace's other novels, the ostensibly realistic coastal location of Baritone Bay—which recalls West Cornwall, Pembrokeshire and California all at once—only exists in 'Craceland', a place that is, according to Adam Begley, 'both strange and familiar, historically specific and timeless' (2003, 184). As Philip Tew suggests, landscape is a 'characterised presence' rather than a backdrop to human agency in Craceland: 'the underlying sense of a primeval, natural quality of the environment recurs throughout Crace's fiction' (2006, 6–7). Baritone Bay might be forced to concede to the bulldozers of the Salt Pines development that Celice and Joseph stumble upon, but the littoral landscape of *Being Dead* is largely understood as a space that shapes itself, regardless of human concerns. It is a landscape composed of Crace's 'raw materials', which includes, but is not exclusively human. This is a site where weather, decay and geology reign in a landscape 'already sculpted out of death'; if they had not been removed by human hands, Joseph and Celice 'would have turned to landscape, given time' (Crace 1999, 207). Crace explains the importance of his phenomenological experience of being in the landscape in an interview with Tew:

> You cannot be in any doubt that I love landscape. My novels are full of it. Landscape is almost a character in them all. But I don't write about landscape because I read landscape books. If I write about landscape it's because at every opportunity, I go out, I walk the coast, or I go up hills, or I go caving or whatever. That's where I obtain my raw materials. (Crace cited in. Tew 2006, 5)

Despite this emphasis on his affective relationship to landscape, the 'raw materials' of experience are transformed into the invented pastoral settings and taxonomically strange ecosystems that we repeatedly find in Craceland, which occupies a zone somewhere between the world-building of the imagination and the worlding of phenomenological experience.

Crace populates *Being Dead* with numerous fictional organisms, which operate as textual 'strange strangers' that flit about in the spectral realm of the novel, disturbing accepted scientific taxonomies. Almost all the creatures and plants that Crace introduces are fictional. Along with the forensic descriptions of the decaying corpses these inventions give a pseudoscientific feel to the narrative, but science does not offer any more of a consolation than religion here. While many of Crace's novels, including *Being Dead*, are relentless in their Neo-Darwinism and their rejection of life after death, his fabricated taxonomies suggest a parody of the scientific endeavor in which both Joseph and Celice, zoologists to the last, seem to put their hope. The narrative thread that records their first meeting has a young Celice in pursuit of Joseph and nature out on the dunes:

> Besides, the period of resting on the ridge, alone, the views, the detail of the
> land, the sour ocean smell, the melancholy drama of being young and unattached
> and not quite warm enough, had reminded her how joyful it could be to have
> the landscape to herself. She put a Latin and a common name to all the plants
> and birds she saw. A family game. By naming them, she doubled their existence
> and her own. This was the pleasure of zoology, to be the lonely heroine of open
> skies and specibags. Science, romance, oxygen. A potent brew. (Crace 1999, 77)

Celice is involved here in a kind of worlding through naming, much like
Crace's own invented taxonomies. Naming not only creates the world around
her, but also affirms her own sense of self, as future zoologist, and human
being, separate from those creatures that daily bear the weight of a 'Latin
and a common name' under the scientist's gaze. Getting her 'notebook out'
and 'listing species', Celice plays the game of nonsense taxonomy, which
is all that is possible in Craceland. She notes a series of real and invented
plants 'broom sedge, spartina grass, redstem, firesel and cordon': 'But as she
walked further out on to the bay the dunes began to concentrate—though not
exclusively—on lissom grass, that misplaced lawn, suburban green most of
the year, as spongy and as welcoming as moss. Its Latin name? *Festuca mol-
lis*' (Crace 1999, 79). The fictional lissom grass appears throughout the novel,
accompanying intimate moments between the couple: sexual intercourse,
then violent death, and finally decay.

It is hard to distinguish real from invented organisms in the novel, and this
is due to the apparent authenticity of Crace's fictional entities. His organisms are convincing for several reasons. First, they offer close parallels with
organisms in the real world; second they display characteristics or affects
that resonate with their names, and finally they are legitimated through the
novel's recourse to Latin. The 'strange strangers' of Crace's taxonomy are,
as Morton suggests, 'uncanny, familiar and strange simultaneously'. Though
they seem to be recognizable, creatures such as the sprayhopper are as radically uncanny as any creature from Lewis Carroll. Moreover, such creatures
do not readily fit as 'part of a series (such as species or genus)' (Morton
2010, 277). We are reminded here that Deleuzian affect avoids 'defining a
body by its organs and functions' or by its 'Species or Genus'; instead bodies
or assemblages are enumerated and analyses by their 'affects' (Deleuze &
Guattari 1988, 257). Crace's fictional taxonomies are not organized according to a Linnaean system, but are instead predicated on the various affects
of the flora, fauna or creatures that he invents: from the 'unscientific local
name' of the sprayhopper, which Joseph sees as 'far more accurate' than its
Latin '*Pseudogryllidus pelagicus*', to the supple swaying 'lissom grass' or
grave-robbing 'swag-flies' (1999, 81). Jean-Jacques Lecercle's comparison
between the nonsensical inventions of the *Alice* books and the Victorian

fascination with natural history and entomology in *Philosophy of Nonsense* is germane here. Nonsense, he writes, has an 'advantage over natural history' in 'that it can invent those species (like the Snap-dragon-fly) in the imaginative sense, whereas natural history can [only] discover what already exists. Nonsense is the entomologist's dream come true, or the Linnaean classification gone mad, because gone creative. ... From the rationality of natural history there is only a short step, in the inscription of nonsense, to madness' (1994, 204). Crace's nonsensical creatures indicate a Linnaean system in overdrive, nature in excess, Morton's 'super natural'. Naming things might seem like a source of power for our zoologists, whose rational thought can suitably organize and control nature, but such discourses can no more stave off mortality than the superstitions ostensibly recorded by Mondazy or the nonsense '*bon viveur* or nectar bugs, which had either too many legs or none' (1999, 109).

Joseph too relies on his zoological knowledge to ward off extinction even if it is of creatures supposedly more durable and less 'marginal' than 'human kind'. He assumes that the objects of his doctoral thesis, the sprayhoppers, will still be there on his return to Baritone Bay. The narrator recalls Joseph admonishing a student at the Institute, 'when she had been too dismissive of the earth's smaller beings'. 'We hardly count in the natural orders of zoology' he tells her:

> They might not have a sense of self, like us. Or memory. Or hope. Or consciences. Or fear of death. They might not know how strong and wonderful they are. But when every human being in the world has perished, and all our sewerage pipes and gas cookers and diesel engines have fossilized, there will still be insects. Take my word. Flourishing, evolving, specializing insects. (93)

Despite his confidence in the persistence of life in a world without us, Joseph finds that the sprayhoppers have disappeared from the coast, in yet another uncanny presage of their human fate. Relying on the rationality of scientific endeavour, 'the doctors of zoology were ill-informed'. 'They did not understand the rigours of the natural world', or at least not the uncanny world of the novel and its taxonomies and natural laws to which they are subject: 'If sprayhoppers could not survive the changes on the coast, then how and why should they?' (96). Like the portentous lissom grass in which the corpses lie for six days leaving behind a 'vegetable ghost' (208), the sprayhopper's disappearance from the coast also signals the demise of the much more vulnerable human species.

Despite Joseph's error, the novel capitalizes on the resilience of the 'flourishing, evolving, specializing insects' that take up residence in so many of its pages, as well as in the bodies of the zoologists. *Talitrus saltator*, commonly known as a sandhopper, would more likely be the real-world crustacean (not actually an insect) for which Joseph has a 'long-term fondness' not least for its 'connivance in his doctorate' (93) but also for the part they play in his initial courtship of Celice: 'They were his Valentine, They were his single rose (Crace 1999, 94). These arthropods are involved in the intimacies of Joseph and Celice's lives from the start, but it is not until the death that the pair become coupled with insect and arthropod lifeforms 'stretched through counterpoints such as the plant and the rain' (Parikka 2010, 74) and the 'swag-flies and crabs' (Crace 1999, 36). If their first encounter is with the mortal touch of 'Mondazy's Fish' then Joseph and Celice enter into another series of intensities when they are 'discovered' by *'Claudatus maximi'*, a 'male' beetle:

> Then the raiding parties arrived, drawn by the summons of fresh wounds and the smell of urine: swag flies and crabs. ... Then a gull. No one, expect the newspapers, could say that 'There was only Death among the dunes, that summer's afternoon.' ... This single beetle had no appetite for blood. . . . He had been feeding in an exposed tangle of roots when Celice fell back. . . . The woman's body only up-ended him and pressed him into the grass. Unlike humans, beetles have armour-plating on their backs. They're not soft fruit. (Crace 1999, 36)

This is a level plane of existence, as the narration treats all life forms according to their affective relations with one another, not via any hierarchy of taxonomy or sentience. Caught up in Celice's death throes, the beetle flees 'her weight and shadow, despite the ancient dangers of the open air' (37). He is less vulnerable than Celice and Joseph, not simply because they were 'soft fruit' and 'lived in tender bodies' (12), but because 'he had not spent, like us, his lifetime concocting systems to deny mortality. Nor had he passed his days in melancholic fear of death' (37).

Insects exemplify Morton's strange stranger, that disturbingly 'intimate and foreign body' at the heart of the ecological uncanny (Dolar 1991, 6). Steven Shaviro argues that 'radical becomings take place routinely in their own lives', particularly through 'pupal metamorphosis' (1995, 48). Most of the creatures taking up residence in the bodies of Celice and Joseph undergo some kind of transformation as part of their life cycle as arthropods, whether full metamorphosis from larva to adult fly, or molting such as the crab. On the fourth day of their period of grace, 'the swag-fly maggots had started to emerge ... from their pod larvae, generated by the putrid heat in Joseph and Celice's innards. Long dead—but still producing energy!' (Crace 1999, 109). The couple undergo this affective change too, a transformation that binds them to the other creatures that they now nourish: after one full day Joseph is already 'losing form, though not enough, just yet, to make him animal or alien' (68). Shaviro's explanation of the metamorphosis of insects also obtains to Joseph and Celice: 'one genome, one continuously replenished body, one discretely bounded organism; and yet a radical discontinuity both of lived experience and of physical form' (1995, 48). The affective relations of a larva to the world are different from the affective relations of the fly, although both produce a similar affective response of disgust for the reader. Moreover, the apparently excessive way (which in itself promotes disgust) in which these creatures devour the rotting bodies is necessary for the transformation to take place. 'The surplus value accumulation of larval feeding gives way to lavish expenditure', as Shaviro explains. 'The body of an insect', like the decomposing human body, is always becoming, and 'perpetually "other than itself" ' (48). Once conjoined with the human in death, this insect assemblage echoes Morton's notion that we are all 'composites of other strange strangers': 'Every life-form is familiar, since we are related to it', and therefore radically uncanny (Morton 2010, 277). The 'unrelenting Rot, Rot, Rot', which Crace's epigraph poem and novel relentlessly puts before the reader suggests the kind of level plane of existence characterized by Morton's composite 'mesh' of interrelated lifeforms. For, 'as you regress from *Zoo.* to *Bot*', as the poem says, what was once recognizably human is all at once abbreviated into smaller entities, some alive, others synthetic: Crace's teleology is perversely, like his narrative, told in reverse as human life (*zoe*) regresses to botfly or synthetic bot, becoming larval (1999, n.p.).

Joseph and Celice have entered 'into composition' with 'the affects of another body', as Deleuze and Guattari describe; they have been 'destroyed by it', 'exchange[d] actions and passions with it' and 'join[ed] with it in composing a more powerful body' (1988, 257). Measured no longer by rational taxonomy or genus, but understood in terms of their affective relations with other entities, 'they'd been passed down through classes, orders, species, to the last in line, the lumpen multitude, the grubs, the loopers, the millepedes, the button lice, the tubal worms and flets, the *bon viveur* or nectar bugs, which had either too many legs or none' (Crace 1999, 109). Their final affective encounter is vegetal rather than insect, however, as the lissom grass is restored to life despite being smothered by their heavy bodies: 'For almost six days the grass had had to live by root alone, scavenging for its nutrients and minerals with its thin threads while its foliage was bleaching in the dark. Celice and Joseph's long and heavy shapes had robbed the grass of its free energy and left a vegetable ghost' (208). The processes of photosynthesis that accompany the renewed plant life are delivered with as much forensic precision as the previous descriptions of decomposition: 'The grass's stored supplies of water and carbon dioxide conspired with the thin light of that misty, cloudy day to make its carbohydrates and put back into the world its by-product of oxygen.' Once haunted by this landscape, Joseph and Celice are a now part of its radically uncanny ecology, turned first to insect-assemblage, then 'vegetable ghost', their traces exhaled by the lissom grass: 'By final light on the ninth day since the murder all traces of any life and love that had been spilt had disappeared. The natural world flooded back' (209).

BIBLIOGRAPHY

Begley, Adam. 2003. 'Jim Crace: The Art of Fiction CLXXIX.' *Paris Review*, 167: 183–214.

Bezan, Sarah. 2015. 'Necro-Eco: The Ecology of Death in Jim Crace's Being Dead.' *Mosaic*, 48: 191–207.

Crace, Jim. 1999. *Being Dead*. London: Viking.

Deleuze, Gilles and Félix Guattari. 1988. *A Thousand Plateaus: Capitalism and Schizophrenia*. London: Continuum.

Derrida, Jacques. 1993. *Aporias: Dying—Awaiting (One Another at) the 'Limits of Truth.'* Trans. Thomas Dutoit. Stanford: Stanford University Press.

Dolar, Mladen. 1991. ' "I Shall Be with You on Your Wedding-Night": Lacan and the Uncanny.' *October*, 58: 5–23.

Freud, Sigmund. (1919) 1953–1974. 'The Uncanny.' *The Standard Edition of the Complete Psychological Works*, Vol. 17. Trans. and Ed. James Strachey. London: Hogarth Press.

Giggs, Rebecca. 2011. 'The Green Afterword: Cormac McCarthy's *The Road* and the Ecological Uncanny.' *Criticism, Crisis, and Contemporary Narrative*. Ed. Paul Crosthwaite. London: Routledge, 201–18.

Gregg, Melissa and Gregory J. Seigworth. 2010. 'An Inventory of Shimmers.' *The Affect Theory Reader*. Ed. Melissa Gregg and Gregory J. Seigworth. Durham, NC: Duke University Press. 1–25.

Lecercle, Jean-Jacques. 1994. *Philosophy of Nonsense: The Intuitions of Victorian Nonsense Literature*. London: Routledge.

Miller, Jacques-Alain. 1994. 'Extimité.' *Lacanian Theory of Discourse: Subject, Structure, and Society*. Ed. Mark Bracher, Marshall W. Alcorn and Ronald J. Corthell. New York: New York University Press. 74–87.

Morton, Timothy. 2007. *Ecology without Nature: Rethinking Environmental Aesthetics*. Cambridge, MA: Harvard University Press.

_____. 2010. 'Queer Ecology.' *PMLA*, 125: 273–82.

_____. 2012. *The Ecological Thought*. Cambridge, MA: Harvard University Press.

_____. 'Ecology.' 2015. *Jacques Derrida: Key Concepts*. Ed. Claire Colebrook. London: Routledge. 41–7.

Parikka, Jussi. 2010. *Insect Media: An Archaeology of Animals and Technology.* Minneapolis: University of Minnesota Press.

Shaviro, Steven. 1995. 'Two Lessons from Burroughs.' *Posthuman Bodies.* Ed. Judith M. Halberstam and Ira Livingston. Bloomington: Indiana University Press. 38–54.

Tew, Philip. 2006. *Jim Crace.* Manchester: Manchester University Press.

Zaner, Richard M. 1981. *The Context of Self: A Phenomenological Inquiry Using Medicine as a Clue.* Athens: Ohio University Press.

Part II

INNER AND (SUB)URBAN LANDSCAPES

Chapter Five

Phantasmal Cities

The Construction and Function of Haunted Landscapes in Victorian English Cities

Karl Bell

In 1882 the clergyman and scholar Augustus Jessop declared city dwellers were, 'as a rule, destitute of faith in the unseen'. He argued that their imaginations had been effectively stunted by having 'nothing before their eyes but the factory with its ceaseless roar of wheels, the furnace, and the mine. These tell them nothing; they testify only of material power'. Jessop suggested that modern urbanization was anathema to the perpetuation of supernatural mentalities because the growing cities of the Victorian period could hold no mysteries. Locals had seen each new street built before their eyes and therefore there were 'no old closets, dim passages, and cranky holes' in which to deposit ghosts (1882, 735 and 737).

Through exploring the haunted landscapes that existed within Victorian English cities this chapter seeks to disprove Jessop's claims. In fact it argues for the opposite, that the nature of urban living in this period stimulated the imagination into constructing and making collective use of a supernatural environment. The suggested ubiquity of Victorian urban ghosts obviously jars with contemporary hegemonic narratives about the spectacular but disenchanted enchantment of the modernizing nineteenth-century city, a discourse best articulated through the literary and urban sociological figure of the flaneur (Frisby 2001, 27–51). Yet imaginatively crosshatched into this disenchanted, physical environment were supernaturally enchanted spaces. These were not intrinsic to a particular urban locality but could be potentially generated anywhere due to the transformative qualities of supernatural associations. The affective power of the supernatural resided as much in its haunting, ever present potential to manifest itself as it did in those particular occasions when it was realized. Ghosts were themselves the best representation of the present but rarely actualized nature of the supernatural. As the geographer Steve Pile notes, 'ghosts seem to pop out of nowhere, but are somehow always there' (2005, 131).

Urban theorists and cultural and psycho-geographers have often been unable to avoid the temptation to resort to a supernatural rhetoric when describing the modern urban experience. The passage of the crowd as a phantasmagoria, descriptions of fleeting, almost spectral encounter with strangers and the haunting (architectural) presence of multiple pasts all suggest how city life offers itself to such allusions.[1] The recent development of hauntological approaches across a range of academic disciplines has clearly demonstrated the ways in which the concept of the ghost freely lends itself to such allusive and abstract theorizing.[2] However, to understand what ghosts and haunted landscapes meant to people in the past, to appreciate the nature of their affective urban geographies, we must engage with the specific historical and cultural contexts in which they were generated and sustained. As such, this chapter eschews a more ambient or discursive spectrality, drawing instead upon ethnographic accounts of Victorian urban supernatural folklore.

This chapter explores three things. First, it considers various environmental and affective influences on the construction of a supernatural urban landscape. Second, it probes the distinctions to be found between outsider/ insider or literary/ethnographic understandings of fantasized urban spaces. Finally, it briefly explores some of the collective and tacitly subversive functions in imagining a haunted urban terrain, arguing that communal ghost stories played a role in mapping and appropriating altered understandings of local spaces and places. In doing so it seeks to suggest some of the ways in which the external, material landscape and internal, subjective feelings and responses met at the confluence of local ghost lore. It should be stated from the beginning that this chapter makes little claim to gauge the extent of belief behind these accounts. One must work with the reasonable assumption that there was a spectrum of engagement, ranging from genuine belief, through the operation of the 'ironic imagination' (whereby one knows that something is not real but chooses to suspend disbelief for the sake of entertainment), to outright scepticism (Saler 2012, 8–20). Nor was any given individual necessarily fixed in their convictions upon that spectrum. Regardless of the extent of belief, something all but impossible to measure in quantifiable terms, the very existence of urban ghost stories suggests that the city dweller's imagination had not withered in a supposedly disenchanted environment. Local ghost lore seems to indicate a certain craving for (re-?)enchantment; by creating and exchanging ghost stories urban communities imaginatively and endlessly enriched particular spaces and places within their local environment.

One may take exception to Jessop's sweeping dismissal of the imaginative capacities of urban Victorians but it is harder to deny his broader awareness of a mental distinction between those living in urban and rural environments.

The urban environment differed from the rural in the ways it influenced the imagination of its inhabitants. As with the formation of any folkloric narrative, the construction of supernatural urban folklore arose from how cities made people feel, from the affective geographies in which they were located and through which they passed. Rural supernatural imaginings tended to be inspired by an agoraphobic sense of vulnerability, whereas the urban supernatural was more likely to be engendered by the unsettling claustrophobia of the built environment and the press of its multitudinous inhabitants (Thelwell 1900–1901, 291–8). If the rural imagination drew upon the supernatural to express unease with the old, remote or dark places on the fringes of human settlement, the urban imagination responded to the unsettling sense of concealed secrets in the heart of expanding Victorian cities.

Some of the affective influences of the urban experience can be teased apart to demonstrate how the nature of the urban environment informed the generation of ghost stories and hauntings. Obscured visual conditions tended to encourage a reimagining of the urban environment, blurring its rigidity to make it more malleable in the mind. London's famous fogs were liable to prompt an imaginative shift towards the fantastical. Writing in the early decades of the twentieth century, H. V. Morton described how to enter the fog was to 'enter into an incredible underworld' in which 'a taxicab becomes something ogreish; a steam-lorry is a dragon spitting flame and grunting on its evil way. ... The fog ... turned London into a place of ghosts' (1933, 34).

The supernatural had long been associated with the night. George Grote's observation in 1820, that in darkness 'the impression of surrounding beings, whom we cannot see, and who are yet acting around us, is fastened upon our minds in the strongest manner', merely reiterated sentiments that date back to Thomas Nashe's *The Terrors of the Night* in the Elizabethan period (Grote 1820, 24; Nashe 1984, 208–50). Night limited and distorted the visual senses, generating uncertainty that made the imagination more inclined to flirt with supernatural notions. Evidence would suggest this cultural conditioning was not diminished in Victorian cities. A. Roger Ekirch has noted how 'night dramatically transformed the communal landscape, investing innocuous landmarks with sinister portent' (Ekirch 2005, 140). This sense of transformation and its resultant unease was expressed in Mark Knights's 1887 reflections on Norwich's nightscape: 'Mysterious almost is the influence of these venerable thoroughfares over the minds ... during the silent watches of the night, when the pale moon sheds athwart them in a flood of silvery light, throwing into picturesque relief hoary towers and pointed gables. Fancy twists ordinary objects ... into forms such as might have belonged to the buried past' (Knights 1887, 14). While having to account for their tongue-in-cheek humour, Manchester's nineteenth-century dialect ballads such as *Dean Church Ghost! A Recitation* and *The Boggart O'Gorton Chapelyord* certainly suggest urban churchyards

were not to be traversed at night for fear of meeting the resident boggart.[3]
A verse in the latter claimed:

> Across the yord o'er th' creawded graves,
> A footroad wonst passed through,
> Which, freely travelt up by day,
> At neet no mon dust goo. (Harland 1875, 537)

This sense of eeriness was not necessarily dispelled by the development of
gas lighting in many urban centres from the early 1820s. Gas lamps provided
a more steady illumination than oil lamps but they tended to create 'sudden
pools of light fringed by blackness' (Ackroyd 2000, 444). As such, the gas-
lit urban street retained a penumbra of darkness that was ripe with potential
mystery and threat. In some cases gas lamps were themselves the stimulus
for urban ghost scares. In December 1872 two lads were charged with making a disturbance following a gathering outside a house in Brixton, London.
The house's faulty gas lighting had given rise to the youths' claims that it
was haunted, and whenever the lights flickered the boys shouted that it was
a ghost. Their cries drew a mob in the street. When the boys knocked on
the front door, the woman inside the house was understandably scared and
refused to answer. When she went to the window, stones were thrown and
people shouted 'There's the ghost!' (*Pall Mall Gazette* 1872, 6).

If various forms of visual obscurity provided conditions that fostered
accounts of ghosts, the converse also had some influence. The encroachment
of new buildings and streets caused older edifices to stand out in a changing
environment, granting these remnants of previous historical periods an anachronistic visual distinction. There seems little mystery in the fact that older
buildings, particularly churches and pubs, tended to acquire ghost stories.
They served as a literal reminder of how the city's pasts constantly haunted
the spaces of the present. Excepting freak circumstances such as a workman's
fatal accident during the construction process, Jessop was generally right in
his assertion that new buildings did not tend to attract ghosts. It usually took
a generation or two, enough for buildings to become familiar landmarks and
acquire a certain historical presence, before ghosts started to take up tenancy.

Like the Victorians themselves, historians have been attracted by the urban
spectacle of the nineteenth century, both its monumentalizing civic grandeur
and the repulsion-attraction of its concealed social horrors. This has generally led to biasing the visual over other sensory experiences of the past. The
city's rich soundscape could also contribute to supernatural 'incidents' and
interpretations. In 1860 the *Manchester Times* reported that 'When strange
noises are heard in a house, we rather say it is haunted than that the material substances are moving about of their own accord ... the supposition of

spiritual interference, though it clashes with our experience, is more in harmony with our nature' (1860, 2). An 1885 article from the same newspaper declared 'it is impossible to say how many a ghost story would long ago have found a satisfactory solution if only attention had been paid to the properties of sound'. Combining the influence of night and sound, it continued, 'sounds are far more audible at night time ... and that what would fail to attract notice ... during the hours of sunlight, would probably be treated in a different aspect when once the darkness of evening has set in' (1885, 5). These visual distortions and aural misinterpretations suggest urban dwellers were just as willing as those in rural environments to resort to and even favour supernatural interpretations when immediate and obvious explanations were lacking. These readings of the environment were entertained even if (or quite possibly because) they resided beyond the boundaries of respectable rationality. For all the fear and anxiety generated by ghosts, the supernatural explanation was an appealing means of retaining or generating a sense of enchantment in an overwhelmingly prosaic, material environment.

Underlying the influence of these various sensory perceptions were psychological impressions derived from living in urban conditions. Dating back to the turn of the twentieth century, a number of theorists have contributed to the notion that the urban experience was (and remains) fundamentally unsettling and potentially ripe for haunting. Georg Simmel's sociological construct of the 'metropolitan man' and his adaptive ability to screen out much of the urban sensory experience highlighted a fear of contact within crowded streets (1997, 174–85). It also suggested that urban dwellers' minds endured a constant and potentially overwhelming barrage of aural, visual and olfactory stimulus. Perhaps more pertinent than Simmel's idea of individual disconnection was Walter Benjamin's emphasis on the imaginary engagement with the city, an environment that he considered to be full of (secular) enchantments informed by perceptions and memories. Benjamin argued that buildings and spaces store memories and meanings 'as pasts that are no longer visible press on the experience of the present' (Tonkiss 2005, 120 and 121). Like ghost stories, these meanings are not accessed in a direct or linear return to the past but via an appropriately attuned imagination. While not focussed specifically on the urban, Sigmund Freud's work on the uncanny, on the familiar and known disturbed into the *unhemlich* (unhomely) and strange, also has relevance here (Freud 2003, 121–62). In evicting people from the comfortable familiarity of their surroundings, ghosts articulated a sense of the unsettled and unsettling nature of the urban experience. They resonated with the fundamental unknowability of the city, an environment defined by surface appearances and concealed secrets. More recently, Anthony Vidler has associated urban unease with the modern city's pathological combination of agoraphobia and claustrophobia, seemingly paradoxical spatial fears that derive from the dual pressure of enclosed proximity amidst the expanding scale of the modernizing city (2002, 47).

None of this unease arose from any inherent quality within a particular locale, but rather from one's psychological experience of, interaction with, and response to the urban environmental experience. Growing urban conurbations ensured one could only ever possess a limited, and, relatively speaking, decreasing knowledge of surroundings and people. The modernizing city was defined by a sense that one always lacked personal control or influence over such a dominant environment. In an atmosphere constantly marked by the limitations of knowledge and a failure of comprehension beyond immediate, daily needs, the supernatural was one way of extending or enhancing a sense of both.

Ghost stories helped articulate how certain places made people feel, the supernatural providing a useful vocabulary for otherness, the unsettled, the unseen and the unsolid. They were a means of expressing the subconscious awareness that cities were not just bricks and mortar but rich psychical landscapes pulsating with resonances that were prone to generating unease. Shared through narratives, these intangible, unsettling feelings and impressions were translated into terms by which others could recognize and talk about them, and thereby cathartically alleviate the apprehension engendered by urban living. Obscured perception, eerie sounds, the distinction and imposing weight of past edifices amidst the modern and the very nature of living in the developing cities of the Victorian period all contributed to the generation of urban ghost stories. Contrary to Jessop's views then contemporaries imaginatively constructed haunted landscapes from whatever sensory and psychological impressions the local environment presented, imposed upon, or inspired within them.

Victorians' experiences of the city generated both genuine unease and the titillation of literary urban gothic imaginings. One can draw a distinction here between 'outsider' and indigenous or 'insider' perceptions of enchanted urban spaces. Such a formulation rifts upon Michel de Certeau's distinction between the conceptualized and experiential city. The 'outsider' view is akin to de Certeau's concept city, laid out and imagined in an encompassing spatial form, as a map, as a model, as viewed from atop a skyscraper (1988, 91–5). Where this particular outsider form diverges from de Certeau's concept is that his city was defined by an impression of order, legibility and comprehensibility, whereas the urban gothic promoted the symbol of the labyrinth, a concept that challenges, militates against and confounds comprehension. The 'insider' view is more akin to the lived city, the city as understood and navigated by pedestrians at street level. De Certeau likened the random routes taken by pedestrians to spatial stories that they tell with their feet and there is a kinship here with the way people wove their ghost stories around 'their' local spaces and places (1988, 97–103). Both 'outsider' and 'insider' perceptions involved projections of the imagination onto the urban environment but those projections took different narrative form. The conceptual 'outsider' view was usually depicted in literary and visual formats, not just as fictional literature (which may or may not feature ghosts) and urban cartography, but via government health report and journalistic social investigation by the likes of Henry Mayhew, Angus Reach and James Greenwood. The 'insider' perception was shaped by localized, ethnographic imaginings, amongst which we must include local gossip, rumour and ghost stories.

Contemporary 'outsider' views were frequently inflected through the lens of urban gothic fantasies. The idea of the mysterious, maze-like cityscape into which the light of civilization had failed to reach was promoted by journalists, fiction writers and medical officials alike, people who were usually social and geographical outsiders to the parts of the city they were exploring. John Philip Kay's *The Moral and Physical Condition of the Working Class* (1832) was an example of a doctor's attempt to grapple with the haunting presence of urban disease in the wake of the cholera outbreak of 1831. Indicative of the 'outsider' view, it portrayed the poverty-stricken districts of Manchester as a gothic underworld. Kay described how his pursuit of cholera, 'this messenger of death', led him into 'mighty wildernesses of building', where one 'must descend to the abodes of poverty, must frequent the close alleys, the crowded courts, the over-peopled habitations of wretchedness' (Kay 1832, 8 and 11). As indicated here, the language of social investigation was frequently one of quest, of a descent into netherworlds and the narrative sketching of grim cartographies of poverty, disease and crime.

Richard Maxwell has argued that this tendency to view the city as labyrinth was prompted by urban modernization itself, for when new, straighter streets were constructed the older, poorer districts that avoided modernizing came to 'exert a new fascination. Here there are many narrow, winding alleys … here, the visitor who is not a native may well feel mystified' (1992, 15). In such circumstances, gothic fantasy became a means of projecting beyond the limits of one's own knowledge and comprehension of these concealed netherworlds. This was best represented in the period's urban gothic fiction, a sub-genre epitomized by G. W. M. Reynolds's massively popular serial, *The Mysteries of London* (1844–1848). Removing the safe spatial and temporal distance of earlier gothic works, Reynolds and his imitators swapped a previous focus on labyrinthine forests and ancient ruined castles for the incarcerating maze of alleys and backstreet courts to be found in nineteenth-century London. Writers and their readers projected their sense of mystery and fear onto these concealed spaces from outside, increasingly from the safety of the suburbs. The motif proved enduring. Fin-de-siècle writers from Arthur Conan Doyle to Arthur Machen continued to perpetuate the notion of the urban labyrinth and its hidden secrets, supernatural or otherwise.

The reason for this persistence may lay in the way urban gothic depictions of the city-as-labyrinth symbolically represented truths about the incomprehensible nature of the modernizing city. Just as ghost stories helped express certain subconscious responses to the urban environment, so the evolving size, complexity and nature of Victorian urban conurbations seemed to actively encourage their re-imagining in terms of labyrinths. This gothic depiction resonated with the way the urban environment made people feel rather than what they actually saw or knew, while its attendant tropes of monstrosity and decay could articulate a host of contemporary social, political and medical anxieties about Victorian urban life. Yet in channelling these urban fears through what became familiar tropes, in vicariously flirting with the gothic horrors of the concealed city, this urban unease could be redirected and safely indulged in a fictional space.

When considering urban space from 'inside', from locals' perspectives, one gets a rather different impression. Local ghost stories were never located in an unknown labyrinth but in specific, known places. These accounts removed the distance and boundaries offered by 'outsider' literary representations. The power of local folkloric narratives came from entwining the supernatural into the material fabric of known neighbourhoods and lived spaces. This was reflected in Victorian street ballads too. Capturing oral gossip and news in doggerel rhyme or simple prose narratives, ballads generally adopted a mocking, humorous tone as they used local ghost scares to criticise popular credulity. A London street ballad, 'The Ghost of Woburn Square', claimed its bizarre ghost had 'escaped from St Pancras churchyard I hear, not liking the company he had got there' (Hindley 1969, 138). Printed in nearby St Giles, the writer or printer ensured the supernatural element was rooted in a real locality familiar to its predominantly local readership.

Churches and graveyards were common and obvious sites for locating folkloric accounts of supernatural encounters. This did not arise solely from the proximity of the dead to the living in the urban environment. Unusual grave features were prone to generating supernatural or macabre tales to explain them. Given Victorian anxieties about bodysnatching, graveyard 'hauntings' were also inclined to arise from the living being mistaken for ghosts, especially at night. In August 1851 rumour spread that a ghost had been seen in Shadwell churchyard, London. For several nights curious crowds gathered and caused a degree of disorder. When two men entered the graveyard to find the ghost they encountered two tea-urn makers who claimed to be doing the same thing. This resulted in a fight as one of the initial ghost seekers thought the men were the body snatchers after the corpse of his father. The 'ghost' was later revealed to be an old woman who lived in a nearby alms house. She had simply taken a short cut through the graveyard one night (*The Era* 1851, 14). The locals' imagination had done the rest. Informed by a vibrant body of popular beliefs relating to graves, corpses and supernatural returns, urban churchyards represented a vestigial sacred space amidst the increasingly secular city (Richardson 2001, 3–29). It is notable in this context that once the older, overcrowded churchyards were replaced by larger municipal cemeteries on the outskirts of cities it becomes harder to find comparable levels of ghost sightings.

This link between ghosts and the macabre meant the sites of urban executions were also frequently tainted by the supernatural, at least until public hanging was ended in 1868. Whether one reads the public gallows as a place where state-sanctioned murder took place or a criminal's rupture in the moral fabric was symbolically redressed and restored, they were places charged with meaning beyond the mundane. Following the hanging of Martha Alden at Norwich Hill, Norwich, in July 1807 local rumour claimed her ghost continued to haunt the site. This generated a crowd of eager ghost seekers who converged on the place of the execution and caused such disruption that some of them were eventually arrested (De Castre 1918, 93–4).

While the macabre dimension made graveyards and the gallows particularly potent sites in the haunted urban landscape, ghosts were just as likely to frequent more mundane locations. In 1863 the *Court Journal* claimed 'the number of so called haunted houses that are closed and have gone to decay in and about [London], under this mouldering and blighting reputation , is ridiculously large. We know of half a dozen such' (*Hampshire Telegraph* 1863, 3). Communal buildings such as pubs, theatres, schools, hospitals, asylums and barracks, buildings that had witnessed the passage and energies of multiple lives, tended to be the specific locations that generated local ghost stories. A district's empty buildings also drew spectres. Writing about his childhood in an Edwardian Salford slum, Robert Roberts reported that 'few houses in our district stood vacant for longer than a fortnight before ghosts got in' (1987, 148). Such was the crowded nature of urban existence that the sense of a void seemed to inspire unease, the locals filling the absence with supernatural tenants. Unlike the geographical remoteness of many rural phantoms, urban ghosts and ghost stories were necessarily woven tightly into the communal spaces of the living (Bell 2014, 60–1).

Lingering in the 'insider' or lived city, the remainder of this chapter will consider some of the communal functions of urban hauntings and the importance of ghosts in mapping invisible, collective, although far from consensual cartographies of local memory and imagination. Like all oral narratives, a ghost story required a function for both tellers and listeners, if not it would find no lasting place in the collective repertoire of local legends. This is not to say that everyone believed or had to believe the story. As previously mentioned, it is reasonable to assume that even within the small community formed around a street or urban district there would be little consensus over the veracity or meaning of a local ghost story.[4] Importantly though the ghost story still became associated with a particular locale in the memory regardless of whether it was believed or not. If the supernatural represented a fictional attempt to project beyond the limitations of the comprehensible in urban gothic imaginings, in local communities it became a means of imaginatively reinforcing and texturing a sense of the known. Rather than flights of fancy from the material world, communal ghost stories served as a collective means of imaginatively enhancing particular sites within a locality. Through briefly considering the spatial, temporal and socio-psychological dimensions of urban supernatural geographies, it will be suggested that ghosts helped articulate an altered and perhaps alternative localized understanding of urban spaces and places.

Ghosts were a means of ingraining collective memories (however false) in the community. The conflating of the known, material environment with a supernatural element created powerful, jarring tensions that served a useful mnemonic purpose. The specificity of a mundane place gave the narrative credibility while its continual retelling reinforced local bonds to specific sites, providing a sense of imagined connection even if the details of the story were invariably altered or embellished with each telling. As such, ghost stories were both rooted in and sustained by their locality.

Ghost stories also tended to be attuned to the melodramatic nature of many urban narratives. Whether in the penny gaff theatres or the serialized literature of the period, melodrama was frequently the preferred mode for imagining the divisions and extremes of wealth and poverty that co-existed in the city (Dentith 1998, 114–18). Its propensity for presenting rather theatrical, two-dimensional portrayals of moral and immoral characters could be found in both urban gothic tales and ethnographic ghost stories. To return from death usually required abnormal, melodramatic circumstances. Most ghosts had or acquired appropriately dramatic backstories which justified their genesis and granted them the power to leave something of themselves beyond death. Usually this resulted from the violence of their murder, suicide or accidental death. The narrative maps formed by ghost stories were frequently those that plotted the stains of past moral wrongdoings and tragedies that had been left upon the material environment in which they supposedly occurred. The ghost's fusion of the past and the present was necessarily a dramatic act and existence, and such heightened dramas made the mapping onto local places all the more memorable.

The external geography of the Victorian city may have been prone to development and change but its associated ghost lore existed in a collective, imaginative space that often proved more enduring in mapping the (mis-) remembered history of an evolving neighbourhood. Ghosts illustrated the multiple temporalities that infused the modern city for they never derived from just one period of history. Yet the historical accuracy of such accounts was not really that important. Nor was the fact that many elements of these local stories frequently conformed to generic narratives that were broadly repeated across oral folktales and literary works alike. What was more important was the way the oral exchange of ghost stories and legends worked a subtle transformation on the way audiences subsequently engaged with their locality. As the folklorist Terry Gunnell notes, local legends 'always involved an alteration of the environment in the minds of the listeners. ... The stories may not be true, but they change the world around us' (2009, 307). Accounts of ghosts and hauntings charged specific locations with supernatural meaning that caused them to be remembered as qualitatively different from their surroundings.

This narrative means of granting significance to particular physical spaces and places offers us a valuable glimpse into how contemporaries imagined and experienced their urban environment. Supernatural urban folklore enchanted the local terrain, drawing tellers and listeners into a web of shared stories that were fixed upon specific locations. The repeated retelling of ghostly accounts helped foster imaginative bonds, both between locals themselves and with the built environment in which they dwelt. While ghosts may have been a popular and long-established means of talking about otherness, in these particular circumstances they can also be read as a means of articulating and mapping a local sense of self, one informed by a narratively enriched comprehension of the local environment. Ghosts made urban localities known to their residents in ways official means of urban cognition such as maps or statistical data could not. They spoke to the epistemological uncertainties that arose from the fusion of the material and subjectively experienced cities, being at once spatially located but phantasmal, there but not always visible. These narrative 'maps' were not as objectively accurate as formal means of recording the city, but they were arguably truer in their psychological resonance.

As this suggests, city dwellers were active consumers and users of urban space, not just its passive subjects. Localized ghost accounts did more than just narratively memorialize and map spatial locations through dramatically fusing past and present, fiction and fact. They also served to imaginatively appropriate particular places and spaces into an altered, supernatural terrain of the community's creation. The imposition of the supernatural onto and into a mundane space disturbed and destabilized the formal, readable surfaces of those locations. A haunted building was no longer simply a house or a pub but something else too. This narrative act of alteration revealed that those formal meanings could be superseded and appropriated. This was a small, empowering gesture against an urban environment that intrinsically asserted the physical solidity and fixity of purpose of each place and space within it. Altering the meaning of localities through ghost stories did not have any obvious influence on a building's formal purpose but through imbuing it with an additional supernatural significance that generally remained unknown beyond the community, locals could still assert a sense of influence over their locality (Bell 2012, 249–56).

This sense of local communal agency was facilitated by the ever-present potential for alternative supernatural readings of the urban landscape. As above examples suggest, mere rumours of a ghost were enough for a community to appropriate a building or a space within their locality as supernatural. Such claims could arise at any time and from any one. These acts were not consciously initiated by the community as a whole. They began with individual 'authors' such as the boys outside the house in Brixton, but they were swiftly absorbed and appropriated by the community through rumour. External civic authorities could do nothing to stem the stories or the changes they wrought in the local imagination. Ghost accounts granted locals the power to imaginatively re-shape their urban surroundings as and when they chose.

Weaving an additional supernatural texturing and comprehension into specific urban sites possessed an element of tacit subversion. These altered topographical understandings were neither recognised by nor conformed to the city that was to be found on maps or in government reports. As entities that were out of joint with both space and time, ghosts were always potent figures of insubordination. By walking through walls built after their death they refused to abide by 'official' spatial ordering or to even acknowledge the solidity of their surroundings. Importantly, and with rare exception, urban ghosts were usually anthropomorphic figures. While rural ghosts may appear as animals, the teeming humanity of the city seems to have conditioned urban dwellers' imaginations to 'see' in a certain way, thus informing expectations as to the form urban ghosts would take. As such, accounts of urban ghosts' spatial transgressions can be understood as assertions of individual agency both in and over the built environment. As a product of the moment in which they were told, ghost stories presented their spectres as members of the contemporary community, and the telling of their supernatural accounts allowed narrators and audiences to vicariously share the phantom's unconscious acts of spatial rebellion.

These imaginative assertions arguably took their most explicit form in communal ghost hunting, a customary practice and popular entertainment that infrequently erupted in Victorian cities (Davies 2007, 90–4). Ghost hunts demonstrate how the mere rumours of the supernatural could still exert a powerful influence in urban neighbourhoods in the nineteenth century. Hunts frequently involved hundreds of people, particularly men and youths who took it upon themselves to protect their neighbourhood. In a scare in Bermondsey, London, in August 1868, arrests had to be made. At the trial the magistrate stated his surprise that 'some two thousand persons should be found to be so superstitious as to surround Bermondsey churchyard for hours on the chance of seeing a ghost' (*Daily News* 1868, 6). The common practice of gathering in large mobs and frequently refusing to be moved on by police officers represented a temporary but highly unpredictable communal reclamation of the streets.

Urban ghost hunts made public and explicit what the telling of local ghost stories did implicitly; both made communal claims upon urban locations whilst injecting a disruptive, supernatural element into the prosaic environment. *The Portsmouth Guardian* provided a particularly elaborate example in September 1854. For two consecutive nights rumours of a ghost left 'the neighbourhood [around Portsmouth's] Jewish Synagogue ... well-nigh impassable', the incident having 'created quite a sensation in the district'. Unusually this was not an anthropomorphic figure. Seemingly mocking the wild rumours in the locality, the newspaper reported that it was 'like a gigantic Cochin China cock, with boots and spurs, and fifty tremendous horns'. Other witnesses said it had 'glaring eyes ... and formidable hoofs ... and fire and brimstone issuing from its mouth' (*Bradford Observer* 1854, 3). Despite sociological arguments about the supposed decline of urban communities and the atomized individual's experience of the modern city, local ghost hunts and storytelling both illustrate a continuing collective response to the supposed eruption of the urban supernatural (Morrison 1995, 129–31).

The scattered accounts of historical urban hauntings that have made it into written records are undoubtedly the mere ruins of a former imaginative terrain, eroded by the transmission from oral to literary form and dissipated as urban communities changed over time. Yet in a way this was always the nature of urban supernatural geographies. The phantasmal city was never a unified whole that extensively co-existed within the material fabric of the mundane city. Its potential to exist was everywhere and anywhere within the urban environment but its tendency to manifest and be understood in a localized context meant it was always fragmentary and scattered. It was defined by those mere outcrops of the supernatural that intersected with and at best were temporarily embedded within specific, material locations. As befits its phantasmal nature, such a terrain would emerge into the communal consciousness, transforming and distorting the spaces and places with which they became associated, and then, as memories or stories faded, recede again. Like the modernizing, physical city within which it was entwined, such a terrain could never be comprehended in its totality.

This chapter has briefly attempted to tease out some of the various components of urban space—visual, aural, spatial, the temporal, the psychological, sociological and the imaginary—to enable us to start to comprehend the importance of a disjointed haunted landscape to Victorian city dwellers. Challenging the now somewhat clichéd notion of the city as a palimpsest, ghosts did not simply scrawl supernatural fantasies over the hard surface of its physical spaces. Their accounts blurred the mundane and the mysterious. Supernatural spaces were not so much layered as fused and melded, at least for the duration of the story, at most for as long as that story continued to circulate within the urban community from which it had emerged.

It is of course possible for us to quantitatively map the historical accounts of ghosts in specific urban localities. Existing projects like the online Paranormal Database represents a good online attempt to do just that.[5] However, mere spatial plotting tells us little about contemporaries' deeper imaginative engagement with their urban surroundings. More meaningful and more interesting is the vast socio-psychological hinterlands that lay hauntingly beyond those simple points of interface between supernatural and physical landscapes. Ghosts frequently become a means to talk about or at least represent something larger than themselves. In this particular case, they appear to offer some spectral hint of the rich terrain of imagination, memory and feeling that was enfolded within the Victorian city.

NOTES

1. See, for example, Pile (2005, 1–24 and 131–64).

2. Key examples include Jacque Derrida, *Spectres of Marx: The State of the Debt, the Work of Mourning, and the New International* (New York; Routledge, 1994); Avery F. Gordon, *Ghostly Matters: Haunting and the Sociological Imagination* (Minneapolis; University of Minnesota Press, 1998); Maria del Pilar Blanco and Esther Peeren (eds), *Popular Ghosts: The Haunted Spaces of Everyday Culture.* New York: Continuum, 2010.

3. A copy of the *Dean Church Ghost! A Recitation* is located in the Pearson Ballad Collection, Manchester Central Library, Vol. 1, 158.

4. For an example of mixed reactions in an urban locality see 'Window Smashing in Norwich; or The Mad Pranks of a Glazier's Ghost', *Norwich Songs, Ballads, Etc* (Norwich Millennium Library ref. C821.04 XL, Vol. 4, 111.
 5. See http://www.paranormaldatabase.com.

BIBLIOGRAPHY

Ackroyd, Peter. 2000. *London—The Biography*. London: Chatto and Windus.
Bell, Karl. 2012. *The Magical Imagination: Magic and Modernity in Urban England, 1780–1914*. Cambridge: Cambridge University Press.
Bell, Karl.. 2014. 'Civic Spirits: Ghost Lore and Civic Narratives in Nineteenth-Century Portsmouth.' *Cultural and Social History*, 11: 51–68.
Bradford Observer. 21 September 1854. 'Ghost in Portsmouth.' 3.
Daily News. 1 August 1868. 'The Police Courts—Southwark.' 6.
Davies, Owen. 2007. *The Haunted: A Social History of Ghosts*. Basingstoke: Palgrave.
De Castre, William. 1918. *Norfolk Folklore Collection*, Vol. 3. Great Yarmouth Library ref L398.
De Certeau, Michel. 1988. *The Practice of Everyday Life*. Berkeley, CA: University of California Press.
Dentith, Simon. 1998. *Society and Cultural Forms in Nineteenth-Century England*. Basingstoke: Palgrave Macmillan.
Ekirch, A. Roger. 2005. *At Days Close: A History of Nighttime*. London: Phoenix.
The Era. 17 August 1851. 'Laying a Ghost.' 14.
Freud, Sigmund. 2003. *The Uncanny*. London: Penguin.
Frisby, David. 2001. *Cityscapes of Modernity*. Cambridge, UK: Polity Press.
Grote, George. 1820. 'Essay on Magic.' British Library manuscript reference Add. 29531.
Gunnell, Terry. 2009. 'Legends and Landscape in the Nordic Countries.' *Cultural and Social History*, 6: 305–22.
Hampshire Telegraph. 12 September 1863. 'General Domestic News.' 3.
Harland, John. 1875. *Ballads and Songs of Lancashire, Ancient and Modern*. London: Routledge.
Hindley, Charles. 1969. *Curiosities of Street Literature*. Welwyn Garden City: Seven Dials.
Jessop, Augustus. 1882. 'Superstition in Arcady.' *The Nineteenth Century*, 733–55.
Kay, John Philip. 1832. *The Moral and Physical Condition of the Working Class*. 2nd edn. London: James Ridgway.
Knights, Mark. 1887. *The Highways and Byeways of Old Norwich*. Norwich: Jarrold and Sons.
Manchester Times. 13 June 1885. 'Mysterious Sounds.' 5.
—. 22 September 1860. 'Ghosts of the New and Old School.' 2.
Maxwell, Richard. 1992. *The Mysteries of Paris and London*. Charlottesville: University Press of Virginia.

Morrison, Ken. 1995. *Marx, Durkheim, Weber—Formations of Modern Social Thought*. London: Sage.

Morton, H. V. 1933. *The Heart of London*. 15th edn. London: Methuen.

Nashe, Thomas. 1984. *The Unfortunate Traveller and Other Works*. London: Penguin.

Pall Mall Gazette. 17 December 1872. 'Summary of This Morning's News.' 6.

Pile, Steve. 2005. *Real Cities*. London: Sage.

Richardson, Ruth. 2001. *Death, Dissection and the Destitute*. London: Phoenix.

Roberts, Robert. 1987. *A Ragged Schooling*. Manchester: Manchester University Press.

Saler, Michael. 2012. *As If: Modern Enchantment and the Literary History Prehistory of Virtual Reality*. Oxford: Oxford University Press.

Simmel, Georg. 1997. 'The Metropolis and Mental Life.' *Simmel on Culture*. Ed. David Frisby and Mike Featherstone. London: Sage. 174–85.

Thelwell, M. 1900–1901. 'The Power of Darkness.' *The Eastern Counties Magazine*, 1: 291–8.

Tonkiss, Fran. 2005. *Space, the City and Social Theory*. Cambridge, UK: Polity Press.

Vidler, Anthony. 2002. 'Bodies in Space/Subjects in the City.' *The Blackwell City Reader*. Ed. Gary Bridge and Sophie Watson. Oxford: Blackwell. 46–51.

Chapter Six

'The Girl Who Wouldn't Die'

Masculinity, Power and Control in The Haunting of Hill House *and* Hell House

Kevin Corstorphine

In the first century AD, Pliny the Younger writes a letter to Sura where he describes a haunted house. The motifs of his description would remain relatively unchanged over the next two millennia:

> There was at Athens a large and spacious but ill-reputed and pestilential house. In the dead of the night a noise, resembling the clashing of iron, was frequently heard, which, if you listened more attentively, sounded like the rattling of fetters; at first it seemed at a distance, but approached nearer by degrees; immediately afterward a phantom appeared in the form of an old man, extremely meagre and squalid, with a long beard and bristling hair, rattling the gyves on his feet and hands. The poor inhabitants consequently passed sleepless nights under the most dismal terrors imaginable. This, as it broke their rest, threw them into distempers, which, as their horrors of mind increased, proved in the end fatal to their lives. (2006, 68–9)

Similar narratives reverberate through the earliest folk tales and European literature, but coalesce most notably in the emergence of the Gothic novel in the late eighteenth century, usually identified with the publication of Horace Walpole's *The Castle of Otranto* in 2014. 'Graveyard' poets such as Walpole's friend Thomas Gray 'wrote poems infused with melancholia and littered with ruins: crumbling monasteries and castles' (Reynolds 2013, 86), cementing the link between the faded grandeur of old buildings with a sense of supernatural mystery.

The late twentieth century saw the development of what Dale Bailey identifies as a distinct 'contemporary haunted house formula [which] took shape in the 1970s and 1980s' (1999, x). This might include popular novels including, for example, Robert Marasco's *Burnt Offerings* (1973), Jay Anson's *The Amityville Horror* (1977), Stephen King's *The Shining* (1977), and Anne Rivers Siddons's *The House Next Door* (1978), and has recently been revived on the screen with the success of films such as *Paranormal Activity* (2007) and *The Conjuring* (2013). What the contemporary haunted house story takes for granted is a reliance on the terminology, aesthetics and morality of the late nineteenth century, particularly the Spiritualist tradition and the Victorian ghost story that drew on its world view. As Mark Llewellyn points out, 'relatively little has been done to assert the... connective threads surrounding shadows and ghosts of the Victorian period in the present as a re-articulation of the Victorians' own fascination with séances, spectres and other spooky things' (2009, 24). The emergence of a new wave of 'neo-Victorian' fiction in recent years has provided a means through which to explore and respond to the period, but it is shot through with a postmodern sensibility that creates a further distance from its subject matter.

This chapter will identify two novels as bridging this gap in both time and tone, and shaping the haunted house formula as we have come to know it: Shirley Jackson's *The Haunting of Hill House* (1959) and Richard Matheson's *Hell House* (1971). Both of these novels are striking in the way that they look backwards, even as they attempt to reinvent the ghost story within the scientific and political contexts of their own time. The result reveals much about how these kinds of narratives portray identity and history, and situate them within space and place. The setting of both novels is contemporaneous with their publication, but the events they describe take place some 60 or 70 years after the building of the houses that inform their narratives. In this sense the novels are not just haunted by the ghosts they portray, but by the broader sense of the 'spirit' of a past age. Llewellyn points out that 'through pastiche and re- visioning, through the mesmeric nature of rereading, the ghost writers of the present are playing an ambiguous game with a contemporary readership hungry for the summoned spirit of a Victorian fiction they believe in' (2009, 42). Jackson and Matheson, writing before the emergence of modern neo-Victorian fiction, were likewise summoning the spirits of the past in order to play narrative games within an ongoing tradition. It is a story that begins more than a century before the publication of their novels.

In 1848 the Second Great Awakening was sweeping the United States, with new religious movements springing up and gaining adherents. Western and Central New York gained the nickname 'the burned-over district' because so many people had been converted there was no more fuel (i.e., people/souls) for the 'fire' of evangelism. It was in the midst of this fervour that two adolescent girls named Kate and Margaret Fox decided to play a prank that would end up steering not only the course of their lives but those of thousands of others. Claiming to communicate with the spirit of a peddler who had been murdered and buried in the basement of their home, they demonstrated their technique of asking questions to which ghostly rapping noises would indicate yes or no. An investigation by scholars from the University of Buffalo suggested that they were able to produce the knockings themselves, by cracking the joints in their lower bodies. A confession by Margaret in 1888 confirmed this explanation, which was quickly circulated in newspapers and even a book titled *The Death-Blow to Spiritualism*, published the same year. It was, however, far from a death-blow. Margaret retracted the confession, and spiritualism continued to attract devotees over the coming decade. This was much to the frustration of sceptics like Harry Houdini, who devoted his later years to exposing fraudulent psychics. One member of the Society for Psychical Research, Ada Goodrich Freer (writing as 'Miss X'), later attempted to work out why this case should prove so enduring, despite having been so thoroughly debunked:

> A special feature of the Hydesville phenomena was the claim of the Fox girls to the power of communicating with the departed [...] The idea of communication with those who are gone can be indifferent to none; it must attract or disgust, it must be food for heart-hunger or offend the most tender sensibilities of all who consider it. (1899, 3)

Freer distinguishes this kind of paranormal activity as of a different order than the older traditions of the malevolent spirit and the raising of the dead. In this she was extremely accurate. These ideas have endured, but are largely confined to horror fiction. The idea of mediumship, with its promise of making contact with departed loved ones, continues to exert an appeal over ordinary people, however much that may frustrate the sceptic who denounces the practice as fraudulent. Faith, of course, has never relied on the trivialities of evidence.

Also, in 1848, Catherine Crowe's popular book *The Night Side of Nature; or, Ghosts and Ghost Seers* appears, laying out Crowe's own views of the supernatural alongside various stories of 'real' hauntings. The title reflects a key tenet of spiritualism; that these phenomena are part of the spectrum of what should properly be considered 'natural'. As she says, 'I do not propose to consider them as supernatural; on the contrary, I am persuaded that the time will come, when they will be reduced strictly within the bounds of science' (1848, 5). Indeed, the need to reconcile science with the 'supernatural' would come, over the next few decades, to capture the imagination of artists and intellectuals across the world. The Society for Psychical Research (SPR) was founded in Britain in 1882, followed by the American equivalent in 1885. A century after these events, Spiritualist beliefs continued to fascinate, as they do into the twenty-first century. Nineteenth-century aesthetics have come to constitute a kind of shorthand for the supernatural. As Barry Curtis notes in his study of haunted houses in film, 'the Victorian house has itself acquired the recurrent persistence of a ghost in popular film' (2008, 45).

Indeed, the titular house of Shirley Jackson's *The Haunting of Hill House* was built 'some eighty-odd years' (1999, 75) before the events of the novel. If we assume that the story is contemporaneous with its publication, then this means at some point in the 1870s. The protagonist is Eleanor Vance, who comes to stay in Hill House at the invitation of Dr Montague, who has chosen her because of an event in her childhood when stones rained down on her house, possibly as a result of a poltergeist manifestation. He also invites Theodora, a bohemian artist who has displayed psychic ability by correctly identifying hidden cards in Montague's laboratory, and Luke Sanderson, a dissolute liar and petty thief who is heir to Hill House through his aunt. The 'psychic' phenomena that occur throughout the novel not only affect these characters individually, but also the ways in which they interact with each other in the confined space of the house. This is a staple theme of Gothic horror, but in particular that of the 'old dark house' genre, used to describe films popular in the 1920s and 1930s such as *One Exciting Night* (1922) and *The Cat and the Canary* (1927). The key characteristics of these films are drawn together in James Whale's film *The Old Dark House* (1932), based on J. B. Priestley's novel *Benighted* (1927), where three travellers take shelter from a storm and are taken in by a family of eccentrics. The plot itself harks back to classic Gothic, in particular, Charlotte Brontë's *Jane Eyre* (1847).

It is the era of these films, the 1920s, which Richard Matheson chooses to look back at with his version of the story, *Hell House*. Matheson's novel was published 12 years later than Jackson's and, although it shares themes with *The Haunting of Hill House*, displays a distinctly different sensibility. The 'Hell House' of the title, or Belasco House (after its creator, Robert Belasco), was built in 1919 and witnessed scenes of debauchery and death over the course of the Roaring Twenties. There is a more overt acknowledgement of the historical horrors that have occurred than in *The Haunting of Hill House*. Hugh Crain, the original owner, created a book for his daughter to teach her about the seven deadly sins, and filled it with lurid illustrations of Hell. Robert Belasco had them played out in reality. Throughout the course of these novels Jackson and Matheson tend towards the opposing categories of terror and horror respectively. These were laid out by Ann Radcliffe in her 1826 article 'On the Supernatural in Poetry':

> Terror and horror are so far opposite, that the first expands the soul, and awakens the faculties to a higher degree of life; the other contracts, freezes, and nearly annihilates them. I apprehend that neither Shakespeare nor Milton by their fictions, nor Mr. Burke by his reasoning, anywhere looked to positive horror as a

source of the sublime, though they all agree that terror is a very high one; and where lies the great difference between horror and terror, but in uncertainty and obscurity, that accompany the first, respecting the dreader evil? (Radcliffe, ix)

This famous distinction, drawing on Edmund Burke, leads to a history of criticism that rests on the basis that horror 'shows' where terror 'tells'. Ellen Moers expands on Radcliffe's distinction to theorize a distinctly 'female' Gothic, although her own analysis of Shelley's *Frankenstein* as 'a horror story of maternity' (1976, 220) shows that women can certainly write in the horror mode. Matheson's *Hell House* can in many ways be seen as a novel that vividly illustrates that which was only hinted at by Jackson. There is a perverse satisfaction in its evocation of the grotesque, but at the loss of the subtlety that characterizes *The Haunting of Hill House*. It is interesting to note that this 'female' subtlety, traced from Radcliffe through to Jackson, is also expressed brilliantly in Henry James's 'The Turn of the Screw' (1898), showing, as with the case of Shelley, the importance of separating sex from gender in terms of authors. Nonetheless, the governess of James's Bly, haunted by either the ghost of Peter Quint or her imagination of such, conforms to Anne Williams's claim that 'the Female Gothic plot is a version of "Beauty and the Beast"' (1995, 145) where the protagonist's romantic fantasies of transforming monstrosity with love are fulfilled. In James, as with Jackson, the danger of such fantasies is exposed.

The title of this chapter is taken from the self-consciously Gothic opening to *Hell House*. The protagonist, Dr. Barrett, is on his way to visit an old newspaper mogul called Deutsch. Deutsch is dying, and wishes to finally establish the existence or not of the afterlife, before he is condemned to face it. He promises one hundred thousand dollars as payment for proof either way. Barrett, a sceptic, despairs of the fact that 'the old man's chain of newspapers and magazines were forever printing articles on the subject. "Return from the Grave!"; "The Girl Who Wouldn't Die"—always sensational, rarely factual' (1971, 9). These evocative titles are reminiscent of the American Gothic tradition, and indeed both could be applied to Poe's 'The Fall of the House of Usher' (1839), but are also obviously parodic. This itself puts *Hell House* in a long tradition of Gothic parodies such as Jane Austen's *Northanger Abbey* (1817), where the young protagonist, Catherine Morland, is recommended seven 'horrid novels' that might suit her lurid tastes in fiction. Indeed, in the opening paragraph Dr. Barrett is almost cast as the female Gothic 'heroine', describing himself as feeling 'rather like a character in some latter-day Gothic romance' (1971, 9). The novel is clearly modelled on *The Haunting of Hill House*, with even the similar title serving as homage to Jackson's novel. It is the original, however, which has attracted most critical attention, including feminist analyses focusing on Eleanor's troubled relationship with her mother and growing madness in the face of her inability to fit into the models offered to her by society. From this point of view the novel reads as a kind of version of Sylvia Plath's *The Bell Jar* (1963) in a spooky mansion. Matheson's novel is decidedly less subtle, certainly more exploitative and arguably misogynistic in its gleeful torture of women. It is worthwhile to note that his earlier novels, including *I Am Legend* (1954) and *The Shrinking Man* (1956), offer intriguing critiques of masculinity, and *I Am Legend* in particular clearly questions the way in which its protagonist, Neville, treats women (albeit vampires) as callously as he does during his experiments.

Barrett, at Deutsch's bidding, joins a team of researchers consisting of himself and two mediums, one 'mental' and the other 'physical'. In addition, his wife Edith insists on joining them. Together, they move into Belasco House, which Barrett describes as 'the Mount Everest of haunted houses' (1971, 15). There is some debate, though, over how it has come to be haunted. Florence, the mental medium, claims that 'we'd be mistaken to think of the house as the haunting force [...] quite evidently, the trouble is created by surviving personalities' (52). This is in response to Fischer, the physical medium who has returned to Hell House after a previous investigation that killed two of his previous team and drove a third insane. Barrett points out that the house has not lived up to its reputation, to which Fischer replies, 'It hasn't taken our measure yet' (52). Both Barrett and Fischer place an emphasis on 'it': the house, granting it an anthropomorphic sense of agency. Manuel Aguirre, in his study of horror fiction, *The Closed Space*, argues that the identification of the house itself as the horror is the dominant mode of the modern haunted house story: 'The first thing that we learn about the modern Haunted House is that it is alive. It is not just inhabited by some ghostly presence, as *Otranto* was: rather, the force that lurks in it is *part of* the house itself. [...] The house in modern terror fiction is not a haunted but a *haunting* house' (1990, 190). Here Aguirre is specifically discussing, among others, *The Haunting of Hill House*, where Barrett's equivalent character, Dr. Montague, claims that 'it might not be too fanciful to say that some houses are born bad' (1999, 70). Although this becomes a tagline for the 1999 remake of Robert Wise's superior film adaptation *The Haunting* (1963), he actually escapes from giving a definitive answer to the question of whether hauntings are due to nature or nurture:

> Hill House, whatever the cause, has been unfit for human habitation for upwards of twenty years. What it was like before then, whether its personality was molded by the people who lived here, or the things they did, or whether it was evil from its start are all questions I cannot answer.... No one knows, even, why some houses are called haunted. (Jackson 1999, 70)

For whatever reason though the house is not haunted by ghosts as such, but as Aguirre points out, is itself the haunting force. Montague claims that 'the evil is the house itself ... it is a place of contained ill will' (82). Hugh Crain, the original owner of Hill House, had built it as a family home, before the death of his wife, and then his second wife, then the third (more on this later). It is strongly implied that some evil has taken root here, but nowhere is it made as explicit as *Hell House*'s explanation for how the Belasco House became 'unfit for human habitation'. When Barrett's wife, Edith, asks him how Hell House got its name, he tells her that it is 'because its owner, Emeric Belasco, created a private hell there' (26). After a childhood characterized by chopping a cat into pieces at age five and sexually assaulting his sister at age ten, he was sent to a private school where he was molested by a teacher and later invited the man to his house, after which the older man hanged himself, presumably due to Belasco's influence. He grew into a six-foot-five man known as the Roaring Giant, and studied widely in philosophy, religion, and languages. In the 1920s, he began to host parties. These began as evenings of fine dining and philosophical debates, but soon descended into drug-fuelled orgies, and then to murder. 'A literal re-enactment of de Sade's 120 Days of Sodom' (60) was followed by a Roman circus at which 'the highlight was the eating of a virgin by a starving leopard' (61). Eventually the guests reverted to living like animals, 'rarely bathing, wearing torn, soiled clothes, eating and drinking anything they could get their hands on, killing each other for food or water, liquor, drugs, sex, blood, even for the taste of human flesh, which many of them had acquired by then' (61). They are all later found dead, apart from Belasco, who was not in their number.

It is taken as a starting point that these horrors are somehow the root cause of the current state of the house. How this should have come to be is the crucial part of the investigation. Barrett is a sceptic with regard to the spiritual, but is nonetheless scientifically open to the possibility that something is really happening. His belief system can be summed up in a conversation with Deutsch's son, who insists, perhaps reasonably, that his investigation is a waste of the family fortune. At the younger Deutsch's insistence that there is no such thing as the supernatural, Barrett replies in the affirmative, but adds that 'the word is "supernormal". Nature cannot be transcen—' (14) before Deutsch angrily cuts him off. That everything, including ghosts, can be considered to be part of nature, is a tradition in thought that is really cemented in the late Victorian period, in the urge to reconcile the enduring idea of haunting to newly uncovered scientific findings. Jackson's novel explicitly pays homage to this tradition, noting that 'Dr. Montague's methods with regards to Hill House derived from the methods of the intrepid nineteenth-century ghost hunters; he was going to go and live in Hill House and see what happened there' (Jackson 1999, 4). *Hell House*, however, takes these references even further.

In a study of the 1973 film version of the novel, retitled *The Legend of Hell House*, Murray Leeder points out the significance of Dr. Barrett's name:

> Barrett is almost certainly named for William Fletcher Barrett (1844–1925). Like his fictional namesake, he was a physicist who devoted the latter part of his career to psychical investigation. This Dr Barrett was one of the founders of the Society for Psychical Research, the London-based organization founded in 1882 for the purpose of scientific investigation of psychic powers, mediumship, haunted houses and the like. (2014, 36)

William Fletcher Barrett visited Boston in 1884, and addressed a group of intellectuals from Harvard alongside local clergymen. He urged the formation of an American branch of the SPR to further the work into reconciling the realms of the spiritual and material worlds (Blum 2007, 82). He was there on the invitation of William James, the eminent psychologist and brother of Henry, who was fascinated with spiritualism, and did indeed go on to be a founding member of the American branch of the SPR the following year. In a 1909 essay he writes that 'It is hard not to suspect that here may be something different from a mere chapter in human gullibility. It may be a genuine realm of natural phenomena' ([1909] 1986, 363). James was foremost a scientist, and this reconciliation with 'nature' was the crucial test.

Although drawing inspiration from these very earnest scientific enquiries, *Hell House* is very much a sensationalist horror story. Whether the forces are supernatural or 'supernormal', the investigators are tormented by them throughout, and Matheson seems to take great relish in describing, among other things, a sexual assault perpetrated by the medium Florence upon Edith, where she tells her (unconvincingly in the circumstances) that, 'men are ugly, men are cruel. Only women can be trusted' (1971, 232). The depths of depravity are truly realized in the house's chapel, where a huge statue of Christ has been desecrated by having had a phallus modelled onto it. This falls from the wall and crushes Florence, penetrating her violently in the process. At this point she has seemingly already been raped by a ghost, and the somewhat unkind implication is that she has brought this on herself, inviting sexual corruption through her initial naivety. If Christianity is the motif, then Florence is surely Eve, providing the Devil with a means through which to corrupt. The master of this particular Hell is definitely a male presence, although not quite what the investigators might have suspected.

After all the violence and death, Belasco is finally discovered. He is dead, and his corpse shows evidence of what kind of man he was. The 'Roaring Giant' was, in reality, extremely short, and had his legs amputated in order to wear prosthetic ones to make him appear taller. He had sat down with a pitcher of water and allowed himself to die of thirst, 'his final achievement of will' (1971, 299). There had been a ghost, but only one: Belasco's. One spirit that had been controlling all of the events, manipulating the residents of the house into believing that there were other, more sympathetic spirits at work. Belasco may have had physical shortcomings, but had been a man of great wealth and power. The wealth was inherited from his father, who was a munitions manufacturer. Florence suggests that this bloody history might have made him feel guilty, but Barrett refutes this: 'Belasco never felt a twinge of guilt in his life' (56). Here the novel departs from *The Haunting of Hill House* in important ways. This has left the realm of the psychological in providing a comprehensive, although far-fetched, explanation for everything that has happened. Barrett's goal of understanding the 'supernatural' through scientific means is actually achieved, although he dies, mutilated and drowned by an invisible force, before this is discovered. Barrett had come armed with a machine called the 'Reversor', which he had hoped would cleanse the house of psychic energy. The implication is that this would have worked, had Belasco not shielded himself in a lead-lined room.

In contrast to Belasco's lack of guilt, it is Eleanor's guilt which drives the narrative of *The Haunting of Hill House*. It is noteworthy, then, that both novels allude to a strange real-life case of supposed haunting: the house of Sarah Winchester in San Jose, California. In Jackson's novel, Dr. Montague points out the odd shape of the house, which causes the guests to become lost and confused throughout. He suggests that perhaps 'old Hugh Crain expected that someday Hill House might become a showplace, like the Winchester House in California' (Jackson 1999, 105). Hill House has been constructed with every angle slightly wrong: as system that reflects the twisted mind of its creator as well as subtly affecting the minds of the residents. The reference to the Winchester House is more oblique in Matheson's novel, but there is a likely connection with detail that Belasco acquired his wealth through being heir to a munitions fortune. Dr. Barrett tells the group how the fortune represented 'proceeds from the sales of rifles and machine guns' (1971, 56) and when asked by Florence if this made Belasco feel guilty replies that 'Belasco never felt a twinge of guilt in his life' (56).

There are strong connections to the Winchester House in both the construction of the houses and in the theme of guilt. The mansion now known as the 'Winchester Mystery House', and run as a tourist attraction, was built by Sarah Winchester, wife of William Wirt Winchester, who had made a fortune from selling his family's famous Winchester rifles. The Winchester rifle, in particular the 1873 model, was so popular that it would later gain the nickname of 'The Gun that Won the West'. On inheriting the money, Sarah apparently became convinced that she was being haunted by the spirits of the rifle's many victims, mostly Native Americans, and built the house continually from 1884 to 1922, remodelling rooms and extending it over and over again. It is now a commercially run tourist attraction. The rooms lead into one

another, and in other places to dead ends. The chimneys don't always extend
out of the roof, and there are staircases that lead to nowhere. A report in *The
American Weekly* from 1928 (reproduced on the house's website) describes it
in the following way:

> When Mrs. Winchester set out for her Séance Room, it might well have dis-
> couraged the ghost of the Indian or even of a bloodhound, to follow her. After
> traversing an interminable labyrinth of rooms and hallways, suddenly she would
> push a button, a panel would fly back and she would step quickly from one
> apartment into another, and unless the pursuing ghost was watchful and quick,
> he would lose her.

This could have come straight out of a Gothic novel, but also hints at a specifically American form of haunting: the guilt of the past. The 'old Indian burial
ground', of course, is a staple of American horror fiction. Leslie Fiedler's
seminal *Love and Death in the American Novel* identifies a lurking trace of
the Gothic within the American Dream. Fiedler notes that alongside slavery,
'the slaughter of the Indians, who would not yield their lands to the carriers
of utopia [...] provided new evidence that evil did not remain with the world
that had been left behind' (1997, 143). As Teresa Goddu convincingly argues
in a similar vein, '[American] gothic tells of the historical horrors that make
national identity possible yet must be repressed in order to sustain it' (1997,
10). The Winchester House speaks of a moment in history when the myth
of Manifest Destiny was giving way to an awareness of the horrors underpinning its enactment. Belasco, however, is immune to any sense of liberal
guilt. Morally he is the bastard love-child of Aleister Crowley and Ayn Rand,
expressing his will so fully that it overcomes death. Although Belasco built
secret panels into his house in order to hide his corpse, he represents the polar
opposite of Sarah Winchester because he embraces, rather than runs from, the
horrors of his past. Both houses have something in common though, representing the shape of an individual's imagination brought into being, complete
with its dark corridors.

The differences between these figures raise questions of gender and its representation in the Gothic. Anne Williams, expanding on the line of reasoning
discussed earlier, suggests that there are distinct 'male' and 'female' modes
in Gothic writing, although these do not necessarily correspond to biologi-
cally male or female authors. She claims that in male Gothic, women are seen
as objects of the male gaze, and dangerous objects of sexual temptation at
that, creating 'unconscious resentments against the feminine' (1995, 109).
In female Gothic, however, the gaze is a more positive force, as 'her perception enlarges her world, opens up the possibility of discovering good, and of
finding what she seeks' (145). It is tempting to read Jackson's *The Haunting*

of Hill House as a pessimistic updating of the female Gothic narrative: like the heroines of these novels who end up happily married, Eleanor fantasizes that 'journeys end in lovers meeting' (Jackson 1999, 39) but in her case finds only madness and death. *Hell House* is actually more in line with Williams's theory, as Edith and the traumatized Fischer defeat Belasco by confronting his spirit and hurling insults at him, destroying him with their knowledge of the truth.

Other female characters in these novels are characterized by a comical credulity. Like Sarah Winchester, whose belief in Indian spirits was inspired by sitting with a medium, *Hell House*'s Florence holds firm Spiritualist beliefs and even manifests a 'spirit guide' called Red Cloud. These beliefs are shared by Dr Montague's wife in *The Haunting of Hill House*, who bustles in and declares 'You've been here nearly a week and I suppose you've done *nothing* with planchette? Automatic writing? I don't imagine either of those young women has mediumistic gifts?' (1999, 181). Mrs Montague is a humorous character who continually nags her husband. To Dr Montague's lack of enthusiasm, she also turns up with a mysterious male companion, Arthur, who seems to exist solely to be bossed around by her. Mrs Montague's idealistic beliefs about the healing power of pure love may portray her as somewhat foolish, but she does not suffer because of this. Florence, however, is deceived by Belasco into believing that the spirit she detects is his son, Daniel, who needs her help. It is this belief that leads her to be raped, possessed and eventually killed. Belasco is a manipulator above all else, and in this is a descendant of Hugh Crain, as well as the older tradition of a brutal patriarch: Bluebeard.

The figure of Bluebeard looms large in these stories, describing as it does a tyrannical patriarch who revels in his absolute mastery of the domestic space. His story is the best known survivor of various such folk tales that had been popular in late medieval and early modern Europe. The version written by Charles Perrault in 1697 has become the standard. In this story, Bluebeard has had several wives. He charms a young lady with his wealth and charisma, and having married her, gives her the keys to his vast house. When he leaves one day, he points out the key to the one room she must never enter. Inevitably, she does, and finds the murdered corpses of his previous wives. The key is magically stained by blood that will not clean off, and discovering this, he allows her only time to reconcile herself to God before he will kill her too. Fortunately, her brothers appear in time to slay Bluebeard and save her. Hugh Crain too, as Dr Montague euphemistically points out, 'seems to have been—unlucky in his wives' (1999, 77). The first was killed as her carriage overturned, before she even reached the house for the first time. The second died of a fall and the third from consumption while travelling with Crain in Europe. Belasco, too, has a chequered history with women involving incest, abuse and suicide. Like Bluebeard, he must have wanted people to come to his house and fall victim to his machinations. He had even left a recorded message for future visitors with instructions: 'Go where you will, and do what you will—these are the cardinal precepts of my home. Feel free to function as you choose. There are no responsibilities, no rules. "Each to his own device" shall be the only standard here. May you find the answer that you seek. It is here, I promise you' (1971, 38). His philosophy is likely a reference to Aleister Crowley's law of Thelema, and specifically his famous maxim that 'Do what thou wilt shall be the whole of the Law.' This, however, is an illusion. Belasco does not wish to enable visitors to pursue their own goals, but to fall prey to his manipulations. The landscape which he has created is one suffused with masculine authority.

This has clear precedent in the Bluebeard tale. He forbids his young wife from going into the forbidden room, but it is self-evident that he knows she will. Bruno Bettelheim points out how 'it immediately becomes obvious that the female is strongly tempted to do what is forbidden to her' (1991, 301), and reads the story as one about the temptation to sexual infidelity, with Bluebeard testing his young wife. This perspective, however, elides a reading of the story whereby Bluebeard may actively desire this to happen. Edgar Allan Poe, in 'The Imp of the Perverse' (1845), points out that many of our actions are not driven by rationality but in fact 'we perpetrate them merely because we feel that we should *not*' (283, original emphasis). This kind of 'perversity' is evident in the young bride's actions. Bluebeard must be well aware that she will fall victim to her own curiosity. Past experience alone should tell him as much, given the contents of the room. Perhaps the only difference between Bluebeard and Belasco is that Belasco is more honest in his intentions. A sense of confidence in the ownership of their territory allows for transgression within strictly anticipated limits. The young bride may be able to look into the room, but she cannot escape from the castle, at least not without help. Angela Carter brings this out in her revision of the story, 'The Bloody Chamber' (1979), when the bride character speaks to her only ally, a blind piano tuner:

> 'You disobeyed him,' he said. 'That is sufficient reason for him to punish you.'
> 'I only did what he knew I would.'
> 'Like Eve,' he said. (1995, 37–8)

Carter exposes the dynamic of patriarchal authority that runs through all of these narratives. The suggestion is that Bluebeard is a sadistic tyrant, and by extension so too is the God of Genesis. Jack Zipes notes that in Perrault's story, 'the female role is dictated by conditions that demand humility and self-discipline' (1991, 40), pointing out that she is saved when she resorts to prayer. The same might well be said of the tradition of blaming Eve for the Fall of Man, in the service of the attempt to control women and enforce patriarchal values. Carter's story seems to expose this as a kind of perverse power game: something that can be seen in *Hell House*'s Belasco and the way that he manipulates Florence in particular, by appealing to her desire to save 'Daniel' Belasco. In Matheson's bleak narrative the blasphemous statue of Christ punishes, rather than saves.

It would be going too far to say that *Hell House* is, like Carter's story, an overt attempt to revise fairytale narratives. Rather, it functions as a straightforward horror story, and one with overtly misogynist overtones. Contextualization of the novel provides useful points of comparison. Its relentless and brutal treatment of women brings to mind Susan Faludi's argument in *Backlash* (1991), that at times of feminist gains, an 'anti-feminist backlash has been set off not by women's achievements of full equality but by the increased possibility that they might win it' (14). It is notable that *Hell House* is published in 1971, when the previous year had seen the American Women's Strike for Equality. This is a novel where one woman, overtaken by madness, has to be punched on the jaw by a man to help her snap out of it (273) and another slapped in the face 'as hard as possible' (220) when overcome with wanton lust. Notable too is that 1971 sees the publication of a more famous novel about weak and pliable women becoming vessels for demonic male forces: William Peter Blatty's *The Exorcist*. Indeed both novels feature extraordinarily brutal depictions of women's bodies being lacerated by unseen forces. Young women have long been associated with these forces, going back as least as far as the Fox Sisters with their rapping spirits, but in a broader sense to the witchcraft hysteria that swept Early Modern Europe. This, of course, recurred in Salem Massachusetts in 1692, when the seeming possession of two young girls sparked trials which saw nearly three hundred people, mostly women, accused, and 20 executed. The narrator of Nathaniel Hawthorne's 'Alice Doan's Appeal' (1835), looking at Gallow's Hill, where the executions were carried out, expresses perfectly how these events have come to affect the American psyche, and have even scarred the land itself: '[a] physical curse may be said to have blasted the spot, where guilt and phrenzy consummated the most execrable scene, that our history blushes to record. For this was the field where superstition won her darkest triumph; the high place where our fathers set up their shame, to the mournful gaze of generation far remote' (2013, 74). Hawthorne's portrayal of the way in which the sins of the father continue to affect future generations is, of course, heavily influenced by the notion of original sin, filtered by Puritan doctrine, but also shows a sense of self-awareness and criticism lacking at the time of the trials. A more progressive society must live with the knowledge that it rests on injustice, superstition and violence. Importantly, the land itself bears witness to these traumatic events. Roger Luckhurst suggests that '[t]rauma is a piercing or breach of a border that puts inside and outside into a strange communication. Trauma violently opens passageways between systems were once discrete, making unforeseen connections that distress or confound' (2008, 3). Both Hill House and Hell House are affected by their past in a way that expresses this uncanny breach between past and present, dredging up supposedly forgotten horrors.

In *The Haunting of Hill House*, Dr Montague claims 'that the concept of certain houses as unclean or forbidden—perhaps sacred—is as old as the mind of man' (1999, 70). In conflating the cursed and the sacred, he makes a crucial link between the meaning of place and what has previously happened within. Freud noted this in his 1913 study *Totem and Taboo*, where he considers the meaning of the word 'taboo', which is Polynesian in origin:

> The meaning of 'taboo', as we see it, diverges in two contrary directions. To us it means, on the one hand, 'sacred', 'consecrated', and on the other 'uncanny', 'dangerous', 'forbidden', 'unclean'. The converse of 'taboo' in Polynesian is '*noa*', which means 'common' or 'generally accessible'. Thus 'taboo' has about it a sense of something unapproachable, and it is principally expressed in prohibitions and restrictions. (18)

In this way it is possible to view the modern perception of hauntings as the expression of an older, and perhaps even culturally universal, theme surrounding these restrictions. Henri Lefebvre, too, points out that 'some would doubtless argue that the ultimate foundation of social space is *prohibition*' (1991, 35). These novels, and many more like them, notably those of Stephen King, use the terms of science as a means to justify the spiritual. King has described Hill House as functioning 'like a psychic battery' (1993, 297), storing up the traumas of the past and unleashing them on vulnerable souls. Indeed the haunted house narrative in general relies on the appeal of the idea that space can be affected by what happens in it. This is an idea crucial to architectural theory. In his book *Architecture and Disjunction*, Bernard Tschumi offers a picture of a man being pushed out of a window with the caption, '[t]o really appreciate architecture, you may even need to commit a murder'. He goes on to explain that '[a]rchitecture is defined by the actions it witnesses as much as by the enclosure of its walls' (1997, 100). Few genres explore this as effectively as horror, which relies for its effect on this conflation of past and present. What has been can come to be again. The ancient evil of Dracula can invade the present, but only if he sleeps in his casket of Transylvanian soil. The villain of the slasher movie never truly dies, but returns for a sequel every Halloween. Belasco's sadistic perversity can persist beyond death to torment a new generation. Despite any dreams of feminist progress, it is implied that the old patriarch will come back to teach his victims a lesson.

Psychoanalysis is central to the modern portrayal of haunting, despite academia's formal rejection of Freudian tenets. Mark Edmundson, in his insightful diagnosis of the Gothic impulse, claims that 'we are commonsense Freudians in much the way that Chaucer's contemporaries were commonsense Christians: we quote Freud all the time without saying so, and often without knowing as much' (1997, 35–6). He points to Freud's claim that on some level we never forgot any trauma, and that this is transformed in the psyche into a dramatic, indeed Gothic, negotiation between the ego, id and superego. In *Hell House*, Belasco plays the part of the authoritarian superego, punishing the innermost desires of the inhabitants of his home even as he draws these desires from the id. There can be no escape because this is taking place not in an outer, but an inner landscape. Edmundson says that 'For Freud, the psyche, however else he may describe it, is centrally the haunted house of terror Gothic. Freud's remarkable achievement is to have taken the props and passions of terror Gothic—hero-villain, heroine, terrible place, haunting—and to have relocated them inside the self' (32). There is a distinct break between the tone of late eighteenth- and early nineteenth-century Gothic, where the terrors are explained either rationally (Radcliffe), or by an embracing of the supernatural (Walpole, Lewis), and *fin-de-siècle* creations such as Stevenson's *Strange Case of Dr Jekyll and Mr Hyde* (1886) and Wilde's *The Picture of Dorian Gray* (1891), where the focus is resolutely inward. That this shift in tone should be contemporary with the birth of psychoanalytic theory, and that both should persist together, is no coincidence. *The Haunting of Hill House* ends with Eleanor's suicide as she drives into a tree, triumphantly thinking about how she will never leave, despite Dr Montague's concerned wish that she does. It is only in her final moments that the horror of her lack of free will becomes apparent: 'In the unending, crashing second before the car hurled into the tree she thought clearly, *Why* am I doing this? Why am I doing this? Why don't they stop me?' (1999, 245–6). Dara Downey points out that 'Eleanor's act is profoundly ambiguous, as it can be interpreted both as an escape and as an attempt to stay. In either case, it is a failure' (2011, 188).

Eleanor's failure emphasizes that the horror story is a closed space, a loop in which its protagonists are trapped. Hell House has a 'happy' ending of sorts, with Belasco defeated and Fischer and Edith surviving. In this regard, it actually represents a step back to the positivist Spiritualist tradition and ghost stories of the nineteenth century, where errant spirits are laid to their final rest by the discovery and resolution of the source of their disquiet. In *Hell House*, Belasco is defeated by the exposure of his weaknesses, ensuring that rational understanding, if not 'pure love', wins out. Fischer and Edith succeed where Eleanor does not, by breaking the cycle. A circular image is appropriate, as while the hauntings are occurring, Hell House, like Dante's Hell, is a circle.

The haunted house is a singular place where space and time are collapsed in on themselves, and slippage can occur. The Winchester House, one woman's guilt projected into architecture, reveals as much about this as any fiction. It is impossible to escape if the stairs lead to nowhere.

BIBLIOGRAPHY

Aguirre, Manuel. 1990. *The Closed Space: Horror Literature and Western Symbolism.* Manchester and New York: Manchester University Press.

The American Weekly, cited in 'The House,' *Winchester Mystery House Website.* Accessed 3 March 2014. http://www.winchestermysteryhouse.com/learn.cfm.

Bailey, Dale. 1999. *American Nightmares: The Haunted House Formula in American Popular Fiction.* Bowling Green: Bowling Green State University Popular Press.

Bettelheim, Bruno. 1991. *The Uses of Enchantment: The Meaning and Importance of Fairy Tales.* London: Penguin.

Blum, Deborah. 2007. *Ghost Hunters: The Victorians and the Hunt for Proof of Life after Death.* London: Arrow.

Carter, Angela. 1995. 'The Bloody Chamber.' *The Bloody Chamber.* London: Vintage. 7–40.

Crowe, Catherine. 1848. *The Night Side of Nature.* London: T.C. Newby.

Curtis, Barry. 2008. *Dark Places: The Haunted House in Film.* London: Reaktion.

Davenport, Reuben Briggs. 1888. *The Death-Blow to Spiritualism.* New York: G. W. Dillingham.

Downey, Dara. 2011. ' "Reading Her Difficult Riddle": Shirley Jackson and Late 1950s Anthropology.' *It Came From the 1950s! Popular Culture, Popular Anxieties.* Ed. Darryl Jones, Elizabeth McCarthy and Bernice Murpy. Basingstoke: Palgrave Macmillan. 176–97.

Edmundson, Mark. 1997. *Nightmare on Main Street: Angels, Sadomasochism, and the Culture of the Gothic.* London and Cambridge, MA: Harvard University Press.

Faludi, Susan. 1991. *Backlash: The Undeclared War against Women.* London: Vintage.

Fiedler, Leslie. 1997. *Love and Death in the American Novel.* Champaign, IL: Dalkey Archive Press.

Freer, Ada Goodrich, 1899. *Essays in Psychical Research.* London: George Redway, 1899.

Freud, Sigmund. 1994. *Totem and Taboo.* Trans. James Strachey. London and New York: Ark Paperbacks.

Goddu, Teresa A. 1997. *Gothic America: Narrative, History and Nation.* New York: Columbia University Press.

Hawthorne, Nathaniel. 2013. 'Alice Doan's Appeal.' *American Gothic from Salem Witchcraft to H.P. Lovecraft: An Anthology.* 2nd edn. Ed. Charles L. Crow. Oxford: Wiley-Blackwell. 74–80.

Jackson, Shirley. 1999. *The Haunting of Hill House.* London: Robinson.

James, William. [1909] 1986. 'Confidences of a Psychical Researcher.' *Essays in Psychical Research*. Ed. Robert A. McDermott. Cambridge, MA: Harvard University Press. 361–75.

King, Stephen. 1993. *Danse Macabre*. London: Warner.

Leeder, Murray. 2014. 'Victorian Science and Spiritualism in *The Legend of Hell House*.' *Horror Studies*, 5 (1): 31–46.

Lefebvre, Henri. 1991. *The Production of Space*. Trans. Donald Nicholson-Smith. Oxford: Blackwell.

Llewllyn, Mark. 2009. 'Spectrality, S(p)ecularity, and Textuality: Or, Some Reflections in the Glass'. *Haunting and Spectrality in Neo-Victorian Fiction*. Ed. Rosario Arias and Patricia Pulham. Basingstoke: Palgrave Macmillan. 23–44.

Luckhurst, Roger. 2008. *The Trauma Question*. London and New York: Routledge.

Matheson, Richard. 1971. *Hell House*. New York: Tor.

Moers, Ellen. 1976. *Literary Women: The Great Writers*. New York: Doubleday.

Pliny the Younger. 2006. *Complete Letters*. Trans. P. G. Walsh. Oxford: Oxford University Press.

Poe, Edgar Allan. 1992. 'The Imp of the Perverse.' *The Complete Tales and Poems of Edgar Allan Poe*. London: Penguin. 280–4.

Radcliffe, Ann. 1980. 'On the Supernatural in Poetry.' *The Mysteries of Udolpho*. Ed. Bonamy Dubrée. Oxford and New York: Oxford University Press.

Reynolds, Nicole. 2013. 'Gothic and the Architectural Imagination, 1740–1840.' The Gothic World. Ed. Glennis Byron and Dale Towshend. London: Routledge. 85–97.

Tschumi, Bernard. 1997. 'Advertisements for Architecture.' *Architecture and Disjunction*. London: MIT Press.

Williams, Anne. 1995. *Art of Darkness: A Poetics of Gothic*. Chicago: University of Chicago Press.

Zipes, Jack. 1991. *Fairy Tales and the Art of Subversion*. London and New York: Routledge.

Chapter Seven

Gothic Chronotopes and Bloodied Cobblestones

The Uncanny Psycho-Geography of London's Whitechapel Ward

HollyGale Millette

Forward and forward and then back, back. ... Time felt like a shove or a jerk. ...
This telling had a stillness, not time stopping, but time hurting. (Ng 1993, 145)

This essay approaches Gothic Whitechapel, as a land surveyor: marking, squaring, noting and deconstructing the territory of serial killing and
haunting. It offers what could be called a historiography of its haunting.
Methodologically, Whitechapel is analysed here using gothic tropes of violence, necropolis, gender and conflict to evidence a geographic performance
of haunting. Haunting is crucial to my argument because it draws on historical text to illuminate and make visible context and recover what is lost or
what we have been forced to forget. This 'spectral view' of history 'no longer
relies on the presence of living witnesses to communicate events between
generations, but makes the ghosts of history independent, haunting anyone
who crosses their paths' (Peeren 2007, 86–7). This essay maps the urban
site at the time of the Whitechapel Murders using Bakhtin's construct of the
chronotope—a place wherein space and time collapse. Here, this refers to
how Whitechapel 'is cast as that which is beyond modern time and space'
(MacIntyre & Nast 2011, 1473–4)—a hyper-exploited entity whose ghosts
are its most valuable currency. Ghosts are perhaps the best illustration of the
collapsing of space and time, as they are spectres that exist outside of those
parameters and rely on their invisibility to affect. Bakhtin (1981) first presents his chronotope as Einstein's 'time-space' (Vice 1997); however, while
Einstein's theory is grounded in the constant of light velocity, his is grounded
in the constant of history. His work was relative to the fiction he was interpreting, but cultural studies and fiction differ so this essay will favour a
more interdisciplinary approach than Bakhtin applied. At a more theoretically abstract level, my use of chronotope prefigures more recent calls for a

'historical-geographical materialism' (Soja 1989) and complements calls for the 'spatio-temporal turn' (Harvey 2003; Jessop 2006). This materialism is best explained in how the chronotope intervenes to help us map the presence of myth via conflict (Holquist 1990) because it reveals different causal forces operating simultaneously (here, e.g., the slum, alienation, gendered spheres, class fear, immigration, competition) in both outer and inner spatio-temporal patters. Capturing such complex causation in a place necessarily implies capturing the complexities of spatiality across time and this is an example of where cultural historians and narrative material must work in a 'space-time envelope' (Richland 2008, 10) in order to evoke the history of a geography; the settings where the truths of these inter-subjective encounters can be more accurately imagined. Foucault, in his own linguistic take on the collapsing of space and time, uses cultural geography to insist that spaces *do* things *for* people (2001, xix). Whitechapel captivates because of its ghostly traces and because it 'is about haunting in a paradigmatic way; it is neither pre-modern superstition nor individual psychosis, rather a generalizable social phenomena' (Gordon 1997, 7) precisely because the psycho-geography of Whitechapel is unresolved and ghosts are the repressed elements of unre-solved experience. Haunting is counter-intuitive in that repairing it cannot be done without violence, and so it is consistently recycled in productions capitalizing on its residue without ever reaching resolution. Like Anthony Vidler, I am 'preoccupied by traces and residues' (1992, xiii) but acknowl-edge that given the ideological function of the Gothic is to deal in them it would be problematic to re-present such distinctions or elide and compensate their effective effacement. Therefore, this writing struggles to remain self-aware so as not to enact a sort of complicity with the material or with its history—and it nowhere follows the route of Ripperology. Neither does it foreground the murderer either in form (nowhere is this person gendered) or function, and I attempt to resist a tendency towards 'ruin porn' in discussing its space. Nor will I be anchoring the history of Whitechapel in a discourse of prostitution or of late Victorian moral battles. These were—and still are—a reality for Whitechapel, but to foreground the business that the murdered women were conducting at the time of their deaths would, in the context of the space, result in unintentional effacement. Methodologically, chronotopes are both heteroglot in method and 'multi-voiced' in historiography, which is useful here as landscapes cannot be 'read' as monoglot texts because they are three-dimensional and so 'a dialogical approach to "reading" them is more faithful to their reality. The chronotope, then, becomes the gateway to a dialogical approach to narrative truth-telling about the landscape' (Lawson 2011, 391). As an analysis tool, chronotopes act as theoretical bridges that enable us to take account of parallel space-time frames in history and culture, which, in turn, sheds a unique light on real events (Clark & Holquist 1984,

278–9). Using them allows us to discuss spatial and temporal representations as linked, and as linked cultural material. As a concept, the chronotope affirms that time and space are inseparable and co-mingle, but where Bakhtin gives priority to the element of time in his concept, here, I am prioritizing space. Also, Bakhtin's work focused on the space-time settings that frame any historic event in the literary narrative, but this does not necessarily present a paradox in this work once one accepts Bakhtin's argument on his own terrain and then applies it, methodologically via analogous chronotopic bridges, to non-fiction—in this case, psycho-geography. In point of fact, one of my assumptions is that the Whitechapel Murders have passed into myth and are, therefore, partly fictionalized and 'shielded from overall criticism, precisely because they take the form of histories, the individual facts of which are thoroughly documented' (Lawson 2011, 397). That said this writing is more accurately concerned with Whitechapel being a place of collapsed time that perpetually lives with gendered violence and loss. It considers the impossibility of using the mythic distillation of a single signifying moment of violent rupture to suture the symbolic of a space that has had the maternal cut out of it. In other words, if the maternal presence in the Oedipal scene is what makes violence bearable, what haunting happens to the psycho-geography of a place when that is cut away? Specifically, it considers how and why the perpetrator of a now mythic Gothic crime and the philanthropy that flooded the area following it were gendered male, while the blood of the victims have since gendered the Ward itself as both female and martyred. My interest in Bakhtin and the chronotope began with David Harvey (1996) who cites numerous examples of the definition and production of space-time used in everyday space. Harvey seeks to unite chronotope and the everyday in order to redress the Marxist tendency to abstract politics from everyday life, and this writing follows this approach. Theoretically, I also use Freud's thoughts on the uncanny and Marx's discourse on exploitation and alienation to discuss the death of Whitechapel as a space, which I then overlay with the power conflict in the matrilocal everyday of the area in order to map gendered arguments of haunting. I end by casting attention on how post-structuralism intersects with neoliberalist neo-Victorian re-mediations of Whitechapel to co-opt its violent psycho-geographic legacy, thereby infinitely perpetuating it.

MAPPING DEAD[LY] SPACE—WHITECHAPEL, 1888

The word 'slum' has long had a negative connotation—an epithet, implying something evil, Gothic, strange. In fact the word itself is derived from 'slumber' and was probably affixed to the alleyways and dead-ended passages because, to so many, they were unknown territories, wrongly presumed to

Figure 7.1. Roger-Viollet, 1891 [steelpoint engraving] 'Engraving of the Tenth Murder Committed by Jack the Ripper in Whitechapel.' *Le Journal Illustre*, **13 February.**

be sleeping and quiet. Whitechapel was a slum. It is important to recognize that, like poverty itself, slums are relative things; such a term has no fixity or simple polarity. What it feels like to live in a slum is subjective and the ascription—'slum'—is both stigmatizing and restricting. People who live in slums are regarded as inferior, and so they come to harbour suspicions of the outside world (Clinard [1960] 1970, 26–36). They are isolated from the main body of society and lack entitlement to the rights and common property within it. Control, cloaked in deception, is excised over the physical location, motivation and movement of its populace—the deception lies in the implication that the slum is a place from which its inhabitants can easily escape. This is an illusion, for 'without the money to buy themselves out, or the skills and literacy to agitate for better services, they are stuck almost as firmly as if their neighbourhood were literally surrounded by walls' (Deakin & Ungerson 1973, 217). Reformers, it is true, often sought to put names and faces to the countless thousands, but a direct line of thought never connected those faces with the socio-political disenfranchisement engendered by an unequal labour market. The indigenous poor of Whitechapel who lived close by the immigrant skilled working class 'survived on a hand-to-mouth existence of casual labour interspersed without relief from the workhouse (White 1980, 122). Men worked (when they worked) at the docks, as carriers, as market-porters or hawkers in the street. Women worked as washerwomen, charwomen, street-sellers or unskilled textile piece-workers. Four of the five women who were murdered held temporary positions such as these (*Daily Telegraph* 1888). When such employment was unavailable, petty crime and prostitution kept hunger from the door. Perhaps the most hyper-exploited and, therefore, wasted of human populations is the body of the prostitute. All five victims of the Ripper Murders lodged in the rookery, and four, living in common lodging houses at the time of their deaths, were resorting to 'common prostitution' as a means of making due. The number of prostitutes in the district was estimated at 1,200 (Begg 1988, 29–30), but the figure was probably far higher, because in such areas of extreme poverty many women resorted to casual prostitution from time to time in order to survive; indeed, women in these communities were lucky to avoid sex as a means to end, at all. Unlike the full-time 'streetwalker' the 'common prostitute—an exceptionally vague legal category generally meant to designate women who solicited men in public thoroughfares—was largely invisible (Thompson & Yeo 1972). Precipitated by difficult circumstance, rootlessness, economic vulnerability and broken emotional and family ties, 'poor working women often drifted into prostitution because they felt powerless to assert themselves and alter their lives in any way' (Walkowitz 1982, 21). At the time of the murders solicitation was not illegal, rather police were only concerned with containing the 'common prostitute' to certain areas that would deter collusion between them and local thieves and pickpockets. So there was spatially bounded accommodation made, resulting in a level of permissiveness (Radzinowicz 1948–1968). When prostitution was not enough, it was a choice of starvation or the workhouse. In Whitechapel, bare life was for sale because, as well as being a slum, it was a space of dead labour.

Home, in this construction, becomes a haunted place in many ways, not the least of which is because of the invisibility of mother-work. As ghosts operate chronotopically (spectres that are not only out of time but out of place), and as the haunting of invisible mother-work occurs both subjectively *in* the home and historically *of* the home, spectres of invisible labour present themselves in the recesses of 1888. In this way, Peeren posits, time and space 'can be thought of together as disturbing or spectalizing each other: haunting each other, as it were, as each other's ghosts' (2007, 81) that contrive to make the invisible visible. Women—especially women disenfranchised from monetary stability—labour to stitch together the patchwork of urban facilities into workable solutions for their families and communities. Unlike the middle-class 'Angel at the Hearth', these unpaid entrepreneurs worked along the edges of the patriarchal land-use patterns to keep the machine running. Children of the slum were not their mother's aspirational bodies, but surplus labour bodies in early formation—reproducing the proletariat worker as it was spent—either through death, disease or absence. The East End had a larger than average amount of female heads-of-household and the proportion of single mothers in the slum outstripped those in other areas of London to 10:1. Surveys also showed a larger than average constitution of female traders and 'piece-working' home workers (White 1980, Chapter 3). The picture of Whitechapel that emerges is of place inhabited by various hierarchies of split-subjects, suffering endless alienation, at the radius of which sat a certain disaffectation—the ultimate stressor of disenfranchisement.

Alienation is a central force behind Gothic texts because it emphasized the increasing bifurcation of a dystopian/utopian capitalist map. Stevenson's novella *The Strange Case of Dr Jekyll and Mr Hyde* (1886) is an oft-cited example. Proximity, visibility, invisibility and obfuscation are all key markers in the Gothic text and in the sub-text of the Whitechapel Murders, just as superficiality, anonymity and lack of permanence were key to its social relationships. However, the ability of the inner city slum to deal with the alienation and transition adaption was to be found in its own heterogeneity. As Gans determined, transplanted folk traditions of communal support could be reconstructed in 'quasi-primary' relationships (1963). In Whitechapel there was a hard division in family roles, resulting in husbands and wives leading rather separate lives, but '[p]articular value [was] placed upon kinship and neighbour relations, with perhaps the most significant social relationship being between mother and the married daughter' (Parker 1973, 254). Considering the social relationship of gender (Moore 1988, 13) in the Whitechapel space, working-class life could be described as typified by its 'matriloci'—something that conflicted with the social geographic hegemony in late Victorian culture and the idea of nuclear exclusivity. What constituted 'the family' in Whitechapel were echoes of older rural kinship systems that, ideologically and emotionally, posed a threat to current social hegemony. Industrialization, notes E. P. Thompson (1974), affected the emotional life of first the male and then the female worker, because it excised sociability from the male work environment and consigned it to the home. This caused a much more horizontal kinship space to emerge around the streets and private spaces of Whitechapel—the public house, the street and the lodging house stairwell became the reclamation yard of friendships and family alliances

(Stansell 1982). Further, it can be understood that the forced displacement of the people of the Whitechapel Ward through persistent slum clearances (1846–1886) caused great sociological damage and conflict but threatened the delicate and complex matriloci that had resuscitated necessary kinship networks. There have since been praiseworthy studies conducted that map the socio-political disenfranchisement that accumulated in these areas as a result (Clarke 1986). '[W]omen whose families moved too often for them to participate in neighbourhood networks and/or who were far from kin, could be especially vulnerable' (Rapp, Ross & Bridenthal 1983, 244) and all of the murdered women fell into this category. Unstable urban communities like this were places where relatively few people—the atypical minority—were able to settle. Relatives were not within easy reach and there was little privacy to be had due to the crowded living conditions. The house could easily become a veritable prison—a negated zone. Families and labourers came home after a day of frustration and fatigue to dingy, unhealthy, overcrowded living quarters and had no space to vent so they used the outside space to mitigate this oppression, commandeering front stoops, sidewalks, hallways and alleys as their personal private/public space (Clinard [1960] 1970, 7). Family kinship was not a strong local presence (Willmott 1987, 11–13), which is why a certain Ward communitas developed that both replicated kinship-care among neighbours and challenged the public/private spatial divides of kinship activity. In emergencies, neighbours would often combine to affect a complex interior/exterior support system of mutual aid. Neighbours would exchange food, childcare and other major services such as shelter and comfort during domestic crises, helping during sickness, even assist with feeding or bathing each other's sick husbands (Meachem 1977). Neighbour to neighbour, residents of Whitechapel were chronically sick and mothers shuttled from street to home to street providing care and nurture, matriloci performing as kinship. Mechanisms of everyday resistance arose out of these networks such as neighbours saving neighbours by making up arrears payments (White 1980), Mrs. K. T. (2009, 100) or Annie Chapman's neighbour offering her tuppence for a cup of tea a day before her death (*Daily Telegraph* 1888). Collective action safeguarded private space in the public street. Testimonies at the inquests revealed a network of support and mutual aid among the poor and victims—'We got throwed together a good bit here in the lodging house' (Jones 1975, 50)—a community family that would never but entirely abandon them. Contrary to the illustrations, almost all of the bodies were found by locals on their way to and from work—workers who would have known the women directly or viewed them as 'kin' (*The Times* 1888), workers who, by the end of November 1888, began to fear the walk to work.

Kith and Kin networks also hindered crime prevention. In the Flower and Dean Street area, where the murders occurred, it was useless for police

THE FIFTH VICTIM of the WHITECHAPEL FIEND .

Figure 7.2.   Anon. (1888) 'The Fifth Victim of the Whitechapel Fiend.' *The Illustrated Police News: Law Courts and Weekly Record.* **6 October.**

to chase troublemakers or criminals, 'as the houses communicate with one another, and a man pursued can run in and out' (White 1980, 8). Elsewhere, the slum clearance schemes had left empty lots open to crime and overall the area had become synonymous with violence and urban crime. Whitechapel— a district that sported the lowest number of police to population ration— reported the largest numbers of police assaults. Police were so concerned that by late 1887, they began to disguise their constabulary in plain clothes. Over a hundred policemen from Whitechapel and other divisions were employed in this manner in the summer of 1888 and over fifty plainclothes police were still being used in Whitechapel as late as 1890 (Kelly 1995, 24). Ironically, this lack of visibility would result in the police force being chastised as inef- fectual and dismissive of the area. Violent crime was unilaterally brutal across the gender divide, with many being perpetrated on men by women—still the number of violent crimes against women was far higher. A content analysis of the local papers in the three months prior to the first killing report horrifically violent crimes at a rate of about one per week, including reports of women being individually beaten, kicked to death, chopped up with a butcher's knife, jumped on until dead, stabbed, eviscerated and set alight. That said, the slum itself was not 'evil', nor was a denser population necessarily comprised more delinquents; there was simply more temptations, opportunities and immunities from persecution in them. It is perhaps important to remember that irregular employment, relative poverty and transitory nature resulted in workers being cast as predatory, criminal and dangerous but the internal perceptions towards violence may have been construed differently. As the *Daily Telegraph* suggested, 'men and women had become accustomed to violence' (1888, 3), in the sense that they had normalised the vulgarity of it. Neighbours attended and reported to victim's inquests in a matter of fact manner and their lack of moral gloss or condemnation seemed to stun observers—it was news that for persons living in Whitechapel screams portending violence (especially to women), and the discovery of a mutilated body in a public passageway was unremarkable and vaguely commonplace (*East London Observer* 1888). Historians have located the scant biographies of the women who were murdered such that we are able to situate them—as singular subjects, not homogenous objects—within the mean streets of Whitechapel, but the fact remains that the mean streets of Whitechapel were fairly similar to alley and it is overwhelmingly feasible to suppose that at the time of the murders its residents were numb with 'disaffectation', to borrow from Stiegler (2013)—a particular kind of moral miserabilism that had pervaded the urban neoliberal landscape. This sense of resignation, fatalism and finally apathy led to an intolerance of conventional ambitions, unresolved anger and a generalized suspicion of the outside world (Clinard [1960] 1970, 12). The murderer, the press that popularized him, the police who hunted him and the authorities that then began noticing Whitechapel were all outsiders; they were a threat. In opposition to the matrilocal slum, these outsiders were gendered male, and they were uninitiated in the ways of the slum.

MURDER AND MARTYRDOM OF THE MATERNAL

At approximately 03.20 a.m. on Friday the 31st of August 1888, Mary Ann 'Polly' Nichols (nee: Walker), mother of two, was killed by a cut to the throat in Buck's Row, Whitechapel. She was 42 years old. She was not the pretty young thing full of gaiety and song of modern myth's depiction. She was destitute, displaced, hungry and unlucky. Two months later, five women would be dead and the history of the space would change forever. Annie 'Sivvey' Chapman (nee: Smith), also known as 'Siffey' or 'Dark Annie', was also a mother of two. She was murdered shortly before her 48th birthday, on Saturday the 8th of September. On Sunday the 30th of September through to Monday 1 October the murderer claimed the lives of two more women: 45-year-old mother of two, Elizabeth 'Long Liz' Stride (nee: Gustafsdotter), followed by 46-year-old Catherine 'Kate' Kelly who was a mother of four. In

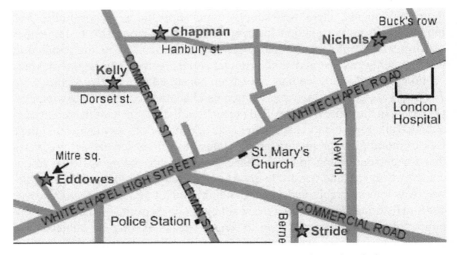

Figure 7.3.   Author's own map, 2016. Sites of the canonical murder victims.

contrast to the previous victims, Marie Jeanette Kelly, known as Mary Kelly or 'Ginger' or 'Fair Emma', was only 25 years old at the time of her death, was murdered indoors on her own bed and had no children. Of the canonical victims, she was the last to be murdered on Friday, 9 November 1888. The women were first garrotted and then eviscerated–in particular their reproductive organs were carefully removed. In real material terms, the subjects of motherhood were murdered and their bloodied ovaries either left on the cobblestones or taken as a trophy. This murder of Whitechapel's mothers would result in the ideological death of the maternal elements of its geography over the next year.

Sir Charles Warren, the commissioner of the Metropolitan Police, would decry the murders as 'unique in the history of our country' (1888, 158), and the London press would give them a hitherto unprecedented display of coverage. The patriarchal and proprietorial press would serve a pivotal role in the turn of events that followed, and by the third murder a moral panic had spread nationally when photographs of the dead women found their way into the more virulent press. The murders were violent, to be sure, and at some level they were a response to a failure to appropriately construct a social identity, but there is much latitude to discuss the further perpetration of violence by the men investigating the murders, reporting on the murders, conducting the autopsies and facilitating the inquests—to say nothing of the commemoration of violence men have committed, and continue to commit today: brutality built on brutality. There is a certain kind of arrogance in this attempt to contain the meaning of the chronotopic of Whitechapel—one that raised the ire of many a commentator when a 'Jack the Ripper Museum' opened in 2015. As Schindel and Colombo comment, 'such attempts at the stabilization of meaning are constantly the site of social contest' (Schindel & Colombo 2004, 5) and result in battles over the labelling of space-time and the imposition of controlled meaning at sites of violence. The excuse made by the exploiters—almost unilaterally male—of the Whitechapel Murders is that this is Heritage History and that their commemorations are 'acts of apprecia-tion.' One Mark Palmer-Edgecumbe is just such a man, who in 2014 snuck a whole museum dedicated to the curating and perpetuation of gendered Gothic violence and martyrdom past Tower Hamlets Council by claiming that it would 'celebrate' women's history in the East End. Unsurprisingly, a furore ensued. To understand the history of the women of the Whitechapel Ward to curatorial museum standard would require understanding that discourses and ideologies are neither given nor immutable, but products of complex processes. Without this, heritage history risks the erroneous replication of the mythologized violence and repeats the repetition of this violence in memes that are devoid of context, positioning or fact. In narratives of time-space compression, we would do well to respect the power of history memory, and identity before opening museums to spin money. That a monument to misogynist gore-history has been erected in the heart of still-deprived Tower Hamlets is the subject of another essay; however, the violence perpetuated by this horrification is the subject of this one. The violence against women that occurred after the murders was, and is, a-social (Klein 1984)—an Arendtian crime of the mind, a crime of the most basic thoughtlessness (Arendt 1978). The precise psychopathy of the murder will never be known, but the violence in men's response to the murders since may well be argued as a response to the fraudulence of their own power—something Arendt denotes as 'Impotent Bigness'—and it both answers and buries the question: 'Whose violence in this situation is allowable? Sanctioned?' In short, it makes female victimhood public property, and threatens to contain the victims perpetually.

While I disagree with Katherine MacKinnon's (MacKinnon & Dworkin 1997) supposition that women are fated to their victimhood and that the eroticization of violence is solely because of man's pathogenic qualities as perpetrators, I do find her argument useful here because she discusses the violence of the psyche (subjective, communal and topographical) of our Whitechapel—violence that makes an abomination of the murder, the murderous act and women's subsequent victimhood. More attention is now being paid to the spatial manifestation of trauma and violence on memory and social melancholy (Schindel & Colombo 2004). As social actors, we comprehend space in relational terms, which is how we can analyse these traces of victimhood and understand how violent spaces still produce affect. This supposes a relationship between remnants and memory, although this is

Figure 7.4. Bell, 2015 [digital photograph] 'Protesters Outside the Jack the Ripper Museum in Cable Street, East London.' 'Jack the Ripper Museum Architect says he was "duped" over Change of plans', Museum Section, *The Guardian*, 5 August.

not often evident or discussed outside of deliberations on the aesthetic and is obfuscated in the very process of memory, which both carries and hides fragments of the past (Croce 2002) while continuing to producing new experience in and of place. Whitechapel's history and our access to its past geographies is not transparent, rather it is thickly constructed and imagined. Thus, the narrative of violence in Whitechapel's past and the historical memory of this narrative becomes central to the construction of what Gregory calls the 'imaginary geographies' (1994) that exceed the everyday of that place and often embody the sublime. Whitechapel, I would argue, has a sublimely theatrical aspect due to the revenants of violence that permeate its memory fabric. Its Gothic trauma still circulates in ways that erupt into the spaces of its present—not as intentional memorial or sideshow carnival, but with a subtle theatricality. Gothic Whitechapel was and remains that class of frightening indebted to the Freudian uncanny: something 'old-established in the mind and which has become alienated from it only through the process of repression' (Freud 1990, 340). When Freud first writes of the uncanny, he uses the word '*unheimlich*', which, literally translated, means 'unhomely', where one is 'not at home in herself'. The home is closed and boundaried; it is where affect is loosed; it is something you keep close ('close to home'; 'home is where the heart is'), and it is a place where secrets are kept, shared and obscured from public view. To be in the uncanny is to experience the reversal of this. For us, this is key, when held up against the ideology of the Victorian separate-sphere ideology. To the middle-class outsider, the slum spilled out into the public zone was politically *unheimlich* because it ought to have remained hidden and did not (224), was unhomely and unwelcoming in affect. And, as haunting is effective when it displaces the home and/or dialogue of the hearth, this manifested in a topography that was particularly susceptible to haunting. Freud's uncanny has three aspects: it is that which is at once strange and unfamiliar; that which suggests a primal mythic topos of the supernatural; and that which inspires sublime feelings (be it of awe, admiration or fear). Freud describes his own experience of this sensation on becoming turned-around in a provincial Italian town, such that he kept circling back to the red-light district by 'mistake'. In his psycho-geographic perambulation, the space behaves as a 'fantasy zone'. 'Fantasy zones such as red-light districts, gipsy encampments, pleasure gardens, the bohemian *demi-monde*, or back-stage at a theatre, gain their potency from the fact that they are a source of conflicting images' (Witchard 2009, 103) that perform this 'uncanny' within and throughout the very fabric of their place. Like these sites, Whitechapel demonstrates an 'uncanny social-science' performance on heavily mediated stage-sets of Gothic horror. Such a position calls into argument how a site is bounded by authenticity, identity and the desire of the voyeur for the sublime—trauma, after all, is invested with a certain degree of narcissism. This voyeur—the participant in a walking tour, let us say—lays claim to the trauma histories and space-time identities it perceives as consumable, but rarely dips into the internal histories and identities as part of that. But then the tourist sees what he or she comes to see. Revenant sites have little fixity; they are open and porous to the multiplicity of the social relations occurring everyday within and without them. Contemporary sites of protest act similarly and they are preoccupied with maintaining this porosity and accommodating their ever-shifting cultural and social relations in order to stage hegemonic resistance, but these are radically celebrated spaces, whereas today's touristic Whitechapel celebrates gendered sacrifice through violence and is, in its fixity, a Conservative patriarchal nightmare, as well as a Gothic one.

GOTHIC MYTH, FEAR AND THE MATERNAL MARTYR

Significantly, the acts of a criminal at large or a serial killer never apprehended become open signifiers in collapsed time and place. Historically, the murders could be a commentary on surplus labour, on the morality of the 'fallen', on lack of capital investment in housing, on immigration and the 'Other', gendered violence or on any other contemporary social ailment that could be mapped onto the 'slum'. Ideologically, the distillation of topographic melancholy could stamp the space 'haunted' in order that we might better cope with the violence that passed there. In either, we give prominence to our feelings of regret and mourning as we consider what we are left with when something ends what touches us, what remains and repeats. In these matters, our consciousness is often occluded, repressed or subjugated; however, our unconscious remains garrulous and open to a melancholic object preserved across time. Melancholia is never lost, as an object is, and it carries on uncontested, unaddressed—just as the Whitechapel murderer was uncontested, unaddressed, yet it is possible to live with this loss if we mythologize it within a singular moment and place of rupture—a heterotopia of haunting, if you will, particular to the British romantic consciousness (Woodcock 2000, 141) that sits neatly in a space-time envelope.

However, in Whitechapel itself space, and the use of space, changed overnight with little time given over to mourning. Immediately prior to the murders the Bryant and May match factory women (and girls) had won a successful strike action undertaken by women for women that was less indicative of a political communitas than the leaking of matrilocal communitas into the workspace. It was no surprise then that when crisis peaked it was the Ward's women who rioted outside the police station—demanding that the victims' bodies be released for them to bury and for the police to either do their jobs or 'they would do them for them'. Police Commissioner Warren admitted his unease—he feared the charging women outside the police station more than unemployed male rioters a few months earlier. The men he could bludgeon, whereas the women—the visible backbone of Whitechapel—were untouchable. The *Women's Penny Paper*—an early feminist organ that was run, written by and circulated for women—baited the commissioner (1888) by stressing the connectedness of all women' (Warkentin 2010, 42)—not all women as victims, but all women as empowered protectors of themselves. Historically women's involvement with state affairs such as policing or community control was strictly forbidden and would, well into the twentieth century, only ever been sanctioned *in extremis* (usually in times of war)—by losing control of the women of Whitechapel outside a local precinct, Warren was publicly admitting a policing failure of the worst kind while foregrounding women's public involvement with state affairs. This was further exacerbated by illustrated reports of women in the Ward taking matters into their own hands and arming themselves.

By then the point at which the overwriting of *e*ffect by *a*ffect in historical psycho-geography of Whitechapel was beginning. Following the murders, women who could choose to stay indoors and under lock and key as much as was possible. Women who were alone or whose business forced them onto the street began to fill the workhouses, and many had left the ward for good by the spring of 1889. Middle-class women and men commandeered

Figure 7.5.   Anon. 1888. 'Ready for the Whitechapel Fiend. Women Secretly Armed.'
The Illustrated Police News, 22 September.

the fear infecting the public spaces of Whitechapel to petition for reform
and recruit local women to adhere to their values of temperance, patriarchy
and morality (Barnet 1921, 306)—actions which only served to acerbate the
already strained class relations in the neighbourhood. The Toynbee Hall, for
all its aid to the locality, led in the opinion that the 'disorderly' and 'public'
lives of the women of the ward were 'more appalling than the actual murders' (Nunn & Gardner 1888). Policing hegemony, the line became that the
murders threatened the safety of 'respectable' local women (Barnett 1888).
This, effectively, put the women of the slum under 'house arrest' and made
them suddenly and entirely dependent on male protection. Prior to the murders, the tendency was for women to be spatially confident, especially when
other people in the locality were around—courage performing as emancipa-
tory. Following the murders, the women of Whitechapel were made to feel
'estranged' from their feelings of comfort and ownership over their everyday
public space. Quite quickly women began to view as dangerous that which
they had viewed as safely familiar the day before. How women 'own' their
space, occupy it or take possession of it by using it repeatedly constitutes a
feeling of being 'at home' (*heimlich*) in their environment (Koskela 1997,
307). Danger is therefore perceived as a cultural construct such that a change
of environment, or any environment that can be constituted as a feeling of

not being at home (*unheimlich*), is perceived as more dangerous than the familiar (Merry 1981; Valentine 1989). Koskela argues that producing this fear, as it was done for the women of Whitechapel, is 'a product of systematic structural violence rather than actual attacks' (1997, 304). In this construct the Whitechapel murderer is transposed into the 'hero' of a crime that intensified the dangers of male violence by convincing women that they were helpless victims (Walkowitz 1982, 569). Doreen Massey has shown how the limitations of women's mobility, both in terms of using space and constructing identity, have been a crucial means of subordination (1994, 179), but certain points of subordination was also visited on the women of Whitechapel by Victorian philanthropy.

The murders invited surveillance from vigilance committees but philanthropists—to mask the repressive activities of past and further slum clearance—also used them (White 1980, Chapter 1). The overall effect of the crimes was to focus attention on the East End, on it's overcrowding and its poverty and on the inadequacies of the (new) police force—leading to the resignation of Commissioner Sir Charles Warren (*The Daily News* 1888). George Bernard Shaw punctuated the situation by cynically observing that middle-class attention—and money—was forthcoming only when Whitechapel's poverty was brought to the headlines (*The Star* 1888). The possibility that the murderer could have been an overzealous social reformer did occur to two prominent medical journals of the day with one speaking openly of the 'good purpose' the murders had served (*The British Medical Journal* 1888; *The Lancet* 1888) and *The Commonweal*—the organ of the Socialist League—prophesied that the fiend-murder would 'become a more effective reformer than all the honest propagandists in the world' (Morris 1888). In truth, the murders did compel the reforming-minded middle class to address the glaring inequalities in the housing and lifestyles of the people in Whitechapel, but the structures that translated this newfound zeal into legislation and charitable housing trusts were, unilaterally, male. 'Masculinity and femininity', Lisa Brush argued, 'are defining dimensions of credibility and power for both reformers and their targets' (Brush 2003, 217). She defines the specific historic choices that contribute to the practice and institutional arranging of reform as 'gendered governance' and notes how it either reflects or opposes the 'governing of gender' that occurs when institutions, policies and practices ask us to accept their definitions before assigning us unequal life choices. In Whitechapel there was a social-spatial incongruence in matriloci that interfered with these 'institutional arrangements' of reform. Thus, the legacy of the five female victims of Whitechapel is more than the reform their deaths may have compelled—they could be seen to have martyred their own matriloci in exchange for it. 'Verily', wrote Henrietta Barnett, 'it was the crucifixion of these poor lost souls which saved the district' (1921, 81–96).

Montgomery (2011) offers three explanations for the persistence of the 'fall' narratives in urban spaces: constant urban decline (the slum space), a moralizing hegemony or doxa (the separate-sphere ideology) and a clash between objective structures and embodied histories over the life course (the murders). She traces how divergent engagements of power relations and culture codes—objective structures that pre-exist individuals and their impressions of the world—imbalance the life-course of a place and latterly affect how the future inhabitants recall urban history. In doing this, she utilizes a kind of morphogenesis—a process of geo-historic optimization that is linked to conditions of stability and of instability. Urban form theory proposes a global theory of engendering forms and their relationships to spatial positions resulting in morphogenetic conceptions of meaning that are then reconstituted through spatial stratification (Marcos 2012). Theoretically, this explains how Whitechapel became reconstituted as haunted in form and representation, but what this essay puts forward is that this haunting was and is gendered consistently reproducing the effect that it names (Butler 1993). Space too is a discursive material as well as a material engaged in reproducing heteropatriarchical imperatives. The death of the women of Whitechapel produced a materiality of victimhood, which conveniently reconstituted the matrilocal space as male and allowed predatory male voyeurs free reign over a hitherto feminized space. True, the 'Male Gothic', as Smith reminds us, is 'characterised by its representation of male violence, female persecution, and semi-pornographic scenes' but these are prone to 'epistemic concealment[s]' (2004, 71) that we must not willingly accept; we must not let violence against women obscure or belittle the real and complex problems with masculinities and gendered economies. The material effect of such a representation is that the bodies on which the crimes were perpetrated have become one heterogeneous body of victim-ised geography. As this geographical body was always already gendered, its victimhood took on that materiality as citational practice; it produced the victim effect it named. Put another way, the materiality of the murdered women (their eviscerated bodies) were an effect of the normative, which in turn consolidated that norm.

BIBLIOGRAPHY

Alesia F. Montgomery. 2011. 'The Sight of Loss.' *Antipode*, 43 (5): 1828–50.
Anon. 1888. 'Reign of Terror in the East End.' *The East London Observer*. 15 September.
_____. 'Sir Charles Warren Defends the Force.' *The Pall Mall Gazette and The Daily News*. 4 October.

_____. 'The East End Murders: Detailed Lessons.' *The British Medical Journal (BMJ)*. 6 October: 768–9.

Arendt, Hannah. 1978. *The Life of the Mind*. New York: Harcourt.

Bakhtin, Mikhail. 1981. *The Dialogic Imagination*. Ed. Michael Holquist. Austin: University of Texas Press.

Barnett, Canon. 1888. 'Letter to Editor.' *The Times*. 16 November.

Barnett, H. O. R. 1921. *Canon Barnett: His Life, Work and Friends by His Wife*. London: Murray.

Begg, Paul. 1988. *Jack the Ripper the Uncensored Facts: A Documentary History of the Whitechapel Murders of 1888*. London: Robson Books.

Brush, Lisa D. 2003. 'Gender and the Uses of History.' *Journal of Urban History*, 29 (2): 216–25.

Butler, Judith, 1993. *Bodies That Matter: On the Discursive Limits of 'Sex'*. New York: Routledge.

Clark, Katerina and Michael Holquist. 1984. *Mikhail Bakhtin*. Cambridge, MA: Harvard University Press.

Clarke, Martin A. 1986. 'Household and Family in Bethnal Green, 1851–71: The Effects of Social and Economic Change.' PhD diss., University of Cambridge.

Clinard, Marshall B. (1960) 1970. *Slums and Community Development*. London: Collier-Macmillan.

Croce, Benedetto. ed. 2002. *The Philosophy of Giambattista Vico*. Trans. R. G. Collingwood. New Brunswick: Transaction.

The Daily Telegraph. 1888. 11 September.

. 1888. 10 October. 3.

Deakin, Nicholas and Clare Ungerson. 1973. *Beyond the Ghetto: The Illusion of Choice*. London: Centre for Environmental Studies.

Dennison, David and Eversley David. eds. *Patterns, Problems and Policies*. London: Heinemann.

Engle Merry, Sally. 1981. *Urban Danger: Life in a Neighbourhood of Strangers*. Philadelphia: Temple University.

Esther, Peeren. 2007. 'Ghost as a Gendered Chronotope.' *Ghosts, Stories, Histories. Ghost Stories and Alternative Histories*. Ed. Sladja Blazan. Newcastle: Cambridge Scholars. 81–96.

Freud, Sigmund. 1990. 'The Uncanny.' *Art and Literature*. Harmondsworth: Penguin Freud Library, 1990.

Foucault, Michel. 2001. *The Order of Things: An Archaeology of the Human Sciences*. London: Routledge.

Gans, Herbert, J. 1963. 'Urbanism and Suburbanism as Ways of Life.' *Readings in Urban Sociology*. Ed. Raymond E. Pahl. Oxford: Pergamon Press. 95–118.

Gordon, Avery. 1997. *Ghostly Matters: Haunting and the Sociological Imagination*. Minneapolis: University of Minnesota Press.

Gregory, Derek. 1994. *Geographical Imaginations*. London: Blackwell.

Harvey, David. 1996. *Justice, Nature & the Geography of Difference*. Malden, MA: Blackwell.

Harvey, David.. 2003. *The New Imperialism*. Oxford: Oxford University Press.

Holquist, Michael. 1990. *Dialogism: Bakhtin and His World*. London: Routledge.

Jessop, Bob. 2006. 'Spatial Fixes, Temporal Fixes and Spatio-Temporal Fixes.' *David Harvey: A Critical Reader*. Ed. Noel Castree and Derek Gregory. Malden, MA: Blackwell. 142–66.

Jones, Elwyn. 1975. *The Ripper File: The Documentary Investigation by Detective Chief Superintendents Charles Barlow and John Watt*. London: Barker.

Kelly, Alexander. 1995. *Jack the Ripper: A Bibliography and Review of the Literature*. London: Association of Assistant Librarians.

Klein, Melanie. 1984. *Narrative of a Child Analysis—The Conduct of the Psycho-Analysis of Children as Seen in the Treatment of a Ten-Year-Old Boy*. London: Hogarth.

Koskela, Hille. 1997. '"'Bold Walk and Breakings"': Women's Spatial Confidence versus Fear of Violence.' *Gender, Place and Culture*, 4 (3): 301–19.

The Lancet. 1888. 6 October.

Lawson, James. 2011. 'Chronotope, Story and Historical Geography: Mikhail Bakhtin and the Space-Time Narratives.' *Antipode*, 43 (2): 384–412.

''''MacKinnon, Katharine and Andrea Dworkin. eds. 1997. *In Harm's Way: The Pornography Civil Rights Hearings*. Cambridge, MA: Harvard University Press.

Massey, Doreen. 1994. *Space, Place and Gender*. Cambridge, UK: Polity Press.

Marcos, Isabel. 2012. 'Urban morphogenesis.' *Semiotica*; 192, 1 (4): 1–14.

McIntyre, Michael and Heidi J. Nast. 2011. 'Bio(necro)polis: Marx, Surplus Populations, and the Spatial Dialectics of *R*eproduction and "Race".' *Antipode*, 43 (5): 1466–88.

Meachem, Standish. 1977. *A Life Apart: The English Working Class, 1890–1914*. Cambridge, MA: Harvard University Press.

Moore, Henrietta. 1988. *Feminism and Anthropology*. Cambridge, UK: Polity Press.

Morris, William. 1888. *The Commonweal*. November.

Myenne Ng, Fae. 1993. *Bone*. New York: Harper.

Nunn, Thomas Hancock and Thomas Gardner. 1888. 'Letters to the Editor.' *The Times*. 6 October.

Radzinowicz, Leon. 1948–1968. *History of English Criminal Law and Its Administration from 1750*. Vol. 1–2. London.

Rapp, Rayna, Ellen Ross and Renate Bridenthal. 1983. 'Examining Family History.' *Sex and Class in Women's History*. Ed. Judith L. Newton, Mary P. Ryan, and Judith R. Walkowitz. London: Routledge. 233–58.

Richland, Justin P. 2008. 'Sovereign Time, Storied Moments: The Temporalities of Law, Tradition, and Ethnography in Hopi Tribal Court'.' *PoLAR: Political and Legal Anthropology Review*, 31 (1): 8–27.

Schindel, Estala and Pamela Colombo. 2004. *Space and the Memories of Violence: Landscapes of Erasure, Disappearance and Exception*. Basingstoke: Palgrave Macmillan.

Shaw, George Bernard. 1888. 'Letter to the Editor: "'Blood Money to Whitechapel".' *The Star*. 24 September.

Smith, Andrew. 2004. *Victorian Demons: Medicine, Masculinity and the Gothic at the Fin-de-Siècle*. Manchester: Manchester University Press.

Soja, Edward. 1989. *Postmodern Geographies: The Reassertion of Space in Critical Social Theory*. London: Verso.

Stansell, Christine. 1982. 'Women, Children, and the Uses of the Streets: Class and Gender Conflict in New York City, 1850–1860.' *Feminist Studies*, 8 (2) (Summer): 309–35.

Stiegler, Bernard. 2013. *Uncontrollable Societies of Disaffected Individuals*. Trans. Daniel Ross. Cambridge, UK: Polity Press.

The Times. 1888. 2 October.

Thompson, E. P. 1974. 'Time Work-Discipline, and Industrial Capitalism.' *Essays in Social History*. Ed. M. W. Finn and T. C. Smout. Oxford: Clarendon Press. 9–77.

_____. and Eileen Yeo. eds. 1972. *The Unknown Mayhew*. New York: Pantheon.

Valentine, Gill. 1989. 'The Geography of Women's Fear.' *Area*, 21: 385–90.

Vice, Sue 1997. *Introducing Bakhtin*. Manchester: Manchester University Press.

Vidler, Anthony. 1992. *The Architectural Uncanny: Essays in the Modern Unhomely*. Cambridge, MA: MIT Press.

Walkowitz, Judith. 1980. *Prostitution and Victorian Society: Women, Class and the State*. Cambridge: Cambridge University Press.

_____. 1982. 'Jack the Ripper and the Myth of Male Violence.' *Feminist Studies*, 8 (3): 542–74.

Warkentin, Elyssa. 2010. '"'JACK THE RIPPER' STRIKES AGAIN"', The "'Ipswich Ripper"' and the "'Vice Girls"' He Killed.' *Feminist Media Studies*, 10 (1): 35–49.

Warren, Sir Charles. 1888. 'Confidential Report to the Home Office, Dated 17 October.' A49301B, Sub. 12, Police Records, 3/141. Folders 158–63. Held in the Metropolitan Archives.

White, Jerry. 1980. *Rothschild Buildings. Life in an East End Tenement Block, 1887–1920*. London: Routledge & Kegan Paul.

Willmott, Peter. 1987. *Kinship and Urban Communities: Past and Present*. Address given at the Ninth H. J. Dyos Memorial Lecture, Leicester, The Victorian Studies Centre at the University of Leicester, 29 April.

Witchard, Anne V. 2009. *Thomas Burke's 'Dark Chinoiserie': Limehouse Nights and the Queer Spell of Chinatown*. Farnham: Ashgate.

The Women's Penny Paper. 1888. 24 November.

Woodcock, Peter. 2000. *This Enchanted Isle: The Neo-Romantic Vision from William Blake to the New Visionaries*. Glastonbury: Gothic Image.

Chapter Eight

(Sub)Urban Landscapes and Perception in Neo-Victorian Fiction[1]

Rosario Arias

'*The Realm of Shells* is essentially a novel about place, about how a place can influence and manipulate people' (Overall 2007a, 9). This is how the author of *The Realm of Shells* (2006) succinctly describes her novel. Taking Sonia Overall's statement about the relevance of place and its effect on people as a starting point, I aim to explore her novel *The Realm of Shells* (2006) drawing on notions of space, memory and 'the felt affect of haunting' of the Victorian past in contemporary culture, as Ruth Heholt states in her introduction. To this end, phenomenology, applied to landscape studies, and the archaeological metaphor will prove to be helpful critical interventions into the neo-Victorian text. Following Yannis Hamilakis's conceptualization of archaeology as the 'multi-sensorial, experiential [mode] of engaging with the world' (2013, 4), this chapter discusses the role of the landscape in relation to the Victorian past, the present and the human through embodied perception. In so doing, it takes sides with a theory of sensoriality which encompasses 'the reconstitution of thinking as another form of felt experience, as sensorial and affective practice, interwoven with all other embodied practices—thinking through the living and sensing body' (Hamilakis 2013, 196).

Landscape and phenomenology have gone hand in hand in the last few years. Phenomenology is the philosophical method that examines how the perceiving subject relates to and interacts with the world, 'the perceived world', of which he or she is inevitably a part. Maurice Merleau-Ponty, the French philosopher who advanced most of his theories in his *Phenomenology of Perception* (1945), claimed that 'we shall need to reawaken our experience of the world as it appears to us in so far as we are in the world with our body' (2002, 239). The senses work together to organize our involvement with the world of things as 'a three-dimensional objective space within which we are located as just another object' (Ménasé 2004, 11). The phenomenological perspective allows for the incorporation of a detached look at an individual experience, which reinterprets and articulates the perceived world, while simultaneously being an intrinsic part of it. This key tension between detachment or distance and proximity is at stake in landscape studies. John Wylie favours a view of landscape 'that emphasizes lived experience rather than detached observation, derived from the work of the phenomenologist Merleau-Ponty (1989) and the cultural anthropologist Ingold (2000)' (Mah 2012, 12). This involves an embodied situatedness, an inscription of the I as subject and object at the same time, an embodied engagement and a being-in-the world as well as a being-with-the-world. The phenomenologist asks questions such as: 'What are the *modes of presence and absence* by which this world manifests itself to me? In what ways do I come to know and inter-act with a world of which I am always, inescapably and ambiguously, a part?' (Garner 1994, 2–3, my emphasis). In this sense, the expression 'the modes of presence and absence' clearly alludes to critical notions such as that of the 'trace', which marks a presence in absence, largely explored by Paul Ricoeur, and that of the 'spectre,' defined by Jacques Derrida, as well as that of the 'phantom', expounded by Nicolas Abraham and Maria Torok. The material 'trace' and haunting (at the crossing of presence and absence) have provided creative and critical forms of landscape remembering:

> The shreds and patches of things, whether treasured possessions or soiled ephemera—handled, venerated or discarded—all the traces of presence of those now absent are worked in such a way so as to show, synchronously, *the absence of presence*, *the presence of absence*, and so … the threshold assumes the status of an enlarged, uncannier zone of indiscernibility and dislocation, disrupting all distinctions. (Wylie 2009, 279, original emphasis)

Wylie has dwelt upon the interrelationship between landscape and phenomenology, its emphasis on presence and landscape and 'spectral geographies,' and its stress on absence and dislocation. Whereas I wish to focus on material traces and memory and their related issues of the corporeal, the sensorial and the affective which capitalize presence, I will also draw on absence, distancing from and non-coincidence between the self and the world to provide a more nuanced perspective on the relationship between self and the world.

Paul Ricoeur, proponent of phenomenological hermeneutics, addressed three types of the 'trace' (the mnesic trace in the brain or cortex, the psychical trace in the unconscious and the written trace) in *Time and Memory* (1985) and in *Memory, History, Forgetting* (2001). The 'trace' dissolves time and space as it is able to travel across time to have a continuous existence in the present, and this duration defines the special nature of the 'trace': it has its origin in the past, yet it continues in the present. According to one critic, 'Ricoeur's emphasis on endurance amounts to an emphasis on preservation. ... The trace is not the past ... but it is a material connection to the past, and while it shows erasure, it also preserves' (Zimmerman 2008, 9). This material link with the past is associated with the phenomenological interest in 'the thing itself', with the essences of phenomena. Because of this, there has been outright rejection of phenomenology since, in the view of some critics, it endorses essentialism and other related positions such as universalism, fixity or timelessness. Phenomenology does not claim that 'individual objects will be seen the same by different subjects, that the act of vision is unconditioned by circumstantial or cultural factors, or that the perceiving subject and its object exist in a kind of privileged ideality' (Garner 1994, 12). Quite the contrary, phenomenology seeks to explore the notion that an object depends on perspectives (it plays with questions of absence and presence) as a phenomenon in any act of perception carried out by an embodied subject: it does not subsume difference, but it attempts to point out 'a set of terms in which experiential difference is manifested' (12). This involves an embodied experience, and seen in this light, phenomenology provides a viable method with which to examine the tangibility of the past, the Victorians, in contemporary culture and the affect their present absence motivates. This is in keeping with a renewed interest in 'bringing to light things previously hidden or lost, unearthing memory, making the invisible visible ... it is the very materiality of memory—its presence, tangibility and there-ness—that [has become] a touchstone' in landscape studies (Wyley 2009, 279) and in criticism, in general, in recent years. Importantly, the language of the senses and sensoriality has contributed to the consideration of the tangibility of the past, the Victorian age included.

Since the beginning of the twenty-first century, there has been a growing body of criticism concerned with Victorian sensoriality and the phenomenological apperception of the Victorian world through the senses, and material conceptualizations of Victorian subjectivity by resorting to the work of Maurice Merleau-Ponty. Critics like William Cohen, David Trotter and Steven Connor, to name just a few, have called our attention to the Victorian sensorium.[2] Patricia Pulham has recently taken lead by discussing the tactile experience in Victorian literature, particularly the influence of John Keats on Oscar Wilde, suggesting that '[i]t seems that touch, whether digital or physical, is an increasingly important tool in mediating the past and the present' (2013, 124). In his *Embodied: Victorian Literature and the Senses* (2009), William Cohen connects the work of Merleau-Ponty to that of Victorian novelists, such as Charles Dickens, Charlotte Brontë and Thomas Hardy, and journalists, in that they similarly focus on the perceived world, the impression (read 'trace') that an object makes on the body of the subject, and 'the fluid exchange between surface and depth, inside and outside, ... the flow of matter and information between subject and the world' (2009, xii). In other words, these writers and journalists pay heed to the flow of matter between past and present, the Victorians and us. Therefore, not only touch, but all the senses, evoked and conjured up in present time, can function as a passageway between past and present, the Victorians and today's culture.

As far as neo-Victorianism is concerned, Nadine Boehm-Schnitker and Susanne Gruss have based their argument on the need to interrelate the visual and the material, which 'will further sharpen theoretical tools' (2011, 2). Material Culture Studies, Thing Culture and Commodity Culture are delineated as theoretical perspectives to address the neo-Victorian experience. And, yet, they still beg for 'a further calibration of analytic approaches to material and visual culture [and pose questions such as] how can material culture— and the material presence of the Victorian in the neo-Victorian—be analysed so as to provide insights into processes of historiography?' (10). The visual and the material fall within the region of the phenomenological enquiry, and, arguably, phenomenology opens up new access routes 'to the individual and social life-worlds within which history arises and manifests itself', as well as includes 'the particular modes of attention engaged by history, the ways in which history is both manifested and constituted in personal and intersubjective fields' (Garner 1994, 10). In this, phenomenology, and its related aspects of absence and presence, subjectivity and objectivity, can be associated with the interaction between past and present in neo-Victorianism.

The phenomenological perspective allows for the incorporation of a look that looks at and looks with the perceived world, while simultaneously being part of it. This comprises the embodied activity of a reader who is both subject and object, being-in and with-the-world. It is indeed through the embodied presence of the Victorians under the contemporary reader's gaze that the Victorian age actualizes itself. Neo-Victorianism appears, then, as an embodied experiential mode. In this, I follow Stanton Garner's *Bodied Spaces: Phenomenology and Performance in Contemporary Drama* which sustains the following: 'The phenomenological approach—with its twin perspective on the world as it is perceived and inhabited, and the emphasis on *embodied* subjectivity … —is uniquely able to illuminate … experiential duality' (1994, 3). Although Garner refers to the act of the performance and the stage, it is possible to consider phenomenology for any experiential duality, as happens in neo-Victorianism, where doubles and the doubling metaphor have turned into key features (being about the Victorian past and the present). One critic also uses the term 'binocular vision' to describe the phenomenological look (States cited in Garner 1994, 15), in that it fosters a dialogue between inside and outside, interior and exterior, past and present. Since the inception of neo-Victorianism, several critics have underlined the doubled nature of the field: Sarah Gamble mentions the term 'binocular narrative' (quoting Jonathan Loesberg) to refer to the way in which we see the

Victorians, from a contemporary standpoint, for example. The emphasis on the doubled nature of neo-Victorianism, 'double act of recollection' (Gamble 2009, 128), doublings (Johnston & Waters 2008, 10) and the double vision of neo-Victorianism (Heilmann & Llewellyn 2010, 210) invites the reader to use his/her 'binocular vision' to read and interpret the Victorian world as an embodied subject, in a reciprocal way. Therefore, a phenomenological perspective on neo-Victorianism offers a conduit, a passageway, through which the matter flows between past and present, the Victorians and the present time, in such a way that reading and interpreting the Victorians in contemporary culture might be considered an embodied act.

Therefore, it seems that neo-Victorianism has taken its cue from this materialist line of Victorian writing in stressing the close relation between subjects in, for example, Sarah Waters's novels or Michel Faber's *The Crimson Petal and the White* (2002), as I have discussed elsewhere. Critics like Silvana Colella have already delved into the relevance of smell in this novel. Boehm-Schnitker and Gruss call the embodied experience of reading this novel where so much emphasis is put on sensorial apprehension, 'vicarious synaesthesia' (2011, 5). However, an aspect deserves closer attention: reciprocity and intersubjectivity.[3] According to Cohen, 'Victorian fiction frequently recurs to the body's materiality in representing interior being' (2009, 11). In turn, neo-Victorian novels seem to display a correspondence between interior and exterior, surface and depth, world and being, and, ultimately, past and present. In this line, Cohen studies Oscar Wilde's *The Picture of Dorian Gray* (1890) from the phenomenological point of view of the auditory corruption that Lord Henry Wotton inflicts upon Dorian: 'Once internalized, however, this auditory corruption expresses itself visually: cast out from his soul and incarnated in the painting, the sinfulness assumes visible form' (2009, 15). In Jean Rhys's *Wide Sargasso Sea* (1966), Charlotte Brontë's *Jane Eyre*'s prequel and one of the founding texts of neo-Victorianism, auditory corruption is perceived in the encounter between Rochester and Daniel Cosway as seen in the following passage: ' "Give my love to your wife—my sister", he called after me *venomously*' (Rhys 1966, 104, my emphasis). Arguably, *Wide Sargasso Sea* is a forerunner (in this as in many other aspects) of the depiction of Victorian embodied subjectivities in contemporary fiction.[4]

Sonia Overall's *The Realm of Shells* (2006) proves to be a case in point as far as Victorian embodied subjectivities in relation to landscape phenomenology are concerned. Clearly, there is an interest in the reciprocal relationship between embodied subjects and the perceived world. Sonia Overall defines herself as 'an avid psychogeographer' (website), which implies that the author considers geographical sites and spaces fundamental in her writing.[5] *The Realm of Shells* is her second novel where she fictionalizes the real story of the Margate shell-encrusted grotto, discovered by Joshua Newlove in 1835 under the family garden. The novel is set in early Victorian England (the 1830s) and is narrated from the perspective of Frances Newlove, an eight-year-old child whose parents open two boarding schools in Margate. Mrs Newlove and her children arrive to Margate by sea and this helps create a certain atmosphere and an emphasis on fluidity or flow of matter and relationships. A child perceives the external world primarily through the senses, and then, onomatopoeias and sound devices abound to convey Frances Newlove's perception of reality. A row between children is described as follows:

> 'Why are you so stuck-up?' say I. 'Anyone would think you were a *gentleman*'s daughter.'
> 'Whose daughter are you then?' says Frances. She sticks out her tongue. 'My father pays *your* father. And your mother. My mother doesn't work for a living, like a school dame.
> Get up and she gets up knocks the board over and the [tea] pieces go up and come down *klat-kli-kli-klaaaat* rolling. My hand up jumps smack-claps her cheek. She *aieeee-eeeee!* Screams yells and finger-claws at me. (2007b, 175–6)

These sound devices (alliterations and onomatopoeias) show the relevance not only of auditory perception in the novel (since reality is perceived by a little girl), but also that of the general soundscape in the novel where sounds flow and matter. In fact, the novel's soundscape helps indicate how the past is conjured up in the novel by means of echoing and reverberating in landscapes, in bodies and, ultimately, in the secret cave, covered with shells. Then, *The Realm of Shells* is a text-sound where the past, as if it were a sound wave, resonates, repeatedly producing echoes and double sound patterns, to indicate fluidity and co-presence of past and present, self and the world. Reverberated sound, understood this way, can be considered as a metaphor of the continuing presence of the (Victorian) past in contemporary fiction, which generates flows and sensorial relationships. In the nineteenth century 'new sounds in office buildings lacked reverberation' (Smith 2007, 54), therefore, echoes and resounds seem to indicate a past that has not gone by as yet. The past is sensed from the point of view of hearing since the novel's emphasis on sound proves to be a medium through which the past is evoked.[6]

The underground cave, incrusted with shells, found by the children Joshua and Fanny, 'serves as their secret hiding place, allowing them to feel truly free and at home' (Sulmicki 2012, 57). In fact, they feel constricted at their place since these children are subject to strict rules and observation. Mr Newlove does not treat his children differently to the other students at their schools and demands respect and deference on their side: 'During all school hours you will refer to your mother as Mrs Newlove, and to myself as Mr Newlove … You will show the same level of respect and deference as other pupils'

(2007b, 52). The separation and absence of human contact that Mr Newlove fosters is counterbalanced by references to tactility encounters, thus producing a tension between distance and proximity. Fanny reacts as follows, when her father's hand reaches her: 'His hand reaches big and lays heavy and hot on my head, His hand! "Bless you, you are a good girl, Fanny"' (2007b, 70). This tension existing between distance and proximity is at stake in the novel, and facilitates sensorial flows, rather than privilege one sense over the other.

It remains clear that Mr Newlove's motto has to do with an educational programme devised to produce useful members of society. Sulmicki relates this formal relation between parents and offspring to the Thatcherite government in the 1980s (2012, 51). Notwithstanding the parallel between the treatment of education in Overall's novel and Thatcher's promotion of 'paternalistic authoritarianism', in my view the novel bears similarities to Charles Dickens's *Hard Times* (1862). Crucially, in portraying authoritarian education based on utility, *The Realm of Shells* seems to echo the Utilitarian ideology illustrated in *Hard Times* and its Philosophy of Fact represented by Mr Gradgrind. His children Tom and Louisa, like Joshua and Fanny in Overall's neo-Victorian novel, suffer from the limitations imposed by a life without enjoyment, emotionally starved (Schlicke 1989, xvii). But this is not the only parallelism between the two novels. Following William Cohen's phenomenological approach to Victorian literature, Dickens found his own particular image for the interaction and interpenetration of interior and exterior: the keyhole, 'at once a figure *for* the eye and the ear and a channel—*like* the eye and the ear—through which information, emotions, and matter pass from the inside of one character into that of another' (Cohen 2009, xiii, original emphasis). The keyhole features in Dickens' *Hard Times* in Book I, Chapter 3, when Thomas and Louisa Gradgrind peep through a keyhole to take a look at the circus (1989, 15), and this embodied act of looking has a powerful impact on the subject who does the looking, and it also has much impact 'on the observed for the keyhole has openings in both directions' (Cohen 2009, 32). Likewise, in Overall's novel a hole, a tunnel, provides Joshua and Fanny (and other children and, later, the adult world) with access to the grotto cavern, made up of wonderful shells:

> 'I've found the treasure. ... It's a secret underground palace.'
> He puts his hand in his pocket and brings out a lump of something, white with shiny bits of pink and grey and blue. *Chalk*, with seashells stuck into it, curved and cupped like a flower. ... 'I've found the realm of shells'. (2007b, 125)

Arguably, the world of the grotto functions as an image for the interpenetration of interior and exterior in a phenomenological sense. In this (early) neo-Victorian novel human subjectivity is represented in bodily form and in so doing, it recalls what Charles Dickens did in his novels. The tunnel is also a site of imagination as it provides an entrance to a multifaceted space, fluid and flee-floating since it receives a number of interpretations in the novel (the grotto is simultaneously sacred, demonic, a treasure trove, a smuggling area, among many other things). This construction remains a mystery: no one has been able to discern what the cavern was built for, or who the people involved in it were. The official website of the true shell grotto underlines the mysterious origins of the grotto's design, 'with humble cockles, whelks, mussels and oysters creating a swirling profusion of patterns and symbols. A storehouse for the imagination' (http://shellgrotto.co.uk/).

In *The Realm of Shells*, the tunnel is a conduit that connects self and the world in such a way that the shell world of the grotto (objects) enters the human body and affects and changes the characters' interior qualities. The tunnel the children make connects interior and exterior, adulthood and childhood, the world of the past and the present: 'Wet-smelling and horrid, Joshua sits, shuffles forward. *You have to swing your legs in* his voice says, all flat and funny. Like talking into a well...He is *inside*, in the darkness' (2007b, 130, original emphasis). The tunnel provides a route to the unknown, to the embodied experience of the object-world of the grotto, which wholly transforms those in contact with it. Seen in this light, the tunnel (and the grotto) offers a complex relationship between self and landscape, understood as 'a series of tensions between watcher and watched, interior and exterior, the invisible and the visible ... set in motion' (Wylie 2009, 278), following landscape phenomenology. In this line, if 'the sensorial cannot be dissociated from the affective' (Hamilakis 2013, 629), according to Ben Anderson, affect is 'a body's "capacity to affect and be affected", where a body can in principle be anything' (2014, 9). Then, the grotto becomes a 'body,' an embodied space or landscape, with the capacity to create new meaning, like a touchstone. In affect terminology the grotto generates 'atmospheres' since etymologically speaking the concept of spatiality is inextricably bound to the word (sphere), in the sense of 'a certain type of envelope or surround ... interlinked with forms of enclosure—the couple, the room, the garden—and particular forms of circulation—enveloping, surrounding and radiating' (Anderson 2009, 80). The shell-encrusted grotto, understood as a 'body', produces atmospheres that appear only in contact with other bodies, and elicit affective responses. For example, Joshua shows the boarder boys the shells and at some point, the bully John Fassum becomes so much affected by the atmosphere of the grotto cave that he wants to take possession of it, and claims ownership:

> 'John Fassum has left so many things in the shell room' say I. 'I think he wants to live in there.'

'He's taking over so' says Joshua. 'He thinks it's *his* secret place now. He's been saying who can come in and who can't. Yesterday he let two of the day pupils in. They're not even in the same class as me ... And—and, Fan, he said that girls aren't allowed any more'. (2007b, 188–9)

Interestingly, John Fassum acquires an authoritarian role, like Mr Newlove, and rules out girls from a space, the grotto, previously related to freedom and imagination. Now that the underground cave has lost its magical power as 'a storehouse for the imagination,' Joshua decides to disclose the secret, and let the adults know of its existence.

The verticalized approach to space in the novel (a distinct division between upper and lower deck since the description of the ship cabin when Mrs Newlove and her children first arrive in Margate) is emphasized when the grotto is found. Then, this two-level narrative structure, below and above ground level, stages the tension between the interior and the exterior, the invisible and the visible. Furthermore, as in landscape phenomenology, the novel is packed with terminology related to sensation, presence, contact and *co-presence* of self and world, while simultaneously indicating absences, gaps and secrets that impede the movement towards presence. Wylie sustains that the 'agenda of making-present, re-presenting, is further characterized in some instances by a pervasive use of *archaeological metaphors*' (2009, 279, my emphasis). The archaeological metaphor utilized in the novel brings to light what has been hidden, what is not seen, what needs salvaging and rescuing. The shell-incrusted grotto evokes the past through the shells that cover the place. The shells (like the fossils) are vestiges from the past and material traces of a presence that was before. At the beginning of the novel Mrs Newlove refers to seashells in a conversation with Davidson, a teacher at the boarding school, in the following way: 'To breathe air and to gather seashells, a perfectly innocent and pleasurable recreation for the children ... After all, Captain, are shells not simple and elegant, like flowers? The very essence of natural beauty. [Davidson] Shells are the h-husks of dead creatures' (Overall 2007b, 29). To Davidson, who knows Hebrew, the 'realm of shells' seems demonic: a hidden world which, according to the Jewish religion, exists in parallel to the tangible one. Whether or not the shells are demonic, what remains clear is that the shells are the remnants of past beings, hidden in an underground space. The archaeological image presented here is attuned to the 'archaeology of the senses', proposed by Yannis Hamilakis, whereby '[a] sensorial archaeology is not a representation of the past but an evocation of its presence, its palpable, living materiality, its flesh' (2013, 199).

Like the shell, the fossil blurs the boundaries of life and death, and conjures up its tangible existence, through the materiality of the 'trace'. Tracy Chevalier's *Remarkable Creatures* (2010) examines the centrality of the

'trace' as the novel deals with the parallel stories of real-life fossil hunters: Mary Anning and Elizabeth Philpot. Drawing on phenomenology, the
fossil is not only a trace, a locus of memory, dissolving space and time, but
also an item, invested with the power to blur exterior and interior, a conduit
of feelings, an embodied presence which underlines the continuity of the
past into the present and the future. *Remarkable Creatures* belongs to what
Virginia Zimmerman refers to as 'literature of excavation', which is based
on the interrelatedness of time and space: 'an object is removed from layers
of Earth that signify the passage of time and re-presents the past' (2008, 3).
The fossil marks the passage of time, but is also a thing of the present: 'the
trace seems to exist outside time or across all time' (10). The trace (the fossil)
bridges the gap between past and present and makes us aware of the depth
of time, opening itself to re-interpretation and significance in the present, as
happens to Mary Anning when she discovers the ichthyosaurus: 'For once
he was quiet, and that made me ask the question I'd been wanting to for
several days now. "Sir," I said, "is this one of the creatures Noah brought
on his Ark?"' (Chevalier 2010, 128). These Victorian remnants are granted
the power to evoke the passage of time which means the combination of past
and present in the object, the item, the trace. In addition, the novel supports
the idea that fossil hunting is an embodied activity: at the end of the novel
Elizabeth Philpot is explicitly compared to a fossil that has been newly found
or re-discovered:

> There *was* something different about her, though I could not say exactly what
> it was. It was as if she were more certain. If someone were sketching her they
> would use clear, strong lines, whereas before they might have used faint marks
> and more shading. She was like a fossil that's been cleaned and set so everyone
> can see what it is. (2010, 298)

That fossil hunting is described as an embodied activity is made clear in the
sensory apprehension of the world manifested by Mary Anning and Elizabeth
Philpot. This embodied activity acquires an added significance in Elizabeth's
comments on her skin, which, from a phenomenological point of view, illustrate the close relationship between inside and outside, inner and outer. In
other words, the skin is the organ of touch; it provides the coat of protection
for the bodily organs and is situated 'at the crossover point between the phenomenal world and all that is contained inside' (Cohen 2009, 65). Elizabeth
refers to the skin of her hands as follows: 'I studied my hands. Despite my
wearing fingerless gloves and applying Margaret's salve daily, they were
rough and scarred, with puckered fingers and a rim of blue clay under each
nail' (2010, 237). Elizabeth's inner truth of her life, always fraught with difficulties and betrayals, is revealed on the surface of the skin. Both novels
can be defined as novels of excavation where the archaeological metaphor

is fundamental in more than one way. In both cases a sensorially inspired archaeology is privileged and a rejection of binary oppositions (subject/object, self/world) is emphasized since sensorial flows of matter, bodies and beings contribute to the evocation of the past.

As mentioned before, the Margate grotto is considered as 'a *secret* underground palace' (Overall 2007b, 125, my emphasis). The children discover its existence by chance and manage to keep the secret for a while until Joshua deems it necessary for the adult world to take over. When the secret is disclosed, the adults take charge of it and their lives are dramatically changed. Imagination is replaced with common sense and pecuniary issues. Mr Da Costa (a villainous character) tries to convince Mr Newlove to buy the land and the house since he would be gaining not only the land and the house 'but all that is buried beneath' (221). The notion of the 'secret' brings about the language of ghosts and haunting, thus counterpoising the proliferation of the sensorial and the affect, dislocating landscape phenomenology and demonstrating that the neo-Victorian novel oscillates between presence and absence. The secret motif haunts the whole narrative. There are several unspeakable secrets. For example, Fanny teaches George (the gardener's son) to read in the underground space of the grotto; Lizzy (the eldest daughter) keeps an illicit relationship with Captain Easter, 'the antagonist of the novel [who] comes inside and brutally wrecks some of the shell designs in search of treasure' (Sulmicki 2012, 57); and Fanny sustains that she is 'good at secrets' (Overall 2007b, 287). Another character of the novel argues that the grotto 'is an ancient temple, and that the shell flowers are *not* flowers but secret code, secret shell writing' (235). From the psychoanalytic point of view, Nicolas Abraham and Maria Torok use the archaeological metaphor to refer to remembering as digging out a secret that is unspeakable. Memory traces, or 'vestiges of perception' (Abraham 1994, 91), indicate the return of the repressed lodged in the crypt but whose symptoms can be felt on the surface/*shell*. The language of spectrality subtly infiltrates the novel through the reference to the secret and the phantom. Abraham and Torok defined the phantom as follows: 'what haunts are not the dead, but the gaps left within us by the secrets of others' (1994, 171). Contrasted to Freudian conceptualization of trauma, the phantom is related to an unnameable event that is passed on to the child, haunted by traces of that unspoken act. As Susanne Gruss has stated, 'it is only in recent years ... that Abraham and Torok are being rediscovered—their concepts of the phantom, the crypt, and intergenerational haunting' (2014, 125). The unspeakable secret, that is finally uncovered, is Mrs Newlove's surrender to Captain Easter's sexual advances who has become the family's creditor. The final scene of the novel proves how the unearthing of the grotto has altered adults in such a way that the whole family becomes affected: Mrs Newlove finds herself unable to stop Captain Easter's sexual advances (witnessed by Frances), and Frances' father prefers to remain blind to Captain Easter's dishonourable behaviour towards his wife. The language related to absence, secrets, gaps and ghosts indicates the tension that the neo-Victorian novel manifests between a metaphysics of presence (through images of excavation, archaeology and landscape phenomenology), and dislocation, separation, and absence (through the language of the secret, haunting and gaps). It is this ambivalent tension of presence/absence that characterizes the neo-Victorian novel in general, and Overall's narrative in particular, thus producing paradoxical, but also complementary, readings into the text.

In this chapter I have examined the role of landscape phenomenology and the tensions between presence and absence, distance and closeness, subject and object in Sonia Overall's neo-Victorian novel *The Realm of Shells* (2006) through the analysis of the ambivalent evocation of the past as both present and absent, close and distant. Phenomenology has provided useful critical interventions into spatial studies, as well as into archaeology. John Wylie recognizes that Merleau-Ponty's concepts of 'embodiment, vision and practice have become a cardinal reference point for landscape phenomenology' (2009, 280), whereas Yannis Hamilakis proposes, in turn, 'an archaeology of the senses' and thus, to redirect attention towards the human body, which offers 'multisensorial modes of being-in and attending to the world' (2014, 9). Through landscape phenomenology and the archaeological metaphor, I have explored how affective material memory of the Victorian past is evoked through a combined approach of presence and absence, encapsulated in the critical notions of the trace, the spectre and the phantom. The language of the senses and affect provides an access route to the dislocation and fracture of the binary opposition between self and world, past and present, portrayed in the novel, privileging co-presence and mutuality. Overall's novel generates life and sensorial relationships and entanglements, as the affect 'connects with the sensorial field as a space of flows and encounters, as a sensorial contact zone' (Hamilakis 2013, 125). The shell-encrusted grotto, at below ground level, functions as a 'body', eliciting responses and producing atmospheres which finally affect those in contact with it. Moreover, the shell (as the fossil) relates that underground world to the material connection to the past, the vestige, the trace of a being that once existed, which has a tangible continuity in the present. At the same time, secrets, gaps and absences signal detachment and non-coincidence between self and world. *The Realm of Shells* operates between these two poles and, in a way, this is in keeping with the doubled vision or nature of neo-Victorianism, as generally agreed by critics. The phenomenological reading of the novel (soundscapes, tactile encounters, the tunnel as conduit between interior and exterior, among other sensorial instances) is undercut by the haunting of secrets and individual trauma. Furthermore, the tunnel through which the characters have access to the underground 'realm of shells' could function as a metaphorical channel, a means of communication between the Victorian past and the present, the Victorians and us, through which whole bodies, affect and matter interact and penetrate. Therefore, a phenomenological perspective on neo-Victorianism offers a conduit through which the matter flows between past and present, the Victorians and us in such a way that reading and interpreting the Victorians in contemporary culture might be considered an embodied act, simultaneously and paradoxically looking with and looking at the Victorian world.

NOTES

1. The research for this chapter has been funded by the Spanish Ministry of Economy of Competitiveness (Research Project reference number: FFI2013-44154-P) and VINS (Victorian and Neo-Victorian Studies in Spain Network) (reference number FFI2015-71025-REDT). An earlier version of this contribution was delivered at the Neo-Victorian Networks Conference (13–15 June 2012, Amsterdam).
2. As I have discussed elsewhere, in the introduction to a special issue on 'The Victorian Sensorium', Wendy Parkins notes that several Victorian writers already referred to the dangers posed by the sensory overload stimulated by the city of London, particularly towards the end the nineteenth century (2009, 1–7).
3. Sugar's reading of Agnes's discarded diaries illustrates one example of close relation between subjects. Agnes's diaries date from the period she was at the convent school in 1865, and the information it contains gives Sugar access to the interior of the child and adolescent Agnes. Gianmarco Perticaroli has defined consumption of things in Faber's novel as 'the site of a real or imaginary co-presence, where the experience of being perceived prevails over the act of self-perception' (2011, 130). Faber's novel employs the diaries as an opening of the self to the world, as a material vestige of the interior which is perceived and apprehended by another embodied self, Sugar, a 'co-presence': 'Now at last Sugar understands: this muddle-headed, minuetting adolescent *is* a lady, as fully adult as she'll ever be' (2002, 553).
4. One has only to remember the overwhelming references to sensorial apprehension in this novel.
5. According to Merlin Coverley, the origins of the term 'psycho-geography' can be traced back 'to Paris in the 1950s and the Lettrist Group, a forerunner of the Situationist International' (2006, 10).
6. For more information about 'the italicized silent protests (not) voiced by the female child narrator', consult Sulmicki (2012, 55).

BIBLIOGRAPHY

Abraham, Nicolas and Maria Torok. 1994. *The Shell and the Kernel: Renewals of Psychoanalysis*. Chicago and London: University of Chicago Press.

Anderson, Ben. 2009. 'Affective Atmospheres.' *Emotion, Space and Society*, 2: 77–81.

Anderson, Ben.. 2014. *Encountering Affect: Capacities, Apparatuses, Conditions.* Farnham and Burlington: Ashgate.

Boehm-Schnitker, Nadine and Susanne Gruss. 2011. 'Introduction: Spectacles and Things—Visual and Material Culture and/in Neo-Victorianism.' *Neo-Victorian Studies*, 4 (2): 1–23.

Chevalier, Tracy. 2010. *Remarkable Creatures*. New York: Dutton.

Cohen, William. 2009. *Embodied: Victorian Literature and the Senses*. Minneapolis and London: University of Minnesota Press.

Coverley, Merlin. 2006. *Psychogeography*. Herts: Pocket Essentials.

Dickens, Charles. (1862) 1989. *Hard Times*. Oxford: Oxford University Press.

Faber, Michel. 2002. *The Crimson Petal and the White*. Edinburgh: Canongate.

Gamble, Sarah. 2009. '"You Cannot Impersonate What You Are": Questions of Authenticity in the Neo-Victorian Novel.' *LIT: Literature, Interpretation, Theory*, 20 (1–2): 126–40.

Garner, Stanton B. Jr. 1994. *Bodied Spaces: Phenomenology and Performance in Contemporary Drama*. Ithaca and London: Cornell University Press.

Gruss, Susanne. 2014. 'Spectres of the Past: Reading the Phantom of Family Trauma in Neo-Victorian Fiction.' *Neo-Victorian Literature and Culture: Immersions and Revisitations*. Ed. Nadine Boehm-Schnitker and Susanne Gruss. New York and London: Routledge. 123–36.

Hamilakis, Yannis. 2013. *Archaeology and the Senses: Human Experience, Memory and Affect*. Cambridge: Cambridge University Press.

Heilmann, Ann and Mark Llewellyn. 2010. *Neo-Victorianism: The Victorians in the Twenty-First Century, 1999–2009*. Basingstoke: Palgrave Macmillan.

Johnston, Judith and Catherine Waters. 2008. 'Introduction: Victorian Turns, Neo-Victorian Returns.' *Victorian Turns, Neo-Victorian Returns: Essays on Fiction and Culture*. Ed. Penny Gay, Judith Johnston and Catherine Waters. Newcastle upon Tyne: Cambridge Scholars. 1–11.

Mah, Alice A. 2012. *Industrial Ruination, Community, and Place: Landscapes and Legaciones of Urban Decline*. Toronto: University of Toronto Press.

Ménasé, Stéphanie. 2004. *Foreword to The World of Perception*, by Maurice Merleau-Ponty. London and New York: Routledge. vii–viii.

Merleau-Ponty, Maurice. 2002. *Phenomenology of Perception*. London and New York: Routledge.

Overall, Sonia. 2007a. 'Facts into Fiction—*The Realm of Shells* and the Margate Shell Grotto.' *The Realm of Shells*. London: Harper Perennial. 9–13.

_____. 2007b. *The Realm of Shells*. London: Harper Perennial.

_____. 2016. Sonia Overall website. Accessed 24 February 2016. http://www.sonia-overall.net/.

Parkins, Wendy. 2009. 'Trust Your Senses?: An Introduction to the Victorian Sensorium.' *Australasian Journal of Victorian Studies*, 14 (2): 1–7.

Perticaroli, Gianmarco. 2011. 'Neo-Victorian Things: Michel Faber's *The Crimson Petal and the White*.' *Neo-Victorian Studies*, 4 (2): 108–32.

Ponty-Merleau, Maurice. 2002. *Phenomenology of Perception.* Trans. Colin Smith. London and New York: Routledge.

Pulham, Patricia. 2013. 'Eyes that Trace like Fingers: Keats, Wilde, and Victorian Statue-Love.' *Rivista interdisciplinare di studi romantici*, 5: 133–49.

Rhys, Jean. 1966. *Wide Sargasso Sea.* Harmondsworth: Penguin.

Ricoeur, Paul. 1990. *Time and Narrative.* Vol. 3. Chicago and London: University of Chicago Press.

Ricoeur, Paul.. 2006. *Memory, History, Forgetting.* Chicago and London: University of Chicago Press.

Schlicke, Paul. 1989. *Introduction to Hard Times*, by Charles Dickens. Oxford: Oxford University Press. vii–xxii.

Smith, Mark M. 2007. *Sensing the Past: Seeing, Hearing, Smelling, Tasting, and Touching in History.* Berkeley and Los Angeles: University of California Press.

Sulmicki, Marcin. 2012. 'Women and Children Last: To What Extent Are Houses Homes in Neo-Victorian Novels.' *Ex-changes: Comparative Studies in British and American Cultures.* Ed. Katarzyna Więckowska and Edyta Lorek-Jezińska. Newcastle upon Tyne: Cambridge Scholars. 46–60.

Wylie, John. 2009. 'Landscape, Absence and the Geographies of Love.' *Transactions of the Institute of British Geographers*, 34: 275–89.

Zimmerman, Virginia. 2008. *Excavating Victorians.* New York: State University of New York Press.

Part III

BORDERLANDS AND OUTLANDS

Chapter Nine

W. G. Sebald's Afterlives

Haunting Contemporary Landscape Writing

Daniel Weston

W. G. Sebald sought out ghostly presences in place but he has now also become one for other writers who follow after him. He haunts contemporary place writing *en masse*, and in particular that of East Anglia where *The Rings of Saturn*, his most regionally located prose narrative, takes place. As artist Jeremy Millar notes, 'he is now a layer of that history of which he writes' and 'a very definite part of that landscape' (interview in Gee 2015). Sebald has been an important and influential figure for authors writing about landscape over the past decade, with a significant number drawing heavily on (and some outright adopting) his idiosyncratic mode of engaging with place and of writing about that engagement. His influence—openly admitted by many and less explicitly signalled by a greater number still—has been pervasive in practice across a range of creative disciplines: the sample of work indebted to Sebald that I will discuss in this chapter encompasses visual art, exhibition curation, film, poetry and prose writing. In this chapter I ask where Sebald's example can be felt in the work of a number of writers and practitioners in order to assess what kind of report it produces and also what senses of a place it might preclude. In addition, reflections on visits to the Suffolk landscapes and places on the itinerary of *The Rings of Saturn* are briefly incorporated. My own sense of these places is markedly different from that communicated in the book. This disjuncture does not merely reaffirm the already well-established point that Sebald's accounts are subjective and semi-fictionalised, but speaks to the pervasive influence of his genre-defying texts in landscape writing today. Following consideration of texts where Sebald's inflections can be discerned, I evaluate the benefits and drawbacks of his spectral presence and ask what happens when haunting—in the form of a set of recognizable literary tropes deployed repeatedly across a genre—reaches a point of saturation.

Sebald's influence has not only been on creative practitioners of landscape writing and art but also on attendant critical articulations. His four prose narratives of place—*Vertigo* (originally published in German 1990, translated 1999), *The Emigrants* (1992, 1996), *The Rings of Saturn* (1995, 1998) and *Austerlitz* (2001, 2001)—have received significant attention from literary critics and cultural geographers alike, and have been one of the testing grounds upon which dialogues between the two disciplines have been forged. For cultural geographer John Wylie, Sebald's work 'has been a specific source of inspiration for recent geographical engagements with landscape writing'; furthermore, *The Rings of Saturn* in particular 'has come to stand as something of a model for contemporary cultural geographies of landscape' (2007b, 207). This interdisciplinary gravitation towards Sebald is important in itself for a book (and book series) such as this, but even more apposite for this chapter is the fact that this interest is founded on these texts' significant role in establishing the generic conventions of contemporary landscape writing: like the ghost of metre that T. S. Eliot finds present in even the most free verse, Sebald haunts this lately rejuvenated literary mode as a presence upon which younger writers sound their own accounts. Indeed, the current revival of interest in narratives of this kind explains the recent consolidation of conventions: Wylie has said that 'whereas landscape art is a familiar and rich visual tradition, there is in contrast no generally understood or accepted literary genre named "landscape writing"' (2010, 48). Sebald's importance has been one of the case studies upon which a definition to fill this hole has been arrived at. His impact is thus most apparent in form, style and atmosphere. Wylie continues: 'Sebald is perhaps most notable and influential for his elaboration of an innovative literary form, one incorporating elements of existential memoir, autobiography, travel writing, cultural history and phantasmagoria. In and through this format Sebald conjures a strange metaphysics of landscape' (2007b, 207). The literary ticks that Sebald's writing is known for and the combinations that it formulates are those that many others have taken up.

Many of the hallmarks of Sebald's narratorial persona and his sense of place can be checked off with a brief reading of the opening few sentences from *The Rings of Saturn*. The (literary) tradition of peripatetic, pastoral retreat familiar from the Romantics and much farther back can clearly be seen here, but so can the way Sebald reframes certain poses anew:

In August 1992, when the dog days were drawing to an end, I set off to walk the county of Suffolk, in the hope of dispelling the emptiness that takes hold of me whenever I have completed a long stint of work. And in fact my hope was realized, up to a point; for I have seldom felt so carefree as I did then, walking for hours in the day through the thinly populated countryside, which stretches inland from the coast. I wonder now, however, whether there might be something in the old superstition that certain ailments of the spirit and of the body are particularly likely to beset us under the sign of the Dog Star. At all events, in retrospect I became preoccupied not only with the unaccustomed sense of freedom but also with the paralysing horror that had come over me at various times when confronted with the traces of destruction, reaching far back into the past, that were evident even in that remote place. (2002, 3)

Here is the solitary (usually male) walker retiring from work to find release in countryside pursuits and engage in earnest reflection. The book's trajectory is quickly away from urban Norwich towards the ever more rural. The solitude of this figure is further emphasized by the 'thinly populated countryside' or the 'remote place' that is selected for visitation, and, it might be added, by the eliding of those encountered there in the written account. However, the characteristic gesture outwards, drawing links from the terrain crossed and places called upon towards a larger European and world history, mitigates this gesture of retreat. The text is constantly swinging between the minutiae of place—seemingly researched in great detail before the trip—and a much bigger picture. Some of the connections forged are clearly prompted by sites visited and the lives and events that haunt them; others are only tangentially linked, relying more heavily on the narrator's pre-existing fascinations, and begin to inaugurate the text's key themes (not the least the 'traces of destruction' present from this opening onwards). The almost cabbalistic search for patterns bespeaks a strong agenda brought to the engagement with place.

The pairing of withdrawal and connection is not the only oxymoron here: the combined lightness and heaviness of mood is also a characteristic combination. The narrator is at once 'carefree' and his sense of emptiness dispelled, and at the same time beset by 'ailments of the spirit', paralysed by horror. (Movement and paralysis form a third pairing.) Melancholy characterizes the narrator—sombreness coupled with creativity—under a saturnine influence signalled in the book's title. The astrological reference here to the journey taking place during the sultry, hot days of late summer that coincide with the rise of Sirius, the dog star, exemplifies the learned, scholarly antiquarianism that fills out the text's frame of reference. In short, the text is, as the publisher's back cover classification indicates, fiction and autobiography before it is travel writing. That is, the sense of place that emerges from its pages is highly particularized. These particularities play out across a broad sample of contemporary place writing.

The Rings of Saturn, then, is a text whose narrator constantly ponders 'across what distances in time ... elective affinities and correspondences connect', and for whom 'my rational mind is ... unable to lay [to rest] the ghosts of repetition that haunt me with ever greater frequency' (Sebald 2002, 182,

187). That elective affinity is the process driving much of this narrative of place which has led Jessica Dubow to find that for Sebald 'all places are posthumous' (2011, 189). She coins the term 'negative phenomenology' to describe the way in which Sebald's work (and others) is characterized by 'a perceptual capacity that answers not to the appearance of anything or enfolds any passage from the unknown to the known, but which demands a constant dispersion, a temporal abyss into which immediate visibilities slip the moment they are glimpsed' (191). The traffic is always from the cues in place towards histories now absent from this place or any other. Sebald's places are not, for Dubow, lifeless as a result; rather, they are 'one in which lifelessness is the signature of historicity' (191). This particular form of affect, I would argue, carries the corollary that there is a constant slippage of attention away from the experience of a place. History overburdens the moment of engagement. It is a feature that runs through Sebald's texts and those who follow him. The effect is felt in the content of those accounts and their tone.

Selecting a particular site visited in *The Rings of Saturn* adds definition. The passage describing Orford Ness exemplifies the narrating persona's typical reading of place. Orford Ness is a shingle spit joined to the mainland of the Suffolk coast at Aldeburgh and stretching down over the mouth of the river Alde as far south as Orford. For much of the twentieth century it was administered by the Ministry of Defence and was the site of an Atomic Weapons Research Establishment base where testing took place. As such, it was off limits to the public until the closure of the facility in the 1970s and thereafter took on, not least for Sebald, an abandoned, haunted air. In a passage from *The Rings of Saturn* that imitates a journey across the river Styx, the narrator pays a ferryman to take him across from Orford to the Ness, a place 'people still mostly avoided' and where those who went 'became emotionally disturbed for some time' (Sebald 2002, 234). On arrival, his response is typically melancholic:

> It was as if I were passing through an undiscovered country, and I still remember that I felt, at the same time, both utterly liberated and deeply despondent. I had not a single thought in my head. With each step that I took, the emptiness within and the emptiness without grew ever greater and the silence more profound. (234)

The themes recurrent from the text's opening are clear: a feeling of liberty and heaviness (despondency) combined; desertion (here, silence); emptiness; and elective affinity with environment (within/without alignment). If one walks out towards the military installations, the trajectory is clear—'ahead lay nothing but destruction'—and wandering amongst them prompts a further extension of the narrative of decline and destruction: 'the closer I came to those ruins, the more any notion of a mysterious isle of the dead receded, and the more I imagined myself amidst the remains of our own civilization after its extinction in some future catastrophe' (235, 237). This is reverie much more than reportage.

Orford Ness is no longer the 'undiscovered country' of *The Rings of Saturn*. The site is now a National Nature Reserve managed by the National Trust. The ferry ride now brings visitors to a jetty where they are met by volunteers who provide guidance and a map of routes around the spit's features. It is still likely to be bleak and windy more days than not, and the crumbling buildings to possess a resemblance to those in the Zone of Tarkovsky's *Stalker*, but it is definitely not abandoned or unpeopled. You might exchange a word with other walkers you will almost undoubtedly pass, and if you arrive back at the jetty in-between scheduled ferries then the volunteers might invite you into their heated hut where they drink tea and chat about their grandchildren. They might ask you to add any interesting bird sightings to the daily record or give you advice on cycling further up the coast. You might be forced to revise your notion that the numerous rivers stretching inland without crossings close to the coast serve to isolate villages there, seeing that in fact this fosters closer communities. In short, tracing Sebald might prove a surprising endeavour when the atmosphere of textual representations does not now match a first-hand engagement with place.

And yet, Sebald's writing has had a powerful fixing effect on literary and artistic representations of the area since his death—it is the atmosphere of his text more than any other facet that permeates subsequent creative projects. *Waterlog* was an exhibition of contemporary art staged at Norwich Castle Museum and Art Gallery and then at The Collection in Lincoln in 2007. Steven Bode's catalogue notes describe how from these two regional galleries 'the project set out to explore the wider landscape of the east of England, with the idea of the literary journey as one of its overarching themes. A guiding presence throughout was the figure of W.G. Sebald' (Bode 2007, 6). He goes on to elaborate the nature of this 'guiding presence': 'Sebald's elliptical style—digressive, poetic, reflective—sets the tone of the project as a whole, in which artists' forays out into the surrounding landscape uncover unexpected affinities and connections embedded in the history and geography of the region' (6). Each contribution worked through 'a richly evocative terrain that is unusually flooded with both water and memory, and the accumulated flotsam of history, and whose ghosts, to which Sebald was particularly attuned, are everywhere you look'. The contributing artists share with Sebald 'a unifying sensibility', 'an outlook, and a set of preoccupations' (6, 7). The commonalities identified here are constitutional, structural and stylistic. They are about what stance is brought to the engagement with place, what scholarship accompanies and colours that engagement and the artistic techniques by which that engagement is communicated. The resulting predisposition is to see the landscape in exactly the same 'richly evocative' way.

The same might be said for Grant Gee's film *Patience (After Sebald)*, which, to give it its full title, details *A Walk through 'The Rings of Saturn'* (2012). Coupling interview footage with Sebald's publishers, friends, collaborators, and with creative practitioners interested in his work and following in his footsteps, on the one hand, and location footage overlain with readings from the text, on the other, the film acts both as a documentary about Sebaldian representations of place and an intervention in that field itself. In the latter of these two guises, it looks for an aesthetic coalescence of the landscape of the book—textual and photographic—and that of the same places today. Thus, in a repeated motif, a still image displaying one of the grainy photographs found in *The Rings of Saturn* fades softly into fixed-point film footage of the same spot (in the same composition and framing) years later. The audio accompanying these visuals comprises relevant passages from the book interspersed with a suitably haunting and unsettled soundtrack written for the film. Those interviewed, as well as Gee's editing and selection of interview footage, demonstrate an awareness of the issues attendant upon allowing Sebald to dominate depictions of a region and procedures of a genre of artistic production, but this awareness is not communicated obviously in the aesthetics of the film itself. There is little to disrupt Sebald's distinctive and quite mannered mode.

Turning to literary representations reveals a similarly strong Sebaldian influence. Of course, this is not all pervasive but it is regularly recurring. I elect here to select paradigmatic examples rather than a list-like survey of instances. Blake Morrison's *Shingle Street* (2015) treads ground familiar to readers of *The Rings of Saturn*. The first and longest poem of Morrison's collection, 'The Ballad of Shingle Street', has an endnote attached to it acknowledging but also attempting to mitigate the influence of Sebald. 'The setting is loosely based on the eponymous Suffolk village', Morrison writes, conforming to a Sebaldian itinerary for literary or artistic visitation, selecting this site for the narratives it might tell over and above the myriad others in the region, and then awarding it the precedence of a collection's title poem to sound the dominant notes (2015, 57). The village is just south of Orford Ness and appears just before it on Sebald's journey. The other two poems in the collection named for places are 'Covehithe' and 'Dunwich'—also Sebald's haunts in *The Rings of Saturn*. Morrison quotes Sebald describing Shingle Street as 'the most abandoned spot in the entire region ... which now consists of just one wretched row of humble houses and cottages, and where I have never encountered a single human being', but then counters this perspective with reference to another source, resident Tim Millar's 'affectionate essay' (referred to in these patronizing terms by Morrison) (Sebald 2002, 225;

Morrison 2015, 57). Millar is not quoted as Sebald is, and Morrison's poem does not repopulate Sebald's deserted village. The scales are clearly tipped towards the Sebaldian narrative of this place.

The poem itself bears this out. Opening with an epigraph on loss from John Donne's *Devotions*—a signal comparable to Sebald's own signature penchant for antiquarian quotation—and an exhortation to 'watch your step' on treacherous Shingle Street, the poem is focused at least as much on historical decay as on the place's present guise. Indeed, landscape features and animals become metaphorical markers of that spectral history: 'The rolling seals / Are charcoal grey / As though burnt or singed by grief. / Like ash-streaked mourners, half-possessed' (Morrison 2015, 2). And:

> A soft pink light
> Sneaks up the beach
> As if each stone were ringed with fire,
> As if each pebble stored the heat
> Of past disasters, past defeats.
> And in the dusk they tell the tale
> Of burning boats and blistered flesh
> (2)

The event referred to is the rumoured (though officially unconfirmed and likely fictional propaganda) failed German landing at Shingle Street during World War II, at which hundreds of soldiers supposedly died when their landing crafts were met with a wall of fire. The same story is, of course, made reference to by Sebald. For the narrator of Morrison's poem, the effect by which the landscape bears witness to this story (and requires visitors to do the same) is compelling: 'you can't help but watch and hear / And smell the oil and taste the fear / And feel your skin scorch in the heat' (2015, 3). In later phases, the poem shifts the focus to a different focal point for this narrative of loss and decline: answering the contemporary concerns of climate change, coastal erosion comes to the fore. In Morrison's construction, the forces of climate and weather are actively malevolent—'The waves maraud, / The winds oppress'— with the land as victim—'The earth can't help / But acquiesce'. On this 'receding ground', 'nothing's sound' (4). Though this inflection is new, or newly urgent in the current milieu, the same observations are present in *The Rings of Saturn*, where at Dunwich Sebald dwells on the earth lost to sea (Sebald 2002, 155–9). Indeed, the curiously fraught sensibility, along with accompanying heightened language and tendency to simile and metaphor, overlay immediacy of engagement with Shingle Street as a real location.

Place writing in prose also wears the extensive influence of Sebald, perhaps to an even greater extent than other forms already considered. In particular, the so-called New Nature Writing that has mushroomed since about the mid-2000s has consistently conferred attention on Sebald's places and set out to recover their arcane and obscure histories in a Sebaldian manner, even if there is a tonal distinction to be drawn. Robert Macfarlane, perhaps the best known of the coterie of writers at the heart of this movement, has certainly conferred attention on East Anglia (like so many others in the genre). *The Wild Places* visits locations akin to those in Sebald; goes to those places in ways that bear comparison—the lone, male walker in reflective mode; and is similarly structured—slipping between passages of tactile, first-hand engagement with place and scholarly disquisitions on local (and not so local) history. The introductory remarks of the passage describing Macfarlane's visit to Orford Ness are strikingly Sebaldian:

> Lying just off the Suffolk coast is a desert. Orford Ness is a shingle spit twelve miles long and up to two miles wide. It is unpopulated, and in hundreds of grey acres, the only things moving are hares, hawks, and the sea wind. (2007, 241)

Here is the likening of the close at hand to the far away, the (artificially?) depopulated scene, and the sombre, bleached pallet of colour. The telling of the town's history falls into the familiar pattern of decline at the hands of a seemingly malign power beyond human control: 'In the eleventh and twelfth century, Orford was a thriving port, protected from the North Sea by the comforting arm of the Ness. Then that arm turned murderous.' The gradual extension of the spit led to the port silting up until it was unreachable for larger ships. 'Orford was turned into a small-boat harbor only, dead to trade' (Macfarlane 2007a, 255). The weather on the day of this visit is characteristically bleak—'as we stepped from the ferry onto the pontoon on the Ness's shore, it was clear that the Ness was in a wild state'—and the landform's ex-military buildings have their established psychological effect: 'That day, everything I saw seemed bellicose, mechanized' (255–7). If in these ways, Macfarlane is, wittingly or unwittingly, held under the spell of Sebald just as much as others among his contemporaries, this is not his final position.

Macfarlane is perhaps most interesting as a failed follower of Sebald: he had planned to write a book around following in Sebald's footsteps, and had undertaken some of the necessary walks, but later abandoned the project. At the time of the *Waterlog* exhibition, Macfarlane was working on this scheme and contributed an essay describing it to the exhibition catalogue. In that essay, he reflects on Sebald's processes and on his own. Contrary to most commentators, he sees Sebald not primarily as a writer of place: 'If he was anything, Sebald was a biographer. ... For he walked his subjects back to life—or he walked himself forwards into death (it can be hard to tell which). He travelled the routes formerly taken by his subjects, visited the sites they did' (Macfarlane 2007a, 79). The shift in genre here carries with it a shift in the expectations for engagements with place. For Macfarlane, it also prompts questions: 'What does it mean to haunt the haunter, to footstep a footstepper? For several months now, I have been following Sebald. ... I have started to remake certain of the walks that Sebald (or his narrators) take in each of his four main books. ... I am turning Sebald's own methods back onto him' (2007b, 81). Macfarlane goes on to offer a preliminary answer to his own question: 'I have come to think of Sebald's work, and of my own on Sebald, as versions of revision: both in the sense of re-seeing and re-writing. ... Following in the footsteps of a previous traveller might lead one not to replicate but to innovate' (83).

To speculate, the project may have been abandoned because Macfarlane came to recognize that the innovation he speaks of would have been possible only within certain fairly narrow parameters if Sebald were going to be, in any sense, 'followed'. The reverberation of Sebald's work in those who follow after him risks becoming mere involution thereby reducing the variety of our engagement with place. Macfarlane also discusses the project in interview for Gee's film *Patience*. By this point, he has ceased work on it and accounts for this fact by drawing attention to discrepancies between the representations of these places and the facts he finds on the ground as he walks the route of *The Rings of Saturn*: 'I really wanted it to be a grey day [in Lowestoft]' but 'I was having too much fun to footstep Sebald. ... My memory of that walk is one of delight and a refusal of the walk to conform to my idea of what it should have been' (interview in Gee 2015). Either the Sebaldian manner is too much of a constraint for new writing or it simply does not match reality. In any case, Macfarlane's decision to draw a halt to the undertaking and turn his writerly attention elsewhere rather than to write a contrary account leaves the Sebaldian aura of these places intact and unchallenged.

Iain Sinclair, another prolific and well-regarded figure in the field, though of a different school to Macfarlane's nature writing, has also engaged explicitly with Sebald's writing. Sebald appears occasionally in glancing reference in Sinclair's writing of place, though it is more often the urban Sebald of *Austerlitz* rather than the rural Sebald of *The Rings of Saturn* to be found there. Sinclair's territory is London, and particularly the eastern districts, and thus overlaps with the zone of interest in Sebald's final novel: Liverpool Street Station and its surrounds, Whitechapel, and the Jewish East End. In 2013, Sinclair published a pamphlet titled *Austerlitz & After: Tracking Sebald* in a small print run with an independent press. It consisted of sections cut from his book length text *American Smoke: Journeys to the End of the Light*, published in the same year. That Sinclair elected to exorcise this material from his chief project of the time perhaps suggests an attempt to not re-tread familiar ground or to contain and resist the seductive reading of these places found in Sebald's texts. The publication of the pamphlet nonetheless testifies to attentiveness to Sebald, especially as the printing of only 300 copies suggests a personal interest rather than a particularly commercial venture. *Austerlitz and After* comprises reflections on these London Sebald haunts and—characteristic of Sinclair—a walk with an informed insider to the topic (Sinclair, unlike Sebald, most often walks in company). In this case, the co-walker is Stephen Watts, poet, Sebald associate-collaborator and part-model for the Austerlitz character. Sinclair buys into the 'atmosphere' of Sebald's Liverpool Street, which is an accurate rendering of the station as Sinclair remembers it before its redevelopment (thus facilitating an observation of what is lost in the process of 'regeneration'—a key trope in Sinclair's writing):

> Sebald's description in *Austerlitz* of the abandoned Ladies' Waiting Room may have been finessed but it caught the atmosphere of the pre-development Liverpool Street with preternatural accuracy: a sleepwalker's castle of locked doors, ramps without function, cancelled corridors; intimidating spaces in which the lost souls of the city took up residence on hard benches. (2013, 11)

Though his accession to the mood of Sebald's writing and the vision of places haunted by the lost tallies with what has been seen in other's writing, there is also a greater awareness of Sebald as a writer of fiction here—Sinclair pointedly observes that details are 'finessed' to serve novelistic ends. Further, Sinclair describes a typology of the typical Sebald narrator: 'My sense of the Sebaldian voyage [is] of a man who is not quite well, walking through a landscape of coincidences and elective affinities in search of a sepia photograph of a discontinued self' (18). The awareness of this subjective perspective as a distinct pose is much more central to Sinclair's response than that of others.

Sinclair is also circumspect when, in later phases of the pamphlet, he comes to reflect on the process of tracking Sebald. He is critical of the way in which 'tributes' to Sebald have settled into a recognizable set of conventions (a genre):

> Tributes to Sebald, especially *The Rings of Saturn*, became a genre, an English cultural industry, expediting footsteps that were never there, unpicking the play of meticulously crafted fictions, making them ordinary. And bringing the faithful to places like Snape Maltings, for readings, recitals, concerts, confessions. A quiet cult of managed melancholy and weekend breaks in moody winter resorts. (Sinclair 2013, 23–4)

The apparent failure of subsequent re-visitors and writers to recognize the fictionality of Sebald's texts plays a large part in this critique, as does the pious nature of the response and the melancholic posture that commonly accompanies it. The final sentence quoted here also signals the importance of location in the rise of a 'cult' of Sebald: the East Anglian coast might feel out-of-the-way (in Sebald's own terms, already seen above, a 'remote place', 'thinly populated countryside') but it is also easily accessible for a weekend retreat from the metropolitan centre, London, and the scholarly university city, Cambridge. Thus, its repeated visitation by a largely urban literary set gesturing at the pastoral finds focus, as Sinclair describes, in homages to Sebald. Networks of connection clearly underpin this very English 'cultural industry'.

Interviewed for Gee's film *Patience*, Sinclair extemporises on the wider process that is happening in general as writers and artists revisit sites associated with a dominant figure such as Sebald. He is concerned with the commodification of places such as Orford Ness. There is, he observes, a moment in the history of such places before they are commodified with artists 'deposited there to make works [of art] that give a kind of poetic to these dangerous, dirty, difficult spaces. And the first ones in have a kind of real charge and then it becomes very processional and very bleached of energy in some ways' (interview in Gee 2015). Hostile to commissioned artwork and the sanctified meanings of place that it tends to reinforce, Sinclair expresses a problem inherent to any act of following a figure such as Sebald. Ghostly presences and their revenance sap energy and life from depiction and representation; furthermore, not only is work produced thus lifeless, it also contributes to a process of recovery and sanitization, endorsing certain narratives of a place and tacitly marginalizing others. As Sinclair also notes, the issue is not limited to Sebald and Suffolk: 'the country is black with people going on walks to write books' (interview in Gee 2015). The texts produced deal with different places and present the small histories thus recovered, but their narrative arc and tropes are usually familiar. Sinclair does not, however, propose a resolution. Whether or not artists and writers should consciously attempt to resist the tropes established by those who have gone before is left as an unresolved question. Though detractors from Sinclair's position would no doubt note that he is himself intricately tangled within the web of revisiting that he identifies, his questioning attitude towards the whole process is nonetheless one that it is worthwhile to share.

The questions that Roger Luckhurst asked as long ago as 2002 of the spectral lens through which place is often seen—why has spectrality become a master trope, what are the drawbacks of granting it such precedence—have never really gone away (2002, 527). Luckhurst's concern is that a recent 'Gothic revival' might amount to no more than 'self-referential involution'. He voices a suspicion of 'the very generalized economy of haunting': 'Unable to discriminate between instances and largely uninterested in historicity (beyond its ghostly disruption), the discourse of spectralized modernity risks investing in the compulsive repetitions of a structure of melancholic entrapment'

(534–5). The problem is compounded, for Luckhurst, 'because the spectral infiltrates the hermeneutic act itself, critical work can only replicate tropes from textual sources' (535). He worries that critical purchase to arrest the turn inwards cannot be achieved. These concerns seem particularly apposite for the afterlives of W. G. Sebald in contemporary landscape writing. His ghostly presence is felt broadly as a generalized atmospheric and tonal default position in engagements with place, particularly in writing re-treading the East Anglian landscapes with which he has become associated in seemingly indelible ways. As has been seen, those who might question his accounts and wish to write otherwise, or who find the process of homage and revisiting problematic, have mostly chosen to look elsewhere rather than offer a very different account of these places.

As Steve Pile observes, in any write up of an engagement with place, 'since only particular things are noticed, those that are have special significance', any representation can 'trace only specific histories'. Writers are alike in this particularity of focus: 'Doesn't everyone have their own stories to tell?' (Pile 2002, 122–3). And yet, it seems that many writers of East Anglia, and (to broaden the point) of English place writing of the last few years more generally, have the same story to tell, and that story is markedly similar in structure, form, tone and atmosphere to Sebald's fictional story. Sebald is not himself the originator but his vision has proved compelling. For some, too compelling. Perhaps a laying to rest of this particular ghostly presence is now necessary. What was so attractive about Sebald, for creative writers and critics alike—in Wylie's terms, his 'is production of an at once innovative, oblique and multi-faceted literary form', a 'unique compound'—has now settled into a set of conventions that can be ticked off with all too much ease in any number of those who have followed him (2007b, 174). The best way to process Sebald's legacy might now be to repeat his act of turning away from genre in order to reinvigorate place writing once more.

BIBLIOGRAPHY

Bode, Steven. 2007. 'Forward.' *Waterlog: Journeys around an Exhibition*. Ed. Steven Bode, Jeremy Millar and Nina Ernst. London: Film & Video Umbrella. 7–8.

Dubow, Jessica. 2011. 'Still-Life, After Life, *nature morte*: W. G. Sebald and the Demands of Landscape.' *Envisioning Landscapes, Making Worlds: Geography and the Humanities*. Eds. Stephen Daniels, Dydia DeLyser, J. Nicholas Entrikin, and Douglas Richardson. Abingdon: Routledge. 188–97.

Gee, Grant (Director). 2015. *Patience (After Sebald): A Walk through the Rings of Saturn*. London: Soda.

Luckhurst, Roger. 2002. 'The Contemporary London Gothic and the Limits of the "Spectral Turn".' *Textual Practice*, 16: 527–46.

Macfarlane, Robert. 2007a. 'Afterglow, or Sebald the Walker.' *Waterlog: Journeys around an Exhibition*. Ed. Steven Bode, Jeremy Millar and Nina Ernst. London: Film & Video Umbrella. 78–83.

Macfarlane, Robert. 2007b. *The Wild Places*. London: Granta.

Morrison, Blake. 2015. *Shingle Street*. London: Chatto & Windus.

Pile, Steve. 2002. 'Memory and the City.' *Temporalities, Autobiography and Everyday Life*. Ed. Jan Campbell and Janet Harbord. Manchester: Manchester University Press. 111–27.

Sebald, W. G. 2002. *The Rings of Saturn*. Trans. Michael Hulse. London: Vintage.

Sinclair, Iain. 2013. *Austerlitz & After: Tracking Sebald*. London: Test Centre.

Wylie, John. 2007a. *Landscape*. Abingdon: Routledge.

Wylie, John.. 2007b. 'The Spectral Geographies of W. G. Sebald.' *Cultural Geographies*, 14: 171–88.

Wylie, John.. 2010. 'Writing through Landscape.' *Process: Landscape and Text*. Ed. Catherine Brace and Adeline Johns-Putra. Amsterdam: Rodopi. 45–64.

Chapter Ten

Reivers, Raiders and Revenants

The Haunted Landscapes of the Anglo-Scots Borders

Alison O'Malley-Younger and Colin Younger

Shadow-worlds and shadow-lands are those inhabited by spirits, of what is left when the body is turned to dust, or something that we can experience of another world when we are alive. They represent that which we do not understand, but what we feel must be there—an afterlife, or a refusal to allow the dead to be totally forgotten, because the dead have helped make us what we are. (Beckensall 2005, 8)

It has almost become a critical commonplace to suggest that Scotland is a haunted landscape. Since G. Gregory Smith coined the term 'Caledonian Antisyzygy' in 1919, scholars have sought to address an aesthetics of representation which Smith describes as a 'combination of opposites that define the "polar twins of the Scottish Muse" as a national cultural pathology which is fissured, schismatic and haunted by its own history' (Smith 1919, 19). Nicholas Royle, for example, asserts that 'the uncanny comes from Scotland from that auld country that has so often been represented as "beyond the borders", liminal, an English foreign body' (2003, 12). Following Royle, and entering into a subject which is subject itself to much scholarly debate, Monica Germana argues that this uncanniness results in a 'default mode' in Scottish writing which is 'Gothic', due, in part to the fact that Scottish literature 'addresses its own cultural terrain in terms of fault-lines, wounds to the body, cracks to the psyche' (2011, 1).

A significant development in this research results from Colin Manlove's revisiting of Smith's model in his introduction to *An Anthology of Scottish Fantasy Literature* (1996). Manlove's assertion, to paraphrase in brief, is that Scottish fiction, based on a living tradition of folk and fairy tale, has influenced the Scottish writing tradition to the extent that it subverts traditional assumptions of the real. 'There is' according to Alan Bisset, 'something/

someone/somebody that haunts the fringes of the Scottish imagination ...
perhaps the whisper of history, pain, feudalism, legend, all or none of these
things, but undoubtedly Scotland's is a fiction haunted by itself, one in a
perpetual state of Gothicism' (2001, 6). According to Manlove, Scottish writing, emerging as it does from a complex colonial relationship, espouses this
'gothic', fantastical view of history. In short, it revisits what Cairns Craig
describes as events that are conventionally left out of official historiography, which indeed must, as David Hume observes, be 'buried in silence and
oblivion' for the construction of the history of 'a civilised state' to take place
(cited in Craig 1996, 68). This results in what David Punter describes as 'an
alternative, more [haunted] view of history', disputing the notion that history
has come to an end and can simply be buried—as Fukuyama, for one, would
have it—which enables 'a deeper engagement with the difficulties of the
present' (2002, 107, 124). In sum, according to Punter and Byron, Scottish
history is an 'inevitable' result of its 'suppressed, stateless culture' (123–4)
and the literature which emerges in relation to it is driven by a logic of haunting which voices a paradoxical 'impossibility of escape from history, with the
recurrent sense in Gothic fiction that the past can never be left behind, that it
will reappear and exact a necessary price' (2004, 55).

SHADOWLANDS

This brings us somewhat circuitously to the epigraph and the subject matter
of this chapter—the haunted *shadowlands* of the Anglo-Scots borders. As the
epigraph implies, shadows, insubstantial and intangible are nonetheless real,
and, in parallel to the process of research, are cast only when an object is
illuminated. This suggestion (which the writer of the epigraph relates to the
landscape of Northumberland) is analogous to Jacques Derrida's theory of
'Hauntology' (first described in *Spectres of Marx* in 1993), and the spectral
flux of shadows that surround our material being, holding us in intangible
webs of the past, the present and the future. Hauntology (a portmanteau pun
on hauntology/ontology) relates to nothing less than our state of being. As
Derrida speculates:

> What is a spectre? What is its history and what is its time? The spectre, as its
> name indicates, is the frequency of a certain visibility. But the visibility of the
> invisible. And visibility, by its essence is not seen which is why it remains
> *epekeina tes ousias*, beyond the phenomenon or beyond being. (1994, 100)

Here, ironically, and no doubt deliberately haunted by the spectre of Plato,
Derrida identifies the essence (if one such exists) of his hauntological

dictum: spectres, like shadows, can only be identified by their absent presence. To summarize (if it is possible to summarize the ludic philosophizing of Derrida), every text is haunted by an elusive spectral presence, which cannot be apprehended through the senses but only through intellectual inquiry. The spectre, (an accreted collection of ideas and beliefs which are denied in an attempt to fix meaning) exists neither wholly in the past nor in the present, but being-with spectres is necessary to our sense of what history has made us, and, indeed our construction of meaning per se: 'and this being-with spectres would also be, not only but also, a politics of memory, of inheritance, and of generations' (1994, xviii), thus, as Derrida suggests we must always 'let them speak or ... give them back speech' (221). This *spectropoetical* hermeneutic refers to interpretative exhumations, which allow us to disinter layers of allusions, analogies and other literary devices to see how the spectral past continues to haunt the present. The challenge posed by hauntology is thus to seek residual energies (or shadows) from the past which invite our construction of meaning.

THE BLOODY BORDERS

It is in this sense, at least in part, that the landscapes of the Anglo-Scots borders are haunted, and every story is a ghost story. The border landscape has historically reverberated to the clamour of warfare. By the time the infamously troublesome Border Reivers[1] began their forays and feuds in the medieval period, the borders had already been the locus of internecine combat and bloodshed beginning in the Dark Ages. Hadrian's great wall (designed to contain the *barbaric* Picts) left an indelible scar across the Tyne/Solway line, on the northern countryside, since it was constructed. The subsequent centuries saw repeated bloodshed between the Saxons of Bernicia (the coastal region between Berwick and Warkworth), and the Celtic kingdom of Reged, which covered the remainder of what we understand as the Anglo-Scots borders today. The borders of this newly created kingdom stretched from the Humber to the Forth, after successive bloody battles between the kings of Dalriada (now Scotland) and the kingdoms of Deira and Bernicia (now Northumbria) in the south. Raids from the Heathen Welsh armies of Cadwallon resulted in savage warfare with the armies of the Christian King Oswald in the seventh century. As the century came to a close, the Northern landscape became the backdrop to brutal massacre, plunder and carnage with the 793 arrival of the Vikings: 'bloodthirsty and abominable barbarians [and] enemies of society capable of indefensible outrages of arson and slaughter' (Morris 1998, 73).[2] Following this fatal phalanx of ravaging destroyers, borders history continued in a blood-stained pattern of hostility, feud and cyclical, reciprocal violence between Norseman, Norman, English and Scot, with successive territorial battles between the latter, including William Wallace's invasions of 1296–7; Bruce's merciless harrying of the region, wherein he 'swept down with fire and sword' on the marches; and the Anglo-Scots Wars, during which Edward I pressed all the able-bodied into service with the mandate that *'les gentz de Norhumbrelande'* including *'barouns, chivalers et autres prodes hommes et tote le communaute del conte'* fight on the side of the crown. 'It was now', according to John Sadler, in this 'welling tide of blood ... that the ubiquitous reiver and mosstrooper crept into existence ... and as Northumberland became an embattled landscape, the gaunt, stone towers raising their blunt profiles across the moors and dales, castles, towers, peles and bastles became the order of the day' (1988, 41).

Medieval warfare was a gory and gruesome business. Most cavalrymen and infantrymen expected to receive loss of limbs, teeth, eyes, ears and blood. Ralph Percy, brother of Hotspur, almost bled out at the battle of Otterburn, but lived on to fight again. These grim clashes proved a fruitful source of material to the balladeers who sought to stir regional pride and immortalize the heroic attributes of the fallen. One such, 'The Hunting of the Cheviot' (which may have resorted to some poetic licence), recounts the tale of how one from the Widdrington family fought on after having his legs hewn off at the knees: 'For when bothe his leggis wear hewyne in to, Yet he knyled and fought on his kny' (Childs 1904, 396).

As many scholars, among them Margaret Carter, have argued, the term 'Gothic' was used 'from the eighteenth-century ... to describe the Middle Ages, especially in their barbaric and superstitious aspects' and Gothic literature includes 'eighteenth-century fiction modelled on medieval romance, as well as later works growing out of the tradition' (1987, 5). It is worth noting though that Gothic did not appear out of a vacuum, but was influenced heavily by folklore, and, in particular Ghost Lore,[3] of which there was a burgeoning pantheon, particularly in the medieval period (the time of the collection of Percy's *Reliques of Ancient English Poetry*). Broadsides, ballads and woodcuts contained gory details of ghostly visitations to a medieval mind-set that accepted the reality of spirits returning from the dead. As Stephen Greenblatt says, 'the border between this world and the afterlife was not firmly and irrevocably closed. For a large number of mortals—perhaps the majority of them—time did not come to an end at the moment of death' (2001, 18). The Supernatural Ballads, amongst them 'Tam Lin' and 'Thomas the Rhymer', reflect these beliefs. Witch lore was also rampant, as was the belief in revenants—visibly decayed corporeal rather than ethereal beings who returned from the grave to torment the living. Such beings based on pre-Christian Scandinavian tales are recorded in the history of the region, and it is speculated that they provided the muse for ballads such as 'The Demon

Lover' (latterly appropriated by Walter Scott). Unsurprisingly this smorgas-bord of supernatural folk belief fed into collections of ghost stories such as Howard Pease's 1919 anthology, dedicated to Walter Scott, and imagina-tively titled *Border Ghost Stories*, which includes tales of ghostly Reivers, spectral Danes and doppelgangers. The illustrated front matter shows a steel-bonneted mosstrooper astride a horse, looking out across what appears to be a Northumbrian landscape. Below it is an extract from the seventeenth-century Lyke Wake Dirge which reads:

> This ae nighte, this ae nighte
> Every nighte and alle;
> Fire and sleet and candle light
> And Christe receive they saule.
> When thou from hence away are paste
> Every nighte and alle;
> To Whinny Muir thou comest at laste
> And Christe receive they soule

(1919, n.p.)

The lament wishes the departed a safe passing into a thorny moor, to purga-tory, and thence to heaven, and includes reference to the rite of 'Dishaloof' practiced in the borders (of which more later). Notably it takes place in ghostly topography, between life and death with the moor being seen as a por-tal between life and death—a gothic borderland, within a Gothic borderland.

This spectrality of the borderlands is symptomatic of a history of unre-solved issues and unfinished business. Littered with the detritus left by repeated bitter battles, and a colonial storm of progress which rendered them both buffer and frontier, the borders became a cryptic palimpsest of ellipses and silences from which ancestral voices cry out for retribution and reprisal, and the silenced borderland bogeyman, located at the fringes of civilization, threatens to contaminate the present with his primitive, anachronistic return. As Derrida points out, 'it begins by coming back' (1994, 11).

HAUNTED BORDERLANDS

In what follows we intend to take a diversion from a solely Caledonian car-tography with which this chapter opened, to the haunted landscapes of the Anglo-Scots borders, a *terra contentiosa* historically described as an unre-deemed and irredeemable gothic wilderness, paradoxically unconfined by stable borders or firm moral boundaries wherein anarchic forces are writ large upon the land. These *debateable lands*, described thus since the sixteenth century, are as Walter Scott suggests 'a stage, upon which were presented the most memorable conflicts of two gallant nations' (1803, 1), but, in addition to this, a region wherein folklore has had a profound and unsettling impact on the imaginative perception of the landscape. Home to 'thieves and banditti, to whom its dubious state had afforded a desirable refuge' (1, xxxii).[4] The debateable lands represented a primitive, barbarous and violent breach from the discrete cultural order of the border regions and the laws of the lands of England and Scotland. It is our intention to offer a survey of *Regional Ballads* and *Folklore* and the *Supernatural tradition* (the last a synthesis of the others) as forms of subversion and dissent set against the traditions of verisimilitude and social realism as a manifestation of normative homogenizing Anglicized grand narratives which depicted borders' identity as anachronistic and anomalous in an all-encompassing British tradition. Our purpose is to examine borders' culture through the lens of the spectral, focussing specifically on some exemplary works of borders' writers, and, following Royle's claim for a Caledonian uncanny, to draw critical attention to the fact that due to their superstitions, sublime landscapes and strange inhabitants, the uncanny comes, at least in equal measure, from the haunted landscapes of what we describe as the excluded middle of the Anglo-Scots borders.

The notion of the excluded middle lends itself to the idea of boundaries and thresholds and what lies between. This idea of the 'in between' is particularly apt, not only to the people of the borders, but also the geographical positioning of the terrain; the ballad of the borders (which are transitional in perpetuity) and the genre of Gothic literature which concerns itself with the 'blurring of metaphysical, natural, religious, class, economic, marketing, generic, stylistic, and moral lines' (Hogle 2002, 8–9). Gothic, as Maggie Kilgour suggests,

> is always a boundary breaker which erodes any neat distinction between formats and modes, combining sentimentality and the grotesque, romance and terror, the heroic and the bathetic, philosophy and nonsense. This promiscuous generic cross-breeding is part of the gothic's 'subverting' of stable norms, collapsing of 'binary oppositions', which makes it appropriate for a postmodern sensibility. It appears to offer both a critique and an alternative to our Enlightenment inheritance: as it warns us of the dangers of repressing energies, natural, social, psychic, textual, or sexual, the gothic offers itself a means of expressing otherwise taboo forces. The gothic draws on the modern assumption that it is dangerous to bury things ... by bringing the unspoken to light, it acts as a potential corrective. (1995, 40–1)

In short, Gothic is a boundary-crossing genre, almost uniquely concerned with border peoples and liminal spaces, wherein the threshold 'is already that which it delineates and isolates, and becomes what it defines; or, to put it in different words: the Other takes over and *colonises* its own frontiers' (Manuel Aguirre 2008, 5). The border can therefore be seen as a permeable point of contact between two spheres, which both separates and connects them. Moreover it is home to what can be described as *monsters*; creatures who are, according to Jeffrey Jerome Cohen, 'neither one thing nor the other. Their bodies are chaotic, incapable of complete definition, and, thus, resistant to our complete understanding or control' (6–7).

Besides their corporeal liminality, they are also temporally and spatially liminal: 'boundary creatures, lurking in closets, cemeteries, deep woods, and castles on barren mountaintops. They inhabit spaces and places at the far limits of civilization, locations distant from our daily lives' (2004, 208). Such a suggestion is peculiarly apt to descriptions of the habitat and character of the Border Reivers: shadowy, marginal beings who exist, not only in liminal space, but due to their excision from traditional histories, in liminal time. 'They [monsters of the threshold] cannot', according to Nuzum, 'maintain their existence in history and must relinquish their hold on linear time' (210). Such a suggestion is in accord with Cairns Craig's apothegmatic suggestion that the Scots (and as we argue, the Borderers) are 'outside of History'. They are therefore temporally, historically, geographically, culturally and spatially *gothic*, as is their literature, from the points of view of form and content.

Working from Tony Magistrale's premise that 'no body of literature, even the literature of supernatural terror, can be understood as discrete from the culture from which it arises' this essay locates itself at the 'excluded middle' to examine forms of literature such as the ballad, fantasy, the gothic and the supernatural which were important modes of articulation for writers who are in some degree socially, politically, or regionally marginalized (1992, 3). In this sense Caledonian Antisyzygy can be seen as a parallel to what the anthropologist Victor Turner defines as the liminal or liminoid, a 'betwixt and between' (1974, 108) state inhabited by 'threshold people' (108) in which traditional boundaries no longer operate and conventional taboos cease to operate. These liminal fields in their disorderly and rule-breaking nature are grotesque and uncanny inasmuch as they are 'dangerous, inauspicious or polluting to anyone or anything that does not share a liminal existence' (108). This is in accord with what Fiona Stafford, in relation to the Anglo-Scots borders, describes as the 'duality' of 'Border Vision'—a combination of insider and outsider perspectives (2007, 15) wherein 'the surrounding areas are internally divided' (15). What interests us is the literature which emerged in this context of this liminal Border Vision and how this literature's sustainability lies in its ongoing capacity to register the tensions that lie between shifting borders and behind the surface of culture and identity. These tensions, as we will suggest, can be located in the Lore of the landscape.

SPECTRAL FOLKLORE

The Anglo-Scots borders are a significant repository for folk culture. In common with other societies forced to rely on the resources the land affords them, combined with large doses of their own initiative, Borderers developed a reliance on nature, animal lore and herb lore. In this remote and rural society, the ability to differentiate between poisonous and edible plants was a vital necessity. Equally so, in a world of raids, feuding, and almost continual warfare, without ready access to doctors, an understanding of the curative properties of plants and herbs was (and one might argue is) essential. In short, these people lived off, and with the land, respecting its lore and legends. Unsurprisingly, the legends and memorates[5] of a region become part of a wider folk belief, which can, in turn, mutate into superstitions. The landscape is thus haunted by its lore, and vice versa. Northumberland and the borderlands are replete with such hauntings, as Nancy Ridley observes:

> Whether or not one believes in the supernatural, there is no other county in England so rich in history and legends Northumberland, and on lonely stretches of moorland [...] it is possible to imagine, particularly under the Hunter's Moon, one can see the raiders riding the foray again [...]. Here, where the people take a pride in their past and a belief in the future, old tales are still repeated. The ghosts and boggles are woven into the history of the almost legendary figures of the Mosstroopers, whose careers so often ended on the gallows tree. (1968, 85)

Notably, Ridley relates the haunted nature of the borders to the *locus amoenus*, or spirit of place. The landscape (here elevated to the sublime) in its dark and gloomy moorlands illumined by the light of the moon is inseparable from the ghostly figures who spectrally inhabit it. This complex and varied geography of wild and vast natural scenes, inhabited by banditti and bogles, combined with haunting battle scenes, provided a perfect stimulant to the imagination, and thus, an invocation of the Sublime, and the stimulation of sublime terror.

These folk materials, superstitions and supernatural stories provided a rich vein to be mined by writers of the Gothic such as Walter Scott and James Hogg. In the *Minstrelsy of the Scottish Borders*, for example, Scott cites the 'learned Bishop Nicholson', to acknowledge that 'the natural superstition of our borderers at this day; who are much better acquainted with, and do more firmly believe, their old legendary stories of fairies and witches, than the articles of their creed' (1803, 1: lxxvi). This is endorsed by the Durham born folklorist William Henderson who prefaces his 1866 text *Notes and Folk Lore of the Northern Counties of England and the Borders* with an epigraph from Reginald Scott (a sixteenth-century commentator on the supernatural) to suggest the ubiquity and magnitude of otherworldly beings that haunt the landscapes and imaginations of the border peoples:

> Our mothers maids in our childhood [...] have so frayed us with bullbeggars, spirits, witches, urchine, elven, hags, fairies, satyrs, pans, faunes, sylvan, kit-with-a-candlestick (will-o-the-wisp), tritons (kelpies), centaurs, dwarfs, giants, imps, calcare (assy-pods), conjurors, nymphs, changelings, Incubus, Robin Goodfellow (brownies), the spoorie, the man in the oak, the hellwain, the firedrake (deadlight), The Puckle, Tom Thumb, Hobgoblin, Tom Thumbler, Boucius, and other such bugbears that we are afraid of our own shadows.
> (cited in Henderson 1879, epigraph)

In the following pages, Henderson cites a collection of border customs compiled by a Mr Wilkie, a 'favourite' and protégé of Walter Scott who lived at Bowden near Eildon Hall. These, Henderson suggests, were collected 'at the desire of Sir Walter Scott, for the purpose of being used by him in a projected work on the subject' (1879, ix).[6] Henderson's comprehensive collection includes chapters on 'Life and Death of Man, Days and Seasons, Spells and Divinations, Portents and Auguries, Charms and Spells, Witchcraft, Local Sprites, Worms or Dragons, Occult Powers or Sympathies, Haunted Spots, and Dreams' (ix) and draws on examples of the oral tradition, ballads and proverbs covering the life of the Borderer from cradle to grave. Regionally specific received wisdom ranges from the carnivalesque rites of 'running the braize or the brooze' at riding weddings wherein Mosstroopers 'gallop like madmen' across perilous bogs and dangerous ravines to claim a kiss from the bride at the wedding breakfast, and confer good luck on the couple, to the darker, burial customs of the rhyme of 'saining' crooned by the oldest women present over a corpse as part of the rite of 'dishaloof',[7] and the corpse-watching practice of the lykewake, undertaken to ensure that the soul of the recently deceased is stolen by demons, or Gabriel's hounds.[8] Spells to cure those afflicted with warts, epilepsy, whooping cough and ringworm sit with proverbial wisdom and charms used as antidotes to everything from toothache to goitre and cramp.[9] Bier spirits (Barguests), Bogles, Brownies, Dobies and Muirs disport themselves in haunted spots, Dunters and Powries inhabit peel towers and forts, while the disfigured spinning fays Habetrots[10] and Scantlemabs trick and terrifying unsuspecting mortals who are unlucky enough to cross their path. All of these are rooted in a landscape peculiarly apposite to their continuation, as Henderson points out:

> The universal voice of mankind has ever pointed out certain places as the borderland between the material and the spiritual world [and] truly or falsely indicated deserted houses, marshy wastes, lonely roads, spots where enormous

crimes have been perpetrated, and so forth as haunted ... it is natural then that
with a past rich in historic incidents of the wildest kind, haunted spots should
abound in the North. (314)

For what remains we intend to revisit one such haunted spot, and relate it to
notions of cursing, and thence to the haunted landscapes of 'The Wizard of
the North': Sir Walter Scott.

CURSED LANDSCAPES

In the shadow of Carlisle Castle, in a subterranean passage (or underpass),
on an 80 metre long path, into which are cut the names of all of the Reiver
Riding Graynes,[11] stands an impressive piece of granite, designed by local
artist Gordon Young and made by sculptor Andy Altman. Cut into the rock is
a macabre inscription, 1,069 word-long which reads (in part):

> I CURSE thair heid and all the haris of thairheid; I CURSE thair face, thair ene,
> thair mouth, thair neise, thair toung, thair teith, thair crag, thair schulderis, thair
> breast, thait hert, their stomok, thair bak, thair wame, thair armes, their leggis,
> thair handis, thair feit, and everilk part of thair body, frae the top of thair heid
> to the soill of thair feit, befoir and behind, within and without. I CURSE thaim
> gangand, and I CURSE thaim rydand; I CURSE thaim standand, and I CURSE
> thaim sittand; I CURSE thaim etand, I CURSE thaim drinkand; I CURSE thaim
> walkand, I CURSE thaim sleep and; I CURSE thaim rysand, I CURSE thaim
> lyand; I CURSE thaim at hame, I CURSE thaim fra hame; I CURSE thaim
> within the house, I CURSE thaim without the house; I CURSE thair wiffis,
> thair banris, and their serv and is participand with thaim in their deides. (Fraser
> 1971, 334)

This comprehensive malediction issued by the Scottish prelate, Gavin Dunbar
(c. 1490–1547), Archbishop of Glasgow, against the illicit activities of the
notoriously troublesome Border Reivers (and everyone and anything that had
any association with them) in 1525 ends with the words (translated for ease
of reading):

> And, finally, I condemn them perpetually to the deep pit of hell, there to remain
> with Lucifer and all his fellows, and their bodies to the gallows of Burrow
> moor, first to be hanged, then ripped and torn by dogs, swine, and other wild
> beasts, abominable to all the world. And their candle (light of their life) goes
> from your sight, as may their souls go from the face of God, and their good
> reputation from the world, until they forebear their open sins, aforesaid, and
> rise from this terrible cursing and make satisfaction and penance. (Original
> text, Fraser 1971, 336)

One might argue that these are remarkable, ill-wishing and shockingly occult words coming from a Man of God, particularly during a period in which, when cursing was prohibited as a blasphemous spiritual crime, and condemned by Christian orthodoxy as akin to the deadly sin of despair, inextricably connected to witchcraft (of which more later), and evidence of a contractual relationship with the Devil. Admittedly, this denunciation of cursing became more zealous during the Reformation, and near-maniacal in the reign of James VI of Scotland, I of England. Nonetheless, the Church had decried magic and witchcraft (of which cursing, soothsaying and auguries were considered a part) as diabolical heresies since the patristic teaching of Augustine of Hippo (c. 354–430). Moreover, the practice of *incantatio* related to invocation of cosmic forces by harnessing the powers inherent to the words being chanted.[12] However, there was an ecclesiastical get-out clause for Dunbar, as we shall see.

Although the most extreme, Dunbar's Curse was not the first blight brought upon the Reivers, who became accursed in 1498 by Richard Fox,[13] Bishop of Durham, who forbade all priests to administer the sacraments to them. Cardinal Wolsely again execrated them for unforgivable sins in 1524 after Hector Charlton of Tynedale stole the communion hosts and a firkin of wine from the tabernacle, and served them to his grayne at Tarset Hall. Their expulsion from the religious community under Dunbar's unconditional imprecation commits them to Hell by calling into play supernatural agency (in this case, God) which was perfectly acceptable under the edict of canon law (in which Dunbar was an expert), for grave, deadly and unpardonable sins which are beyond penance, and which can only be pardoned by God. As a matter of interest, Dunbar was also responsible for the burning of seven people for heresy, and was principal signatory on the execution warrant of Patrick Hamilton, Scotland's first Protestant martyr, who took six hours to burn alive for the preaching of Lutheran gospels. As a coda, it is worth remembering that Dunbar's curse has left a lasting legacy on the landscape, as it is, has and continues to be credited with flood, fire and pestilence in the region. While sceptics may laugh at what they see as such credulity, it testifies to Coleman Parson's suggestion that 'the past may be joined to the present by legends and beliefs, by ghosts and haunted places' (1964, 232). The link between present and future may be some form of prediction as it was to the final subject of our discussion: Sir Walter Scott (1771–1832).

THE SOMETIMES WIZARD OF THE NORTH

In his *Recollections of Sir Walter Scott*, the author, R. P. Gillies recalls a conversation in which Scott asserted:

> The most awkward circumstance about well-authenticated hobgoblins is, that
> they, for the most part, come and disappear without any intelligible object or
> purpose, except to frighten people; which, with all due deference, seems rather
> foolish! Very many persons have either seen a ghost, or something like one, and
> I am myself among the number; but my story is not a jot better than the others
> I have heard, which for the most part, were very inept. The good stories are
> sadly devoid of evidence; the stupid ones only are authentic. (1837, 171)

This comment summarizes what can be described as Scott's continuing interest in what might be broadly defined as his rational scepticism towards, yet
continuing interest in the supernatural. This ambivalence, it can be argued,
was an expression of the educated mind during a time of intellectual and
cultural foment, as Sir Herbert Grierson argued in 1934:

> Scott was of the Age of Hume as his treatment of the supernatural, alike in the
> romances and the Demonology and Witchcraft clearly evidences. Any such
> adjustment of the relations between reason and imagination as Wordsworth and
> Coleridge speculated about was not dreamed of in his philosophy. (1938, 5)

Yet, despite, or perhaps because of this ambivalence, Scott repeatedly revis-
ited the theme of the supernatural, in his *Minstrelsy of the Scottish Border*
(1802–1803),[14] and in his subsequent short stories and novels.

If we take Gothic in its original sense as *medieval*, Scott's romances have
an impeccable Gothic pedigree. His interest in the archaic, the antiquarian,
the chivalric and the feudal clearly places him in this generic category. His
collection of the border ballads in his minstrelsy informs a literary landscape,
part feudal and part clannit, inhabited by notorious cattle reivers and freeboot-
ers who became the outlaw heroes of their own tales, and for whom orthodox
religion had been replaced by superstition, as Scott acknowledges:

> Upon the religion of the Borderers there can be very little said. We have already
> noticed, that they remained attached to the Roman Catholic faith rather longer
> than the rest of Scotland. This probably arose from the total indifference upon
> the subject; for we nowhere find in their character the respect for the Church,
> which is a marked feature of that religion. (1803, 1.133–4)

From his reading of these traditional tales he developed his fascination with
the folkloric and the fabled which lends some of his fiction an aura of super-
naturalism. His treatment of witchcraft, for example, as a practice that is
primal, rural and archaic allows us to view him in this way. Likewise is his
fascination with haunted landscapes. As Coleman O. Parsons observes:

> The outdoor haunting of the Waverly Novels is of narrow valleys, stone groups,
> moors and crags—confined, desolate and dangerous spots. Scott makes the

dark possession of forbidden places in the Heart of Midlothian and the deeds perpetrated in them horrifying in proportion to the guilt which he wishes to externalise. Spirits hovering over crags, valley and cairn both commemorate and personify bygone hate. (1964, 125)

Here, as elsewhere, there is a direct connection between the eerie, isolated and essentially sublime setting, the darkness of the deeds perpetrated and the psychological torment of the characters. The settings are sublime, but are not confined to, or focused on, Scotland, but an imaginary composite of highland, lowland and borders, which could be defined as *Scott-land*. Despite Colin Manlove's suggestion that this 'peculiarly Scottish feature' in which 'the location of the fantastic in the real world is often tied in with a precise topography of the Scottish landscape' (Elphinstone 2000, n.p.), we would suggest that while Scott does base his texts in specific terrains and geographies, these are not solely what could be defined as 'Scottish': Indeed, his mythopoeic narratives of loss and hauntings allow him to examine a worldview that could be better defined as a border crossing vision which, for reasons we have suggested, is unequivocally gothic, precisely because of his ability to negotiate confused zones and boundaries which are national, natural and supernatural.

As Stafford notes, 'for Scott, The Borderers were neither Scottish not English, but "kind of outcasts" at odds with both states' (2007, 18). This, she continues, is because border people reside in a mutually permeable frontier region wherein the 'creative centre is split at the core' (18). We endorse this suggestion and also suggest that for Scott the landscape and customs of the people of the borders were inseparable from their stories. By reading (and writing) these stories (which are often bound to very specific geographical locations) Scott is able to look at the liminal spaces between boundaries (such as English/Scottish, civilized/wild) and contradict their mutual exclusivity.

One such tale that can be defined as embodying the genius loci of the border region (for reasons we will recount) is *The Black Dwarf* (Scott 1816). The allusions herein are unequivocally related to the terrain of the borders, and the ballads that spring from this landscape. To wit, most of the central characters in the story bear surnames traditionally associated with those of the Border Reivers. The protagonist, Hobbie Elliot and his sweetheart Grace Armstrong, find themselves in conflict with Willie Graeme of Westerburnflat who is described as a freebooter, a term used interchangeably by Scott when referring to the Border Reivers. The characters' surnames Elliot, Armstrong and Graeme (Graham) are those of three of the most powerful graynes on the Anglo-Scots borders. *The Black Dwarf*, set on Mucklestane-Moor in the Liddesdale hills, is enacted in a locality with which Sir Walter Scott was well acquainted having spent time there searching for ballads to be included in his *Minstrelsy of the Scottish Border*. Scott's choice of setting is apt for the plot and as Parsons proposes 'chiefly expresses the native grotesqueness of folk beliefs' (1964, 105). He summarizes thus:

> Attentive to supernatural tales from childhood, Hobbie Elliott finds the heath 'an unco bogilly bit'. And well may it be, for after sunset it is still 'the ordinary resort of kelpies, spunkies, and other demons, once the companions of the witch's diabolical revels, and now continuing to rendezvous upon the same spot.' (7)

It is worth recalling Scott's now famous dismissal of witchcraft in 'Nobody would believe such folly now-a-days, except low and ignorant persons' (cited in Parsons 1964, 7). Yet his novels and poems are littered with witches, wizards, ghosts and other supernatural beings. It is fair to say that *The Black Dwarf* parallels his own long-held scepticism regarding the otherworldly and his vacillating beliefs relating to positivism and superstition. Herein, Scott compares the ghostly beliefs of the indigenous Borderer (who is identified with primitivism and nature), with the more rational thought processes of the more cultivated Earnscliffe who attempts to rationalize events. This dichotomy can be seen to be rooted not only in the characters, but also tangentially in the landscape itself:

> This dreary common was called Mucklestane-Moor, from a huge column of unhewn granite, which raised its massy head on a knell near the centre of the heath, perhaps to tell of the mighty dead who slept beneath, or to preserve the memory of some bloody skirmish. The real cause of its existence had, however, passed away; and tradition, which is as frequently an inventor of fiction as a preserver of truth, had supplied its place with a supplementary legend of her own, which now came full upon Hobbie's memory. The ground about the pillar was strewed, or rather encumbered, with many large fragments of stone of the same consistence with the column, which, from their appearance as they lay scattered on the waste, were popularly called the Grey Geese of Mucklestane-Moor. The legend accounted for this name and appearance by the catastrophe of a noted and most formidable witch who frequented these hills in former days, causing the ewes to KEB, and the kine to cast their calves, and performing all the feats of mischief ascribed to these evil beings. On this moor she used to hold her revels with her sister hags; and rings were still pointed out on which no grass nor heath ever grew, the turf being, as it were, calcined by the scorching hoofs of their diabolical partners. (Scott 1897, 236)

The physical landscape is sublime and designed to create an atmosphere of terror and dread in conjunction with the dynamics of folk belief and indigenous witch lore exemplified by Hobbie. Further evidence is given for his rootedness in this community of belief when, in a darkly comic moment, he whistles 'the warlike ditty of Jock of the Side' (238) to summon his wilting courage. Here, in his inability to distinguish between natural phenomena (such as the standing stones), and supernatural beliefs (the phantoms of dead witches), Hobbie provides a perfect, Scottian exemplar for the way in which supernatural beliefs were dismissed as tricks of the light and landscape by sceptical Enlightenment philosophers.

Scott's tale offers a blend of the natural, the supernatural and the preternatural with Hobbie representing the somewhat credulous, but nonetheless likeable Borderer clinging to a picturesque, primordial and primitive past, which is peeled back, and explained away by the 'better educated' Earnscliff who 'dashes ineffectual cold water on his warm imaginings, climaxing his scepticism with a rather self-conscious statement: "I am of the opinion that preternatural visions are either ceased altogether or become very rare in our days"' (Parsons 1964, 126). Despite this, and despite the bleak and inevitable fate of the petrified 'Auld Allie' and her 'worricows', the haunting atmosphere of Mucklestane-Moor is, according to Parsons, 'almost consistently maintained' (126), suggesting, perhaps, Scott's dualistic vision, defined by Herbert Grierson as 'a perplexed fascination with, rather than complacent dismissal of, ancestral superstition' (1938, 5).

CONCLUSION

Any foray into the realms of Gothic literature should carry the caution and caveat: 'Reader beware'. Much like the landscape of the borders, the textual terrain is hazardous and pitted throughout with tropes and trapdoors leading to hermeneutical labyrinths into which the unsuspecting can wander. This lends itself to the discontinuity and rupture commonly associated with what David Punter describes as the 'what if?' at the core of the histories of Scotland and Ireland: 'the implicit possibility of a history that could have been "done differently", the possibility of a writing that would now be speaking from a position of political power rather than one of subjugation to the invader, the settler, the conqueror' (2002, 106). This 'what if?' capacity is characteristic of a gothic sensibility defined in part by its resistance to vraisemblance and verisimilitude, but equally so it chronicles the erasure or absence of occluded *national* narratives in a history which 'reflects the voice of a dominant group' (2001, 11). There is, however, as we have suggested, another 'what if?' in this equation. What if there was a border country, of neither England nor Scotland wherein the landscape is haunted not only by ghosts of the past, but also the folkloric foundations of the culture itself? What if, as Penny Fielding suggests, the borders remain an imaginary locality different from either England or Scotland but representing an ideal, romantic space in which national difference itself seems unimportant? (2008, 92). What if there was a Borders Antisyzygy, rooted in the liminal lifestyles and landscapes of the people themselves? Viewed in this way the crucially ambivalent 'what if?' nature of the haunted landscapes of the borders, and their absent presence in Gothic texts, allows for a hauntological reading of history *done differently*. In its convoluted narratives of repetition, recidivism and return, it acknowledges the dual or dubious presence of the past and then opens the past up to different interpretations by appropriating the past in the present in the haunted shadowlands of the Anglo-Scots borders.

NOTES

1. The collective name for the predatory clans of the border region between England and Scotland. Accessed 13 April 2016. http://www.yourdictionary.com/border-reivers.

2. In his 'Gothic Gothicism: Norse Terror in the Late Eighteenth to Early Nineteenth Centuries' (2011) Robert W. Rix makes a convincing case for a Norse provenance in Gothic works, including selected works of Walter Scott. Henderson, in his *Folklore of the North Countries*, also draws a parallel between Northern country superstitions and Nordic myths and legends.

3. For further reading on ghost lore see Thomas (1971, chapter 19).

4. Walter Scott (1803, I, xxxii) uses the term 'Debateable Lands' and the variant 'Bateable Lands' throughout the *Minstrelsy*.

5. Personal experience narratives.

6. Henderson (1879, ix). This 'projected work', it is suggested, relates to Scott's *Minstrelsy of the Scottish Borders*.

7. The Rhyme of Saining:

> Thrice the torchie, thrice the saltie
> Thrice the dishes toom for loffie
> These three times three ye must wave round
> The corpse until it sleep sound.
> Sleep sound and wake nane
> Till to heaven the soul's gane.
> If you want that soul to dee
> Fetch a torch frae the Elleree;
> Gin ye want that soul to live
> Between the dishes place a sieve
> An it sall have a fair, fair shrive.

8. Monstrous, human-headed flying dogs, related to the Celtic Sluagh, and the Wild Hunt. Thought to be the souls of unbaptised children, doomed to haunt the earth until Judgment Day.

9. Included in these charms is carrying a splinter of wood from a gibbet or the paw of a live mole to cure tootache and goitre.

10. Spinning fairies associated with spinning and weaving.

11. Names of families.

12. See Jeffrey Burton Russell, *Witchcraft in the Middle Ages.* Ithaca: Cornell University Press, 1972, 9.

13. Excluded from the sacraments and damned to possession by Satan.

14. Which he based, in part, on Thomas Percy's *Reliques of Ancient Poetry* (1765) which is acknowledged as one of the founding texts for medieval Gothicism.

BIBLIOGRAPHY

Aguirre, Manuel. 2008. 'Geometries of Terror: Numinous Spaces in Gothic, Horror and Science Fiction.' *Gothic Studies*, 10 (2): 1–17. doi:10.7227/gs.10.2.2.

Beckensall, Stan. 2005. *Northumberland: Shadows of the Past.* Stroud, UK: Tempus.

Bissett, Alan. ed. 2001. *Damage Land: New Scottish Gothic Fiction.* Edinburgh: Polygon an Imprint of Birlinn.

Botting, Fred. 2013. *Gothic.* 2nd edn. London: Routledge.

Burke, Edmund. 1759. *A Philosophical Enquiry into the Origin of Our Ideas of the Sublime and Beautiful.* 2nd edn. London.

Carter, Margaret L. 1987. *Specter or Delusion: The Supernatural in Gothic Fiction.* Lewiston, NY: Edwin Mellen Press.

Childs, Francis J. 1904. 'The Hunting of the Cheviot Stanza 54.' *English and Scottish Ballads*, 396.

Cohen, Jeffrey Jerome. 1996. Ed. Monster Theory. Minneapolis: University of Minnesota. The date, 1996, also needs to be added to the parenthetical reference here on page 187.

Craig, Cairns. 1996. *Out of History: Narrative Paradigms in Scottish and British Culture.* Edinburgh: Polygon an Imprint of Birlinn.

Derrida, Jacques. 1994. *'Specters of Marx. 1993.'* Trans. Peggy Kamuf. New York: Routledge.

Elphinstone, Margaret. 2000. 'Fantasising Texts.' Accessed 8 April 2016. http://asls. arts.gla.ac.uk/MElphinstone.html#fn2.

Fielding, Penny. 2008. *Scotland and the Fictions of Geography: North Britain 1760–1830.* Vol. 78. Cambridge: Cambridge University Press.

Germana, Monica. 2011. 'The Sick Body and the Fractured Self: (Contemporary) Scottish Gothic.' *Gothic Studies*, 13 (4): 1.

Gillies, Robert Pearse. 1837. *Recollections of Sir Walter Scott, Bart.* London: J. Fraser.

Greenblatt, Stephen. 2001. *Hamlet in Purgatory.* 2nd edn. Princeton, NJ: Princeton University Press.

Grierson, Herbert John Clifford. 1938. *Sir Walter Scott, Bart.* London: Constable.

Henderson, W. 1879. *Notes on the Folk-Lore of the Northern Counties of England and the Borders.* 2nd edn. n.p.: Folk-Lore Society.

Hogle, Jerrold E. ed. 2002. *The Cambridge Companion to Gothic Fiction.* Cambridge: Cambridge University Press.

Kilgour, Maggie. 1995. *The Rise of the Gothic Novel.* London: Routledge.

Magistrale, Tony. ed. 1992. *The Dark Descent: Essays Defining Stephen King's Horrorscape*. No. 48. London: Greenwood.

Manlove, Colin N. 2013. 'Scottish Fantasy Today.' *Ecloga Online Journal*, 1 (1): 1–13.

Manlove, Colin N.. ed. 1996. *An Anthology of Scottish Fantasy Literature.* Edinburgh: Polygon an Imprint of Birlinn.

Morris, Christopher D. 1998. 'Raiders, Traders and Settlers: The Early Viking Age in Scotland.' *Ireland and Scandinavia in the Early Viking Age*. Dublin: Portland; Four Courts Press.

Nuzum, K. A. 2004. 'The Monster's Sacrifice-Historic Time: The Uses of Mythic and Liminal Time in Monster Literature.' *Children's Literature Association Quarterly*, 29 (3): 207–27.

O'Brien, Conor Cruise. 1992. *The Great Melody: A Thematic Biography and Commented Anthology of Edmund Burke*. United Kingdom: Sinclair-Stevenson.

Parsons, Coleman O. 1964. *Witchcraft and Demonology in Scott's Fiction*. London: Oliver & Boyd.

Paulson, Ronald. ed. 1983. *Representations of Revolution (1789–1820)*. New Haven: Yale University Press.

Pease, Howard. 1919. *Border Ghost Stories*. London: Erskine MacDonald.

Prescott, William Hickling. 1845. *Biographical & Critical Miscellanies*. London: Bentley.

Punter, David. 2001. 'Hungry Ghosts and Foreign Bodies.' *Gothic Modernisms*. Eds. Andrew Smith and Jeff Wallace London: Palgrave Macmillan. 11–28.

Punter, David.. 2002. 'Scottish and Irish Fiction.' *Cambridge Companion to Gothic Fiction* Ed. Jerrold E. Hogle. Cambridge: Cambride University Press. 105–24.

Punter, David and Glennis Byron. 2004. *The Gothic*. Vol. 10. London: Blackwell.

Ridley, Nancy. 1968. *Northumbrian Heritage*. London: Robert Hale.

Royle, Nicholas. 2003. *The Uncanny: An Introduction*. Manchester: Manchester University Press.

Sadler, John. 1988. *Battle for Northumbria: An Odyssey through the Violent History of the Turbulent Border Kingdom*. Morpeth: Bridge Studios.

Scott, Sir Walter. 1803. *Minstrelsy of the Scottish Border: Consisting of Historical and Romantic Ballads, Collected in the Southern Counties of Scotland; With a Few of Modern Date, Founded upon Local Tradition*. 2nd edn. 3 vols. London: Cadell and Davies.

Scott, Sir Walter.. 1897. *A Legend of Montrose and the Black Dwarf*. London: Adam & Charles Black.

Smith, Gregory G. 1919. *Scottish Literature, Character & Influence*. London: Macmillan.

Thomas, Keith. 1971. *Religion and the Decline of Magic: Studies in Popular Beliefs in Sixteenth and Seventeenth Century England*. 4th edn. London: Weidenfeld & Nicolson.

Turner, Victor Witter W. 1974. *Dramas, Fields, and Metaphors; Symbolic Action in Human Society*. 2nd edn. Ithaca, NY: Cornell University Press.

Varma, Devendra P. 1988. *The Gothic Flame: History of the Gothic Novel in England*. Metuchen, NJ: Scarecrow Press.

Chapter Eleven

Haunting the Grown-Ups

The Borderlands of ParaNorman *and* Coraline

Rebecca Lloyd

In his introduction to the recent collection of essays *Animated Landscapes* (2015), Chris Pallant draws attention to the more productive analysis possible in exploring the relationship between landscape and character in animated films over discussions where the focus on character has tended to dominate. The term 'animated landscape' has, where character is the primary concern, usually been taken either to mean the hyper-realist mode of the Disney Studios or something more fantastical. In either case, landscape is figured as a backdrop, static and fixed, against which narrative and character are foregrounded, with no suggestion that landscape itself generates meaning or contributes to character formation and action.

An animated landscape is not 'found', as is the case for live action film, but is purposefully made by animators; Rob DeSue, head of set dressing on *ParaNorman*, notes: 'The team doesn't shoot on location. They create the location' (cited in Alger 2012, 111). Direct human intervention is intrinsic to its very construction. From this perspective, the creative and constitutive force of human presence in the landscape of an animated film simulates the 'real' world landscape itself, now acknowledged as constructed, both in actuality and conceptually (Mitchell 2002; Massey 2005). That is, decisions about design and function of landscape in animation echo how we invest real world landscapes with layers of meaning drawn from our social and cultural understandings about space and place. The landscape in animated film, therefore, stands in a dialectical relationship with characters moving through and across it, opening up 'a theatrical space with mobility and purpose' (Wells 2015, 218). As characters perform, so too does the animated landscape.

My reading of landscape is structured on an analysis of two stop motion animated films, *Coraline* (Henry Selick, 2009), based on the 2002 novel of the same name by Neil Gaiman and *ParaNorman* (Sam Fell & Chris

Butler, 2012). Stop motion animation, analogue or digital, involves the physical manipulation of objects in small incremental movements so that when filmed, they appear to move by their own volition, as if the object were alive. Although anything can be made to move in this way, such as a drawn line, stop motion is primarily associated with the use of puppets, as is the case with *Coraline* and *ParaNorman*. Since the films are stop motion they are actual constructions of children and landscape by adult film-makers, a haunting presence already when the landscape intersects with character. The publicity taglines 'Be careful what you wish for' (*Coraline*) and 'You don't become a hero by being normal' (*ParaNorman*) indicate that these films are supposed to be seen as narratives of self-realization and self-improvement. Certainly, the protagonists undertake journeys and make choices in their struggles to achieve personal and psychological growth by the end of the films. But both films are more than their narrative alone, and I suggest that underpinning the obvious level of story is a significant interest in landscape. It is my argument here that, in these animations, particular characters embody the landscape, and thus landscape is more than 'setting' or backdrop for action.

The films engage with the reciprocal and constitutive relationship between character and landscape in animation, exposing the nature of intervention and investment in that landscape. This is indicated when Henry Selick claims that 'When I first read *Coraline*, I was struck by the juxtaposition of worlds—the world we all live in, where we don't have a choice; and then a better version of all that, where the grass is always greener ... I also loved the fact that the grass-is-greener scenario turns out to be very scary indeed' (cited in Jones 2009, 33). The point that landscapes are 'versions' and that to look more closely at, and through, the façade exposes multiple histories and horrors that are embedded in a landscape is one that runs throughout *Coraline* and *ParaNorman*.

Both films make use of supernatural beings that permeate the diegetic space, haunting and mobilizing their environments in ways that reveal the ideological implications of those landscapes *as* landscapes. But the living protagonists are also haunted by concrete social anxieties about children and adults. *Coraline* and *ParaNorman* raise a critique about how children are defined by attempts to enforce ideals of childhood, and the borderlands of the relationship between adult and child mark and animate the domestic and external landscapes of these films. The cultural boundaries haunting the efforts of Coraline and Norman to negotiate their identities in those landscapes are shown as enforced and policed by adults to fix children in place. But the films also indicate how closure and fixity are illusions. When landscape and character intersect, attempts to establish the boundaries of control are revealed as contingent and unfinished.

Coraline follows 11-year-old Coraline Jones moved by her parents to the Pink Palace Apartments, set in Oregon. Living in other apartments in the house are two former theatrical stars, Miss Forcible and Miss Spink, and an aging Russian gymnast, Mr Bobinsky, who claims to have a group of performing mice. Rehomed and separated from her friends, Coraline is also dislocated from her parents, who are preoccupied with producing a gardening catalogue. Her dissatisfaction causes Coraline to investigate a small door in the apartment that leads, it transpires, from the 'Real World' via a tunnel to the alternative landscape of the 'Other World'. This is a replica of the Real World in form but reconfigured to be as perfect an environment as Coraline might desire. The Other World is presided over by a supernatural being self-named as the Other Mother, and later called the Beldam, who appears as an idealized version of Coraline's Real Mother, except that she has buttons where her eyes should be. The Other Mother creates a doll in Coraline's image as an initial lure, and then offers entertainments and pleasures designed to persuade Coraline to remain in the Other World. If Coraline agrees to stay, she must allow the Other Mother to sew buttons into her eyes. Coraline refuses, having met three ghost children who have suffered that fate, and decides to fight the Beldam. As Coraline rejects the spectacles presented by the Other Mother, they start to disintegrate, and the internal and external landscapes are revealed as dangerous constructions. In the struggle the Other Mother captures the Real Parents, trapping them in a snow globe from Detroit Zoo, and Coraline must save herself, her parents and release the ghost children. A young neighbour, Wybie, and a black cat help Coraline, and she eventually defeats the Other Mother, trapping her body in the Other World and throwing her severed hand into a well in the Real World. The film ends with a garden party for Coraline, her parents and all her neighbours, as Coraline settles for the comforts and shortcomings of everyday existence rather than dangerous spectacle and mistaken desires.

In *ParaNorman* Norman Babcock, also 11 years old, lives in Blithe Hollow, in New England, with his mother, father and teenage sister. As a medium, he can communicate with the dead, making him an outcast amongst the living. At odds with his own family, Norman finds comfort in ghosts, horror films and his collection of zombie artefacts. Blithe Hollow is a commercialized, rubbish-strewn landscape surviving on a claimed history of a witch and her curse on the town, and the focal point of the town square is a statue of a woman as a stereotypical witch with a hooked nose, claw hands, pointy hat and broomstick. The town is celebrating the tercentenary of the execution of the witch, with Norman participating in the school play commemorating the event. During rehearsals Norman has visions of the building burning around him. He is also pursued by his great-uncle, Mr Prenderghast, who although he dies, as a ghost informs Norman that it is the boy's duty to read to the witch to hold the curse in check for another year. Reluctantly Norman attempts this, but it neither placates the witch nor stops the curse, resulting in the raising of the ghosts of the Puritan town councillors who condemned her. Mistaken by the townsfolk for zombies, the ghosts chase Norman until they can tell him that, because he can speak to the dead, only he can finally remove the curse. As the ghosts and the enraged witch become visible across the townscape, Norman finds support from a classmate and his brother, as well as his own sister, who finally value his abilities. Norman ventures into the woodland where the 'witch' was buried, uncovering the truth that she was Agatha Prenderghast, a child and a medium like Norman but executed on a charge of witchcraft by the town councillors. Although she tries to destroy Norman, Agatha finally listens to him as he tells the 'real' story of her loneliness and, pacified, her spirit departs. The ghosts of the councillors can find rest, and peace is restored across the landscape.

Coraline and Norman initially fit Wendy Carse and Nicole Burkholder-Mosco's description of children as the 'most powerless inhabitants of the house' (2005, 216). This powerlessness is also evident across the external landscapes in *Coraline* and *ParaNorman*. Children are expected to be in 'their' place, their identity linked to a location defined as 'appropriate'. Tim Cresswell argues that 'territoriality is an intrinsic part of the organization of power and the control of resources and people' (1996, 12), and for children expectations of their behaviour are reinforced through linking identity and location. Attempts to control transgression surface in processes of inclusion and exclusion, notably in the way in which a person may be defined as 'out of place', a moralizing process (6).

The children are shown engaging with domestic, or internal, and external landscapes. Coraline and Norman have ambivalent responses to these locations, but the actions of adults can be seen as attempts to situate the children and erase resistance. These actions are a nexus of social and cultural assumptions linked to questions of 'public' and 'private' space, but also to how these are embedded in the landscape. Landscape in the diegetic world is revealed to be entirely constructed, as beings that have been banished into or pre-exist the landscape return to destabilize the meanings embedded in their environments, behind which is nothingness. Characters engage with landscapes in ways that they and their landscape merge, each producing the other. There are clear echoes of this in the formal construction and filming of the animations, a point to which I will return.

DOMESTICATED LANDSCAPES

Coraline opens with a shot foregrounding a board bearing the legend 'Pink Palace Apartments', an act of naming that reveals not sole ownership or one's own home, but the site of multiple occupancy where 'home' may be more expediency than realized ambition. Home ownership has often been regarded as indicative of belonging and constitutive of identity, as 'the assumption that where you live—and what type of house you live in—determines your culture, identity and politics' (Hollows 2008, 47). The moniker 'Pink Palace' in suggesting a home for a princess would seem to confirm the location as an ideal of gender and class. Any hope of the dream, however, is undone by the building itself. Initially seen in the distance, in close-up it is revealed as a tattered wooden nineteenth-century house, recalling Norman Bates' house in *Psycho* (1960), atop a mound surrounded by dead-looking plants and dusty and stony paths. It has unevenly pitched roofs, gables and shutters, with steps leading to obscured basement-level accommodation and a rickety staircase winding up to another apartment, also at this point unknowable, in the top floor. The pink remaining in the cracked paint and dirt-stained woodwork shows a house once grand but now decaying, suggestive of the 'historical fault-lines and failures' that mark Gothic conventions (Jackson, Coats & McGillis 2008, 6).

The house serves as an example of the architectural uncanny, an act of interpretation of buildings whereby, Vidler argues, 'they act, historically or culturally, as representations of estrangement'. He notes that such sites do not in themselves 'possess uncanny properties' (1992, 12), and the Pink Palace Apartments in appearance is certainly simply a building that has seen better days. But as Coraline is dislocated from all that she has previously known and found comforting, she is forced into a house that is not a home in an act of estrangement that renders the house uncanny even before she meets the Other Mother. As Coraline wanders through the internal landscape of the Real World house, not just the Jones' apartment but those of their neighbours, she is at a loss. Paul J. J. Pennartz notes in his study of how people understand the atmosphere of a home that '[h]aving nothing to do, when wanting to do something' generates boredom and aimlessness, and a sense of unpleasantness (2006, 101). Coraline is experiencing this discomfort, a mood which her parents do little to ease. Her sense of abandonment is aggravated by what she perceives as the failure of her parents to occupy the house *as* a home. Her Real Father hunches over his computer in his study, and whenever Coraline visits him he dismisses her with invented pointless tasks, such as counting things that are blue. Coraline's Real Mother uses the kitchen not as a domestic setting but to work on the gardening catalogue: the refrigerator is almost empty when they search for some lunch. As Joanne Hollows notes, the distinction between the public and private spaces have been grounded on an idealized separation between the public sphere as the locus of work, while the private sphere is 'the realm of the family, personal life and the domestic' (2008, 2). The estrangement that Coraline experiences at the start of the film appears to suggest that where these boundaries are transgressed, the child has no place and experiences no belonging.

Pennartz suggests that '[p]laces incarnate our experiences and aspirations and are the foci of meaningful events in our lives' (2006, 95–6). At the outset of *Coraline*, we are shown that in the Real World Coraline has been allocated her own bedroom. It is as yet unloved and barely used, however. It contains material artefacts that are 'hers', moved in from her former life. Beside her bed is a photograph of her old friends, and there are a few toys scattered about. These are meaningful in relation to the experiences and aspirations that Coraline has, as Pennartz indicates, but now only as memorials to a past life. The new room is unfinished: depicted in a cold colour scheme of blues and greys, it is still full of packing cases giving a temporary quality to existing in a space that is not yet a place. Coraline is not yet at 'home', so has not made it hers and it lacks identity.

When Coraline follows the passageway between the Real World and the Other World, she is brought into a perfectly formed domestic environment shaped it seems entirely for her. What the Other Mother attempts to build are 'better' or replacement memories for Coraline, feeding from the girl's discontent. Coraline is shown her Other Father in his study. But while her Real Father's room is cold, stacked with partly opened boxes around his table and computer, the Other Father proffers a landscape of colour, pictures, music and entertainment. He invites her in, unlike her Real Father, and has a piano rather than a computer. The piano 'plays me', he says, its mechanical arms and hands controlling him as he sings 'Making Up a Song about Coraline'. This spectacle entrances her, as she is the explicit focus of parental attention in this Other World. Coraline's Other Bedroom is also an idealized version of the Real World. It is fully furnished, and colourful, with flying and speaking toys. Her friends now animated in the photograph wave and call to her.

The Other Kitchen is colourful and warmly lit, full of the sights and smells of food, in contrast to the monochrome barren kitchen of the Real World. The kitchen is a particular locus in the domestic landscape where Coraline is to be lured into the Other World. Standing at the oven is her Other Mother, dressed in neat figure-hugging clothes, with an apron, and wearing bright red lipstick, representing the imagined ideal housewife and feminine mother. The Real Mother has a pale roll-neck jumper, dark trousers and bare face, more a representation of the utilitarian requirements of the world of work. Everything about the Other World is constructed by the Other Mother in an appeal to the conventional life she believes, as does Coraline initially, that the girl desires. The Other Mother offers, in excessive quantities, simple but pleasurable food that children are supposed to like: a plump roast chicken and chocolate cake, unlike the pallid gelatinous 'experiments' produced by her Real Father. The entire domestic landscape in the Other World is designed to appeal to the body and the emotions, as the Other Mother appears to direct all her concern towards satisfying Coraline.

There are two other internal environments: 'wonders' that Coraline is shown. Directed by the Other Mother she visits the apartments firstly of Miss Spink and Miss Forcible, and then that of Mr Bobinsky. In their Other World manifestations, these are transformed into landscapes of entertainment, sumptuous spectacles that are fantastically larger than is possible in the cramped, dark rooms of the Real World. The Other Spink and Forcible perform for Coraline, their fat bodies peeling away revealing gorgeous trapeze artists. This occurs in an astonishing theatre inside their apartment, with a huge proscenium stage, plush red velvet and gold mouldings and an audience of hundreds of dogs. The circus in the attic of Other Mr Bobinsky, reached via a giant popcorn-producing chicken and cotton candy cannons, has an enormous central tent where uniformed Kangaroo Mice perform in a Busby Berkeley-like display. Stoddart discusses how circus performance has figured in 'its reliance on "affective power" rather than cerebral stimulation' (2000, 94), and Tait portrays how it is more 'viscerally thrilling than cognitively understood' (2005, 6). This attraction of the sensational for Coraline as a bodily response to the spectacle of site and performance shows in her widely smiling face and excited applause. But both places become the locus of danger, exposed as facades as Coraline challenges the Other Mother. When Coraline returns to them searching for the ghost children, the Other Spink, Forcible and Bobinsky degenerate into monstrosities: the theatre now houses vampire dog-bats, while the circus mice change into rats, creatures customarily associated with landscapes of fear and horror. A landscape controlled by the adult may provide the sensation of pleasure or terror, depending on whether the child conforms or resists.

As has been noted, 'landscape is the visible and invisible meeting ground of culture, place ˙and space—where identities are exchanged, performed and constructed' (Berberich, Campbell & Hudson 2012, 21). Throughout *Coraline*, competing tensions of the ideal cultural construction of the home environment, a performance of safety and nurture, contrasted with the contingent experiences of actual living, frame how Coraline decides what she really wants and how this shapes her own identity. Although initially delighted by the Other World, when she rejects the perfect domestic landscape offered to her, it starts to decay. What has seemed to be the truth is only the illusion of the visible in that landscape. The purpose of possession underpinning its construction is revealed as the seductive trap of the domestic. This is cultural constructions made by both adult and child, of an idealized identity of home and child. Capitulation entails the loss of life if buttons are sewn into Coraline's eyes. The ideal of the domestic landscape and the home as an escape from the public is exposed as threatening to wholeness and self-identity. When this is rejected, furnishings and beings in the Other domestic landscape decay or are reanimated as threats. Everything, seen more closely, is the dark version of the Real.

In *ParaNorman* the domestic landscape is one that provides some shelter from the external, although it is only partially Norman's home. His bedroom is full of items that reflect his love for horror films, particularly those that depict zombies. He has toys that represent the domesticated monstrous, a site where Norman is in control. His alarm clock bears the legend R. I. P. with a waving skeletal hand, and the walls are covered with posters for films with titles such as 'Brain Eater'. He casually slides his feet into zombie-head slippers and he cleans his teeth with a zombie toothbrush. We see him as if from inside his mirror as he uses the dripping foaming toothpaste that clings to his mouth to present himself in the mirror *as* the monster, the drool forming a fanged maw. In his room Norman is at home with the monstrous. He is far more intimidated by living adults when he is later pursued by his great-uncle, Mr Prenderghast.

Norman's occupation of the house is more comfortable than that of lonely Coraline, adrift in empty rooms. This is because Norman can communicate with the ghost of his paternal grandmother, and he does this when they share the living room watching horror films together. Norman is shown as sitting close to the television screen in the opening sequence of *ParaNorman*, his face full of evident rapture at the images on the screen. The pose is reminiscent of Carol Anne whose attraction to the television in *Poltergeist* (1982) enables the invasion of the domestic space by supernatural forces, but 'invasion' is inflected differently here. The camera pulls back to a wide shot revealing another presence behind Norman, that of ghostly Grandma sitting on the sofa and knitting, an image of familial comfort and care. Her presence is accepted, and their companionable talk is centred on his explanation of the film to her. Here he infiltrates adult and shared space, his knowledgeable conversation with the dead making strange the home where his family refuses to acknowledge the revenant, and so the room is the porous border haunted by actual ghosts and the attempts by parents to dominate their children. When Norman's mother says of Grandma that 'She's in a better place now', he replies 'No she's not, she's in the living room.' His refusal to accept the platitude indicates the distance between his understanding that life and death have no boundaries and the insistence by his parents that the end of the body should be the end of presence in the landscape.

Near to the town cemetery, its broken chain-link fence a permeable boundary, lives Mr Prenderghast, his house a threatening and chaotic place. This partly boarded up building is full of junk, indicative of the hoarder. Described as a 'crazy old tramp' and a 'weird, stinky old bum' by Mr Babcock and Neil, he represents the disturbing figure of the tramp despite having a house.

Cresswell notes of vagrants in American culture that they were presented as 'a mobile body inscribed with multiple signifiers of deviance and transgression' (2001, 20), a notion reinforced when as a ghost Mr Prenderghast materializes from inside a toilet in the school bathroom. At the moment of his death he gains mobility over the constraints of movement through time and landscape, but since Norman comments when he leaves the bathroom 'I would leave it for ten minutes' the man is still figured as the excessive body. Mr Prenderghast's house has a study, a room suggestive of the mind, order and knowledge, but it is not qualitatively different from any other part of the house, which is overrun with vermin. Mr Prenderghast dies here, his corpse in occupation much as he was in life, mere detritus. It is evident that, although this was a home, it is very different to that of Norman; lacking in colour, light and comfort it is held together much as was Mr Prenderghast, patched and infested by flies, and so a reminder that he was his own environment. It is easily invaded by the zombie-ghosts and, although it offers hiding places under tables and behind piles of books, these are shown as ineffectual: material artefacts are no protection from the undead.

EXTERNAL LANDSCAPES

Beyond the domestic sites of both films lies the external world—the wildwood in the case of *ParaNorman*, and the garden in *Coraline*. Much of the narrative of *Coraline* is located in the internal landscapes of the Real and Other Pink Palace, but the external landscapes, the Real and Other Garden and Orchard, contribute to the construction of Coraline by the Other Mother, a landscape architect. Gardens, and garden design, became no longer landscapes of aristocratic privilege but middle and lower class environments in the nineteenth century, 'domesticated' in scale and purpose. They were deemed suitable places for women and children, emphasizing a perceived relationship between the developing child, their interaction with creation and 'the ethics of care', the links reinforced by reference to the Edenic space of innocence and morality. As such, both landscape and child required 'careful training to subdue their rampant tendencies' (Page & Smith 2011, 128). Regarded as an idealized place, the garden was often figured in terms of emotional connections in that 'it becomes a statement of personality and character as much as a stage for practical action' (3).

Coraline is interested in the garden. When she is explaining this to her mother, she is seen framed by the kitchen window. While mother and daughter argue, Coraline plants seeds for pumpkins, peppers and bleeding hearts into pots, plants that provide both sustenance and beauty. Coraline notes the contradiction in the fact that her parents are writing a garden catalogue, but that they hate mud: 'You and Dad are paid to write about plants, and you hate dirt' she grumbles, for which her mother replies, 'Mud makes a mess'. Coraline states, 'I want stuff growing', her plea for 'proper' parental care too. This desire is manipulated by the Other Mother: just as garden designers, engineers and architects have imposed pattern, power and privilege over nature and the landscape, the Other Mother uses display to demonstrate control.

The Other Garden is yet another of the 'wonders'. When she first goes into this fantastical place, Coraline is greeted by the Other Father calling 'Come into our garden' emphasizing her inclusion. He rides a praying mantis tractor, a hybrid machine-insect spraying instantly sprouting bright blue coloured plants, as iridescent humming birds and dragonflies fill the air, and swollen bleeding hearts flowers glow red, illuminated lanterns. The plants in the garden recall those that Coraline has herself been planting, another gesture to inclusion. When her Other Father transports Coraline above the landscape in his monstrous machine the camera pulls back, revealing that the entire garden portrays, in glorious colour, Coraline's own face. The Other Mother makes the garden in Coraline's own image: she is the garden and it is her, in a riot of colour and recognition. But in this Other Garden the supernaturally animated plants, the threat of excess suggested by the snapping snapdragons, are a reminder that Coraline will not thrive here. In an echo of the eighteenth-century proto-feminist condemnation of the pampered treatment of women that 'encourages indolence rather than industrious attempts at improvement' (Page & Smith 2011, 2), the Other Garden is a seductive, destructive landscape, and not the site of healthy growth.

The Other Mother has modelled Coraline as the garden and it as her: she is the landscape. But when resisted, the Other Mother's power over landscape and child fails, and as Coraline moves through the decaying landscape, colours and life drain away revealing, in a white-out, absolute nothingness. This absence of anything is the nothingness that is landscape before intervention, a void of meaning from which Coraline must flee to survive. When order is restored, and the Real Garden is planted with quantities of red tulips by her Real parents and neighbours, it still retains the contours of Coraline's face sculpted by walls, bridge and beds, but now a landscape of 'proper' cultivation. We are reminded that human intervention in the landscape is a presentation of the human as much as of landscape. Both child and planting are ordered and restrained as Coraline accepts the compromises of human existence.

On her first venture into the landscape beyond the house, Coraline searches for an old well, found in a circle of toadstools and mushrooms growing around its mouth. The domesticated landscape is where 'the rampant disorder of vegetation run wild can be pruned and tamed by a civilizing hand' (Page

& Smith 2011, 125). The fungi around the well, then, are indicative of the 'wrong' kind of productive life: not deliberately cultivated it exceeds human control. This is also indicated by the dowsing rod Coraline fashions but which turns out to be poison oak that causes a rash. The rash is curable only by the Other Mother's 'special mud', a substance that identifies her with primal slime. The well itself is an abysmal depthless site that Wybie tells Coraline is where when you look up you can only see the stars even in daytime. Jane Suzanne Carroll's model of the 'lapsed topos' in children's literature indicates that forms with openings reaching into or rising from underground are 'chthonic', because '[t]he underground is the space of the dead' (2011, 143). The well in *Coraline* is certainly such a space: it is where Coraline eventually 'buries' both the key to the Other World and the Other Mother's severed hand, in an attempt to return death deep into the landscape.

In *ParaNorman* Blithe Hollow nestles in a valley surrounded by forest. A town with suburban leanings, with gardens and yards enclosed by the obligatory white picket fences, it is depicted as more closely connected with low-income street culture, the site of abandoned bicycles and food wrappers. It is filled with low-status shops such the Witch's Kitchen café, 'Bewitched in Blithe', a fancy dress emporium where customers can 'become' witches, and billboards and neon signs advertise 'Witchy Wieners', a doubly accented act of commodification, and 'The Lucky Witch Casino'. The town is promoted as 'A Great Place to Hang', the fate of the witch and, by inference, a location more about consumer lassitude than dynamism. This is comically drawn when one townsman, menaced by the approaching zombie-ghosts, finds it hard to relinquish his already purchased bag of 'Greasy Pieces' winding laboriously through a vending machine despite the perceived threat to his life. He flees but returns to grab it because the greatest fear is to abandon paid-for material satisfaction. Although fictional, Blithe Hollow is located in the real state of New England. This siting suggests an intertextual reference Salem in New England, location of the witch trials of 1692 that figure large in American popular culture. Salem itself is nicknamed 'Witch City', with 'a tremendous variety of "witch kitsch"', an entrepreneurial attitude evident since 1862 (Foltz in Berger 2005, 139). This commercialization of witchcraft informs the ways in which the histories of accuser and victim surface and intersect across the landscape throughout *ParaNorman*.

Locally claimed objects, vehicles for mythology, contribute to the formation of social memory and communal identity. Such narratives demonstrate unequal power relations between those who produce mythologies and the subjects of that formation. This is evident in the social relations between adult and child. In Blithe Hollow 'their' witch is a fiction that explicitly ignores the child who was Agatha Prenderghast. Local geography and 'knowledge' about the witch is fixed in the representations of witches on hoardings and advertising, memorialized in the statue purporting to be *the* witch and in the celebrations of remembrance. An act of reimagining enables Blithe Hollow to make money: commercialism enabled by myth constitutes the communal identity. This history performed as social identity is expressed throughout the town, embodied in a bumper sticker proclaiming 'My other car is a broomstick' seen as Norman wanders through the streets.

Few residents have any understanding of original events. At a rehearsal the drama teacher, Mrs Herschel, bemoans the children's lack of knowledge of their town's history. The assumed shared communal 'memory' of the witch is to be enacted but this is history misremembered. Salma, one of the classmates of Norman, complains 'Why is the witch always a hideous old crone with a pointy hat and a broomstick? I don't believe that it is historically accurate'. Mrs Herschel replies 'It's not supposed to be. It's supposed to sell postcards and keychains', a statement that echoes the performance of the 'history' of Salem in the service of the 'historicidal' dimension of contemporary America. Norman witnesses the past irrupt during the re-enactment, searing and seeping through the fabric of the school walls and floor. The burning boundaries of what is claimed as known, in the performance and the built environments of the school and later the Town Hall, reveal hollow darkness underneath as that which has been repressed—the unresolved legacy of fear and ignorance—returns.

Aggie, her true name as she confides to Norman, represents the dangers from inside and outside civilization to the Puritan task of renewal and restoration of the world. This process of purgation allowed threats and fears to be contained and removed. Expelling Aggie from their community is a cleansing manoeuvre, from the councillors' perspective. Transformed and reconstructed into a figure of abject horror, they destroy her, ejecting her body and soul into the wilderness outside the town boundaries. As Salma says, 'People found guilty of witchcraft weren't considered people anymore'. Aggie is ejected from civilization into the place of disorder the councillors believe she represents, in a doomed attempt to police the distinction between both landscapes. Their assurance about civilization is mistaken, understood when the revenants survey, appalled, the modern landscape of neon consumerism and mob mentality.

Misremembered and unknown except through adult voices and histories and commodities, it is in the unwanted, untamed landscape that she materializes in versions of herself constructed by her to haunt and be haunted. The wild wood is not the place of Christian burial but pagan, emblematic of old primal magic, power and sacrifice, and Aggie inhabits and figures this outsider landscape in body and spirit. It is into the forest, represented as an increasingly terrifying and alternative space, that Norman must travel, to face the witch and undo the curse.

As Norman tries to reach Aggie to talk to her, she is in charge of the wild woodlands that represent her and that she represents: the only light emanates from her, bright and blinding, electrically charged rage. Each time he tries to communicate she refuses Norman, increasingly angry until she attempts to destroy him totally. Animating plants, earth and sky to her bidding, she raises tornado clouds and lightening, and splits the ground apart. Trees transform into vengeful anthropomorphic claws, huge shards and splinters with which she tries to impale Norman. Aggie manipulates the ground itself, tearing open bottomless chasms and raising towering peaks, a terrifying sublime that nearly overwhelms. The landscape shown here is created by Aggie alone: as the world around Norman dissolves, there is nothing but darkness beyond the spinning fragments that she animates.

This rendering of the landscape as emotion is reinforced when Aggie is finally comforted by Norman, and as they recount her true story, her spirit departs. Arcadia, where death is ever-present in the binary relationship of dark and light, is recalled as they lean against a tree, sheltered by trunk and branches. Instead of the dark and dangerous forest, the landscape is transformed into the bucolic landscape of the pleasance recalling the rural idyll of physical and spiritual health. Trees are no longer threats, but offer gentle summer shade as warm, yellow tones of sunshine illuminate bright, young green leaves, while birds sing. The scene conjures the pastoral dream of Arcadia as a place and mood of beautiful, soft tranquillity as Aggie dissolves into sleep. Landscape here is a state of being that does not separate the human and the environment. A landscape mobilized by her in her anger now reflects, assists and animates her rest, an Edenic refuge from toil.

Once her spirit is freed, this landscape too disappears, indicating its constructedness: Norman and his family are reconnected in woodland noticeably less sunny than that of Aggie's restoration. The leaves are muted greys and browns, although this place is not the threat that it once was. But the child's body will still be there: even if the truth has been uncovered, and the landscape refashioned, it still contains traces of the history of Aggie. In this, there is the reminder that landscapes are not singular, unified or finished but are the stratified layers of cultural and social myth and memory, none of which are ever fully erased.

ANIMATED LANDSCAPES

James Newton, discussing his model of the 'zombiefied landscape' of *ParaNorman*, argues that stop motion animation is, itself, a form of metaphoric zombification 'in using the artificiality of its process to reinforce the continuity between humans and zombies' (2015, 242–3). But of the

actual diegetic landscape he says 'the stop-motion film retains the distinction between character and setting' because 'a separate aesthetic defines
both character and landscape forged out of the differing materials used to
create them—supple and flexible materials for characters, and more solid
materials used to fashion the elements of the landscape' (243). Clearly this
is true to the extent that puppets must convey the illusion of actual movement while buildings and fields should not move in representations of a
'realistic' world. However, in *Coraline* and *ParaNorman*, the animated
landscape constitutes a significant facet of the narrative, and particularly in
how that narrative explores the place and direct involvement of the human
in that landscape. For Coraline and Norman, their landscapes come alive,
even if in the process of making, the animators use fixed materials such
as plaster and boards for landscape instead of the moulded latex-covered
and jointed armatures, or skeletal cores, for the puppets, that enable
manipulation.

The materiality of landscape is made evident in the companion books
Coraline a Visual Companion (2009) and *The Art and Making of ParaNorman*
(2012), published to coincide with screenings. These books draw attention to
the constructed nature of the films, manifest in the numerous illustrations of
the puppet-makers and scene builders at work, with close-ups on modelled
tulips, the painting of staircases and building bodies to a backdrop of scaf-
folding and lighting rigs. In stills from the *Coraline* companion book, set
builders use sanders and scrapers to prepare the plaster landscape around
the Pink Palace, while the third surrounded by the studio lights and electri-
cal cabling applies artificial grass and spray paint to the same ground. The
animators, frequently referred to in both books as 'creative' individuals
rather than as a faceless 'work force', are variously described as 'artists' and
'crafts' producers, and resemble an army of Victor Frankensteins, often seen
handling the body parts and architectural elements in ways that foreground
the creation of the world. Alger, discussing the making of *ParaNorman*,
notes: 'you are reminded that stop-motion is a physical art that takes place
in three dimensions' (2012, 40), a point reinforced by the use of Rapid
Prototype technology, the 3D printing process used in generating puppets
for both films. So this aspect is never missing from the landscape of stop
motion and contributes, as one of the strata of interpretative forces at play,
to the meaning of the film.

A connection with landscape is clearly important to the film-makers.
Selick's creative decision for *Coraline* to have both parents producing a
gardening catalogue is a departure from the original novel, where Coraline's
mother works on a book 'about native people in a distant country' (Gaiman
2009, 19) and her father reads a garden catalogue to evade work responsibilities (48). This narrative intervention suggests that her parents are more

concerned with generating a commercial product that sells things to grow than they are with 'growing' their child and cultivating their home.

Discourses about witches contribute to the representations of landscape in *Coraline* and *ParaNorman*. Claims to notions of safety within the boundary, while danger lurks outside, are rendered ambiguous, as Aggie, the Other Mother and Coraline all function as witch figures who move in, through and across the landscape. This association of the supernatural and magic with landscape is reinforced by LAIKA's use of 3D Real, a digital-projection format. *Coraline* was the first stop motion film to be entirely shot in this stereoscopic 3D. For Selick this enabled the film-makers to draw the audience 'inside the worlds we create' (cited in Jones 2009, 120), as the image on screen is projected beyond that screen situating and enveloping the viewer in the landscape. The breach in the boundary between audience and film renders both as spectral presences, dialectically haunting each other in the construction of meaning. The use of CG filming and effects, such as the swirling sky over Blithe Hollow, contributes to the supernatural in the narrative and in the visuals where the use of green and purple represents paranormal activity in both films. Although Fell talks of the 'abstract spectral environment' (cited in Alger 2012, 156), Aggie makes the landscape her own by being that landscape. Similarly, the actions of the Other Mother, a being whose existence in time and in the landscape predates and exceeds human presence, compose that landscape as a ghostly form across which traces of her, and her victims, drift. Despite the embodied presence of landscape in both films, however, the effects of the animation form enable the simultaneous disappearance of space, as the layers of digitally animated landscape fade to white or burn away to reveal a black nothingness.

Landscape in *Coraline* and *ParaNorman* is not a lifeless thing, not simply the setting for a narrative. Layers of landscape are animated where representations of time and place are made complex and asymmetrical, reaching back and forth into the past and across space exposing the porous and unlimited dimensions of these categories. Norman and Coraline challenge the falsified and murderous histories constructed by adults. Children, intended to stay in their place, refuse to do so. They transgress and traverse the borderlands, resisting pre-formed identities and locations, prohibitions and prescriptions. As Dani Cavallaro says, such children may 'succeed in conveying a lesson: their ability to live with and interact with the unnameable while their adult counterparts blunder by striving to explain and contain it' (2002, 139). Courtney shouts to the mob in *ParaNorman*: 'You need to stop killing my brother. You're adults'. It is a reminder that grown-ups may fail children. The marginalizing function of moral geography can be transgressed. Children, interred in the moralizing landscape, can and do cross the borders, returning to reveal both their own constructedness, and that of space.

BIBLIOGRAPHY

Alger, Jed. 2012. *The Art and Making of ParaNorman*. San Francisco: Chronicle Books.

Berberich, Christine, Neil Campbell and Robert Hudson. 2012. 'Introduction: Framing and Reframing Land and Identity.' *Land and Identity: Theory, Memory, and Practice*. Amsterdam and New York: Rodopi 17–42.

Berger, A. Helen. 2005. *Witchcraft and Magic: Contemporary North America*. Philadelphia, PA: University of Pennsylvania Press.

Burkholder-Mosco, Nicole and Wendy Carse. 2005. ' "Wondrous Material to Play On": Children as Sites of Gothic Liminality in *The Turn of the Screw*, *the Innocents* and *the Others*.' *Studies in the Humanities*, 32 (2): 201–21.

Carroll, Jane Suzanne. 2011. *Landscape in Children's Literature*. New York and London: Routledge.

Cavallaro, Dani. 2002. *The Gothic Vision. Three Centuries of Horror, Terror and Fear*. London: Continuum.

Cresswell, Tim. 1996. *In Place/Out of Place. Geography, Ideology, and Transgression*. Minneapolis: University of Minnesota Press.

Cresswell, Tim.. 2001. *The Tramp in America*. London: Reaktion Books.

Gaiman, Neil. 2009. *Coraline & Other Stories*. London: Bloomsbury.

Hollows, Joanne. 2008. *Domestic Cultures*. Maidenhead: Open University Press.

Jackson, Anna, Karen Coats and Roderick McGillis. 2008. *The Gothic in Children's Literature: Haunting the Borders*. New York: Routledge.

Jones, Stephen. 2009. *Coraline: A Visual Companion*. London: Titan.

Massey, Doreen. 2005. *Space, Place, and Gender*. Minneapolis: University of Minnesota Press.

Mitchell, W. J. T. 2002. *Landscape and Power*. 2nd edn. Chicago: University of Chicago Press.

Newton, James. 2015. 'The Zombiefied Landscape: *World War Z* (2013), *ParaNorman* (2012) and the Politics of the Animated Corpse.' *Animated Landscapes. History, Form and Function*. Ed. Chris Pallant. New York: Bloomsbury 233–248.

Page, Judith W. and Elise Lawton Smith. 2011. *Women, Literature, and the Domesticated Landscape: England's Disciples of Flora, 1780–1870*. Cambridge: Cambridge University Press.

Pallant, Chris. 2015. 'Introduction.' *Animated Landscapes. History, Form and Function*. Ed. Chris Pallant. New York: Bloomsbury.

Pennartz, Paul, J. J. 2006. 'The Experience of Atmosphere.' *At Home: An Anthropology of Domestic Space*. Ed. Irene Cieraad. Syracuse, NY: Syracuse University Press 95–106.

Stoddart, Helen. 2000. *Rings of Desire: Circus History and Representation*. Manchester: Manchester University Press.

Tait, Peta. 2005. *Circus Bodies: Cultural Identity in Aerial Performance*. London: Routledge.

Vidler, Anthony. 1992. *The Architectural Uncanny Essays in the Modern Unhomely*. Cambridge, MA: MIT Press.

Wells, Paul. 2015. 'Plasmatic Pitches, Temporal Tracks and Conceptual Courts: The Landscapes of Animated Sport.' *Animated Landscapes. History, Form and Function*. Ed. Chris Pallant. New York: Bloomsbury 215–232.

Chapter Twelve

'The Triumph of Nature'

Borderlands and Sunset Horizons in Bram Stoker's The Snake's Pass

William Hughes

The Snake's Pass (1890), Bram Stoker's first published novel, opens with a painterly evocation of a spectacular County Clare landscape. Described at length by the English hero, Arthur Severn, a first time traveller in Victorian Ireland, the whole scene proclaims the sublimity of a coastal region physically and geographically close to the English mainland, yet one which appears strangely alien to the English traveller's perception. Severn's account begins:

> Between two great mountains of grey and green, as the rock cropped out between the tufts of emerald verdure, the valley, almost as narrow as a gorge, ran due west towards the sea. There was just room for the roadway, half cut in the rock, beside the narrow strip of dark lake of seemingly unfathomable depth that lay far below between perpendicular walls of frowning rock. As the valley opened, the land dipped steeply, and the lake became a foam-filled torrent, widening out into pools and miniature lakes as it reached the lower ground. (1990, 2)

'Far beyond', Severn notes, is 'a wildly irregular coastline' bordering 'the sea—the great Atlantic' (2). Above that sea, though, hangs an ominous sky whose colours and variations are seemingly as striking as the land beneath:

> The whole west was a gorgeous mass of violet and sulphur and gold—great masses of storm cloud piling up and up till the very heavens seemed weighted with a burden too great to bear. Clouds of violet, whose centres were almost black and whose outer edges were tinged with living gold; great streaks and piled up clouds of palest yellow deepening into saffron and flame colour which seemed to catch the coming sunset and throw its radiance back to the eastern sky. (2)

The whole majestic vision, which silences even Arthur's loquacious car-driver, Andy Sullivan, is suddenly obscured by a downpour which drives the pair to the shelter of a local shebeen or tavern, within whose walls Arthur learns of the local legends, ancient and modern, around which the remainder of the narrative revolves. Those legends are intimate to the landscape, for they explain both the countryside's ancient geographical features and its more recent economic backwardness and isolation. This isolated corner of the west of Ireland, the literal *finis terre* or final border between Western Europe and the eastern seaboard of the Americas, is as haunted and as defined by its sterile and rocky geographical contours as much as by its lively Celtic twilight of legendary beings, proprietary saints and contemporary demons of finance and exploitation ritually evoked in the demotic surroundings of that most convivial of human refuges, the rural ale house.

Nicholas Daly is fundamentally correct in identifying this opening phase of *The Snake's Pass* with a colonialist thematicization of the countryside. For Daly, Stoker's intensity of description transforms a Western European terrain into 'a landscape that is both mysterious and yet susceptible to the power of the explorer's gaze' (1995, 47). The perceiver—here both an Englishman and a wealthy traveller in unfamiliar territory—effectively *possesses* what he sees: as Daly argues, 'images of an Imperial sublime co-exist with a discourse of visual dominance' (47). Indeed, by the end of the novel, Arthur Severn will *literally* possess both the land and the heroine associated with one of the two estates adjoining the geographical Shleenanaher—the Snake's Pass of the title, rendered in the Irish language—his ownership gained through a combination of chivalric gallantry and financial acumen. He will, likewise, have overwritten a significant component of the native mythology of Christian saints and Pagan serpents, of revolutionary insurgents from France and treasures reputedly buried in the bog, with a new narrative of industry which exorcises the old isolation of the region and relocates it—culturally, financially and, with *relative* success, politically—into a Gladstonian United Kingdom of Great Britain and Ireland, a synergetic and integrated whole which itself aspires to dispel the lingering ghosts of Hibernian dissatisfaction with the Act of Union of 1800.

The implied readership of Stoker's novel, Daly suggests, 'is urban, English and modern', the very epitome, it might seem, of an Imperial class whose interests embrace adjoining as well as distant islands (1995, 58). Whatever the case, however, Daly is forced to concede that this 'discourse of visual dominance' marks paradoxically not the centre but the periphery of the known and controlled world. As a moneyed and erudite traveller, Arthur Severn possesses, but does not own; he perceives but cannot adequately comprehend the uncanny differences he is faced with in this alternately strange and yet familiar country. 'The journey through the wild and desolate landscape', Daly argues, 'marks a transition into an isolate realm where civilised English values don't hold sway' (58). The terrain, the Irish countryside, becomes not so much disputed as liminal. It is seemingly owned through perception and presence, and yet is *not* owned because there is but one colonial traveller in evidence, and that figure is but a point *on* or *in* the landscape rather than a being *of* the landscape, or an organic and integrated participant in the aboriginal culture associated with that terrain.

The relationship of the Imperial to the domestic, and of the exotic to the familiar, is a complex one in *The Snake's Pass*. English values do not 'hold', suggests Daly, yet the presence of an explicitly English perceiver—a sole narrator upon whom readers of all origins and belief are, in consequence of his unique presence, fully dependent—imposes these. The apparent emphasis advanced in Daly's criticism—and indeed, in the writings of other critics—is that Stoker has associated himself with what W. J. McCormack calls 'the London-based exiles as against the home-based revivalists', even where the author's self-confessed support for the Gladstonian compromise of Irish Home Rule might well have been regarded as compromising the Unionist sentiments conventionally associated with his Anglo-Irish Protestant identity and former employment in the British administration at Dublin Castle (McCormack 1991, 845; Stoker 1906: 1, 343). Stoker's attitude, as has been argued elsewhere, is premised not upon a separatist commitment to a discrete cultural identity and national integrity, but rather embraces an idealistic paternalism, integrationist at its heart, and led by an implicit economic, political and cultural superiority on the eastern shores of the Irish Sea. It is easy, therefore, to see Stoker's Irish fiction as one which imposes an idealistic palimpsest of English attitudes upon the vivid Irish canvas of his fictionalized Clare Coast.

This is a neat conclusion, and one which no doubt fulfils many of the cultural and political demands imposed by the heavily postcolonialized discipline of modern Irish Studies. Participation in such a critical discourse demands, it seems, a demarcation which allocates or appropriates styles or images, for example, to the perceived polarities of Unionist or Nationalist, exile or revivalist, popular novelist or polemical fictionalist. Such an approach, though, may veer dangerously close to imposing a closure if not handled carefully and with due respect to the subtleties—and, at times, contradictions—of contemporary context. Deliberately or not, there may be discerned at times a subtle restriction which limits what may be said about Bram Stoker, the author of *The Snake's Pass* as well as of *Dracula* (1897), and indeed which polices the range of authors and fictions to which his writings—arguably Anglicized-Irish or Anglo-Irish as well as cross-generic—may be compared. In the 1960s and 1970s it was undeniably difficult to talk about Stoker's writings other than through the touchstone of *Dracula* and with the aid of psychoanalysis. In the first two decades of the twenty-first century it may well be equally as difficult to discuss this

Irish-born and Irish-educated author without somehow suggesting that his writings about Ireland are premised upon the attitudes of London rather than those of Dublin.

Stoker's writings, however, sit as uneasily in this dichotomized version of the Irish-born writer as 'London-based' or 'home-based' as the author himself does within the culturally troubled world of *The Field Day Anthology of Irish Writing*, the influential but selective and politicized collection in which McCormick's dismissive comment first appeared. To repeat the problematic point here, when writing about Ireland—and about England, too—Stoker remains, perversely, 'home-based' because he is a participant in a range of cultural, behavioural, artistic and political discourses which have currency on both sides of the Irish Sea. As a writer under the scrutiny of critical discourse he, too, is haunted by the mythicized wraiths of his cultural heritage and place of origin.

Certainly, in *The Snake's Pass*, Ireland *is* both exotic and spectacular, and is conveyed through descriptions which might well enforce an assumed sense of distance and unfamiliarity between perceiver and subject. The tourist, though, need not be, strictly speaking, an *English* tourist and nothing else. If spectacle, the spectacle of nature specifically, enforces an alienation or a sense of difference based upon distance, such a position does not necessarily imply anything more than the adoption of a quasi-English identity on the part of the writer, an identity which implicitly conflates the fictional character with the author. It may be argued with equal conviction that the opposition of such cases, where an Irishman writes about rural Ireland, is one imposed not by an eclipsed national identity but through the pressures imposed by participation in an educated urban milieu, a sense of difference which is not incompatible with muted identification.

Stoker's sunset—to return to the opening of this essay—is, in many respects, an *Irish* sunset, the precursor to, and parallel of, a culturally significant Celtic Twilight—a time, as it were, for contemplation and revival following prolonged stress. In initiating *The Snake's Pass* in this way, where a sinking sun and a distant prospect of land and sea induce a thoughtful reverie in the narrator, Stoker is effectively participating in a convention common to both fiction and non-fiction. Such scenes endow the perceived landscape with a personal as well as Imperial or political significance, and serve to integrate the perceiver into the topography, rather than to locate him beyond it or upon it in the manner of a tourist or colonial explorer. The perceiver thus becomes not an outsider but a participant, his destiny implicated in the future of the prospect he possesses through his gaze. The Irish perceiver—specifically the urban, educated perceiver—even when disguised here as an Englishman ambiguously abroad yet still somehow at home—may be paternalist and at times patronizing but is not necessarily imperialist.

This stylistic tradition is not unique to Irish writing, though it is certainly relevant to the type of considered thoughtfulness which Stoker evokes in the reverie which opens his 1890 novel. Consider, as a parallel, a reflective passage contained in Michael J. F. McCarthy's *Five Years in Ireland* (1901), a commentary on Irish events and attitudes between the years 1895 and 1900. McCarthy—like Stoker both a barrister and a graduate of Trinity College Dublin, but unlike him a Roman Catholic—pens his reverie facing the east rather than the west coast of Ireland, though the effect, even in this muted form, is markedly similar to Stoker's earlier fiction. It recalls a sunset viewed five years following the publication of *The Snake's Pass*, and thus one capable of evoking sentiments with regard to the current state of Ireland not dissimilar to those circulating in 1890. McCarthy begins:

> During the splendid June of 1895, I sat on evening on the pier at Howth, looking across the full tide at Ireland's Eye. The glow of sunset reddened the sky from West to North, from Portmarnock and Malahide to Lambay Island. The scene and the time were favourable to meditation.
>
> Beneath that arch of purple and gold lay the plains of my native land, stretching westward to the great rampart of rock and cliff that protects Ireland from the stormy Atlantic. (1901, 7)

There are some obvious similarities between McCarthy's economically phrased reverie and Stoker's somewhat more fulsome fiction. Both authors paint their representations of the sky with a restricted though evocative palette of rich colours, advancing both a poetic intensity and a metaphorical burden englobed in the eye of the beholder. This intensity, moreover, is amplified all the more by Stoker's depiction of the approach of the storm—for McCarthy, the storm exists only in potential, somewhere out in the Atlantic rather than on the immediate fringe of the coastal vantage point occupied by the writer. The major difference between the two accounts, though, is that for McCarthy, writing openly as himself, Dublin Bay is a synecdoche of 'my native land' where, for Stoker's fictional protagonist Arthur Severn, County Clare represents an alien terrain which can be adequately comprehended only when placed against the remembered foil of the tame grassland county and domesticated woodlands of a cloistered youth spent quietly in the south and west of England (1990, 10, 11).

In the two accounts, the intimacy of sunset and sea functions as a crucial catalyst for the introspective confessions that follow. The sunset, in both cases, is deployed as a form of threshold or portal, an opening to a horizon in the distance—a horizon which is fading fast even in the midst of the glamour of its colouring, though one which will in due course receive both illumination and, presumably exploration, as the traveller journeys onward.

McCarthy views the political and social incidents of Irish life between 1895 and 1900 with an indulgent and, at times, paternalistic eye—the eye of an urban commentator perceiving a predominantly rural nation and its localized preoccupation with shifting bogs (1901, 209), sectarian politics (205), education (301), legal intricacies (220–1) and a social hierarchy discretely different from that in existence on the other side of St George's Channel. These Irish preoccupations, in many cases, likewise form the raw subject matter of *The Snake's Pass*, though here they are conveyed with a sympathy none the less imbricated with incidences of melodramatic pathos and grotesque humour. Cultural and political, *Five Years in Ireland* proclaims the achievements of the recent past and hints at the promise of the future. Stoker's account, supposedly that of an outsider relatively ignorant of specific Irish difficulties, lays the emphasis in contrast squarely on to the future—there is no discretely Irish 'burden of the past' in Arthur Severn's narrative of cultural progress and revision, other than what he perceives as a local and national tendency to isolation and underdevelopment. Both *The Snake's Pass* and *Five Years in Ireland* perceive, in Ireland and in the Irish population, a potential for the future, a resource that may be developed—though in Stoker's account such change would appear to come necessarily at the expense of a residual past whose ghostly presence must be duly exorcised in the interests of modernity.

McCarthy, like Stoker, is careful to foreground Ireland's border with the Atlantic—this latter being verbally 'stormy' in the barrister's reminiscence and 'great', but literally tempestuous, in Stoker's novel. The coast and the sunset are, in a sense, intimate in both works, in that they graphically mark the prospect of an open (though dangerous) sea and the physical and symbolic boundary presented by a precipitous coastline. Curiously, McCarthy—writing as a 'home-based' Roman Catholic—is more muted than the Protestant, London-exiled Stoker, when advancing the implications that may be associated with this coastal border. For McCarthy the rampart of the coast *protects* Ireland from the ravages of the sea, and presumably from all that may come *from* that sea—trade, knowledge, influence. Indeed, for McCarthy, the breaching of the rampart of that coast by the Normans in 1172 heralded 'centuries of strife and misery, of darkness, misunderstanding and ignorance' (1901, 7), a lingering hegemony which the writer perceives as being as repressive to the Saxon in England as it was to the Irish Celt (8).

For Stoker—whose fictional Irish characters in this novel are more likely to frequent the west-coast settlements of Westport and Galway rather than the east-coast capital, Dublin—the outer world represents a prospect to be embraced rather than barricaded out. It is significant that the economic and cultural revival of the area around the Snake's Pass is dependent upon both the export of limestone, explicitly identified as a rare commodity in the region, and on the development of a deep-water port which will link the

Shleenanaher with greater Ireland and Great Britain, as well as the more distant trade of Atlantic America—itself a place further west, beyond the sunset, a destination to which one may travel as an impecunious voyager only to return triumphant and wealthy at some future date. There is a tincture of the Victorian myth of the self-made man in this image, too, this being a myth which in itself resists the insularity which Stoker's English hero associates, implicitly and explicitly, with the west of Ireland.

The sunset, as it were, heralds not so much the twilit decline of the present but the dawning promise of a new day to succeed the old—the intimation of better things, of opportunities in the future which build on the achievements of the era just passed. What lies beyond the boundary of the known and present margin is 'a beautiful country', to quote *Under the Sunset* (1882), Stoker's earliest collection of short fiction, 'where the clouds, splendid with light and colour, give a promise of the glory and beauty which encompass it' (1978, 1). For Arthur Severn, at this early stage of *The Snake's Pass*, the sunset and the panorama of land and sea with which he is faced, serve to signify his own recent passage from minority and dependence into the independence associated with the coming of age and inheritance. The prospect of existence as a self-determining independent individual lies before him, a metaphorical new day lying just beyond the close of his present way of life as one dependent upon the charity of an aged relative.

The burgeoning life of the self, in Stoker's fiction at least, may also be closely associated with the destiny of the nation. Stoker's model of an aware self-development does not, however, implicate the aspirations of nationalistic separatism. Arthur Severn is both physically powerful (and as his kingly Christian name suggests) destined to both lead and be *accepted* as a leader—if not in mythological England, like his chivalric namesake, then in a modern, commercialized Victorian Ireland. Severn is, though, an English outsider who will be linked by marriage to native (albeit explicitly Protestant) stock, and whose benign presence will empower those placed economically beneath him only in the sense of what is essentially a neo-feudal relationship. A resident—rather than an absentee—landlord, he will rule somewhat in the manner of a modernized, Anglicized Scottish laird—evading, in this way, the negative political implications that would be caused by a habitual residence in distant London.

For Arthur Severn to assume an acceptable and accepted ascendancy over the native Irish, both Protestant and Roman Catholic, he must, however, confront the cultural and mythological ghosts which haunt the landscape of County Clare. These ghosts—which are variously the lingering legends of ancient history, the apocryphal parables of an historic Christian past, and the residual memories of an unsuccessful rebellion against British or, rather, *English* influence over the island of Ireland—are encoded in both the

contours of the landscape and a still-evocative Irish nomenclature whose enduring relevance must on more than one occasion be explained at length to the non-native aspirant, Arthur Severn.

The process of explanation begins early in the novel. Having observed both the sublime sunset and the cloudy harbinger of the coming storm, Arthur Severn demands of Andy Sullivan, his car-driver, the Irish names associated with some of the local landmarks. The conversation reproduces Andy's demotic west-coast brogue in a colourful, though not necessarily accurate, way:

> 'Tell me, Andy,' I said, 'What do they call the hill beyond?'
> 'The hill beyond there, is it? Well, now, they call the place Shleenanaher.'
> 'Then that is Shleenanaher mountain, then?'
> 'Begor, it's not. The mountain is called Knockcalltecrore. It's Irish.'
> 'And what does it mean?'
> 'Faix, I believe it's a short name for the Hill iv the Lost Goolden Crown.'
> 'And what is Shleenanaher, Andy?'
> 'Throth, it's a bit iv a gap in the rocks beyond that they call Shleenanaher.'
> 'And what does that mean? It's Irish, I suppose?'
> 'Thrue for ye! Irish it is, an' it manes "The Shnake's Pass"' (1990, 14)

Severn's attempt to ascertain why the gap in the rocks is called 'The Snake's Pass' is thwarted by the onset of the storm, although the subject is once again enjoined when the car-driver and his employer seek refuge in the nearby shebeen.

The term 'Irish' here connotes both the linguistic register and the specific meaning of each name, for these features in a landscape—a hill, a pass and the bog which occupies the latter—specifically reference the region's pre-history, its Celtic Christianity and a current tendency towards nationalism, graphically acknowledged through the presence in the shebeen of 'a powerful looking young fellow dressed in the orange and green jersey of the Gaelic Athletic Club' (1990, 19). Historical aspirations of separatism are implicated, also, in the tale which is subsequently told of General Humbert's abortive invasion of Ireland (24). These three key historical myths of the region will need to be progressively overwritten during Severn's intervention into the economic and social present of the West of Ireland, his demonstrable success in implicitly exhibiting a paternalistic and somewhat Gladstonian paradigm which might be profitably applied to the rest of nationalist Ireland.

There is an intimacy between the two narratives through which the naming of the Snake's Pass and the Hill of the Lost Golden Crown are conveyed to the local population assembled in the storm-beset shebeen. Such tales are not so much twice-told as many-times-told. They are familiar traditions to local listeners, a curiosity to outsiders. Yet their ostensibly local significance is belied by the presence of the national saint, Patrick, as a direct participant in the tale of how, having driven the snakes from the island of Ireland, he engaged in a final conflict with the King of the Snakes. The King of the Snakes, a representative of an ancient, pre-Christian Ireland, is not defeated but abdicates in defiance of the Saint's command, burying his golden crown in the unstable bog at the landward end of the present-day Shleenanaher and forcing the gap in the rocks at its seaward end as his sizeable body retreats towards the sea. Explicitly, the Saint cannot claim a total ascendancy over the island he now effectively occupies in the name of Christ. Though the King of the Snakes has gone, his concealed crown remains to represent his enduring hold over land and legend. In defiance, the regal reptile taunts the Saint thus:

> An' till ye get me crown I'm king here still, though ye banish me. An' mayhap I'll come in some forrum what ye don't suspect, for I must watch me crown. An' now I go away, iv me own accord. (1990, 23)

If Arthur Severn's Christian name links him to an evocative figure in *English* mythology, St Patrick enjoys an equal—possibly even a stronger—presence in its Irish counterpart. As a patronal national figure for both Protestant and Roman Catholic communions, St Patrick has the potential to function as a unifying emblem in, and of, Ireland. His action in expelling the snakes from Ireland, though, render him a potent symbol also of nationalist aspirations— witness, in *The Snake's Pass*, the Saint's demand that the King of the Snakes 'lave Irish soil wid all th' other Shnakes' (21). It goes without saying that the Saint was at times deployed as an emblem of Irish nationalist aspirations— one hand-coloured political print of c. 1835–1836 by C. J. Grant, for example, shows 'The Modern Saint Patrick. ... Driving the Vermin Out of Ireland'. The personified and named vermin include not merely 'famine' and 'dis- ease' but also the 'standing army', 'Protestant Church' and 'English Law' (1835–1836, 118).

St Patrick, it would appear, has failed to expel the last of the snakes satis- factorily from the island of Ireland, and it is this fictional weakness—which appears only in Stoker's novel—that forms the interstice through which the English traveller may impose his own modern mythology upon the ancient language, traditions and hostility which define Irish difference. Just as the leg- endary Crown of Gold has become associated in local mythology with a lost chest of French revolutionary gold (1990, 24–6), also reputedly be subsumed in the bog which occupies the present-day Shleenanaher, so the negative figure of the King of the Snakes has been utilized to demonize the reputation of Black Murdock, a gombeenman or unregulated usurer who exploits the precarious financial circumstances of those who dwell in rural backwardness. The assembled locals are vocal in their disdain for this member of their own

Roman Catholic community. Provoked by a passing remark by one elderly storyteller that he was 'not so sure, naythur, that all the shnakes has left all the hill yit!', they exclaim that the remaining serpent—meaning Murdock—is 'a black shnake', one 'wid side-whiskers' (1990, 26). It is surely significant that one of the assembled company concludes, with a clichéd exclamation, 'Begorra! we want St Pathrick to luk in here agin!' (26).

St Patrick, of course, isn't going to look in again, and having failed on the first attempt to rid Ireland of its vermin can promise little more in any return to combat. Essentially, what Stoker has done here is to skew the customary political coordinates of localized Irish politics in favour of what promises to be, in part at least, an interventionist solution to Ireland's historic and contemporary problems. It is not merely that St Patrick, and the rather ancient Hibernian lineage he has come to emblematize through his archaic vestments and ornate crozier—both specifically mentioned in Stoker's mythological account of the expulsion of the snakes (1990, 19)—have proved ineffective. It is, more emphatically, that the vermin have been subtly transformed into a member of the local community, practising moneylending and landowning in a repressive way under specifically Irish conditions of law and custom. Arthur Severn, in other words, must become a nineteenth-century St Patrick, driving out that which is unwholesome, for the good of the Shleenanaher community specifically—and 'for Ireland's good' (240) more generally. If the nineteenth-century King of the Snakes is driven out, the argument follows, all other aspects of cultural snakishness will follow him into oblivion sooner or later.

Severn undertakes his restoration of the region's fortunes initially through a programme of targeted land purchase, first buying Murdock's bog-side property at an advantageous rate, ostensibly to present it to an English associate, Dick Sutherland, whom Murdock had engaged to search the bog for the missing French gold (1990, 123). As he notes, though, this at present sterile and stagnant mass might be ultimately profitable, if drained and in the right hands (121). Sutherland suspects the presence of 'a streak of limestone' beneath the bog (202), and that hard mineral resource is emblematic of a dynamic future that will rapidly lead the economy of the Shleenanaher away from subsistence farming and turf burning and towards a nascent industrial economy. As Sutherland informs Severn,

> A limestone quarry here would be pretty much as valuable as a gold mine. Nearly all these promontories on the western coast of Ireland are of slate or granite, and here we have not got lime within thirty miles. With a quarry on the spot, we can not only build heap and reclaim our own bog, but we can supply five hundred square miles of country with the rudiments of prosperity, and at a nominal price with what they pay now! (1990, 203)

Indeed, with Murdock literally displaced by the novel's conclusion, Severn is able not merely 'to buy the whole mountain' (179), but also much of the surrounding land, resettling its indigenous population further from the centre of his improving activities or else encouraging emigration to Scotland or further afield (179, 203). Those that remain are to have their subsistence agriculture replaced by a new, efficient and business-like model of farms characterized by 'good solid stone houses, with proper offices and farmyards' (203).

This much is economics rather than cultural mythology, though Arthur's final expulsion of Murdock comes not through purchase but by way of a natural disaster which effectively forces the emblematic gombeenman through the cleft of the Shleenanaher and into the ocean in a final, echoing closure of St Patrick's failed attempt. Murdock, who has artificially flooded the bog in order to financially ruin his neighbour, is caught up with his house, his account books and his representative status as an anachronistic and inappropriate emblem of an Ireland whose day is passing and carried out to see by the hitherto stagnant bog—this latter being, too, an emblem of Irish difference. The process, though rapid, is described in detail and through language which is richly symbolic. As Severn recalls,

> The shuddering surface of the bog began to extend on every side to even the solid ground which curbed it ... All things on its surface seemed to melt away and disappear, as though swallowed up. (1990, 229)

A 'silent change or demoralization' (229) sweeps the surface of the land, into which sinks Murdock and his house:

> Then came the end of the terrible convulsion. With a rushing sound, and the noise of a thousand waters falling, the whole bog swept, in waves of gathering size, and with a hideous writhing, down the mountain-side to the entrance of the Shleenanaher—struck the portals with a sound like thunder, and piled up to a vast height. And then the millions of tons of slime and ooze, and bog and earth, and broken rock swept through the pass and into the sea. (230)

The Saint's unfinished mission has been completed, symbolically at least, by a modern Englishman.

The expulsion of the bog purifies the land as much as the removal of the gombeenman and a change in land ownership modernizes local culture upon the implicit regularity of an English paradigm. At the opening of *The Snake's Pass* it is noted that 'The mountain wid the lake on top used to be the fertilest shpot in the whole counthry' (23) until the advent of the unstable bog. With the valley cleansed of the bog's brown murkiness, clean stone and flowing water are revealed beneath, together with the two missing treasures. One is the French gold (239). The other 'an ancient crown of strange form' (241), a Celtic jewel transformed by myth into a serpentine diadem. Its legendary significance is immediately appreciated by Sutherland: it is 'the crown that gave the hill its name and was the genesis of the story of St Patrick and the King of the Snakes!' (242). The literal story of St Patrick has in this sentence been replaced with a theologically tenable one, Sutherland's interpretation implicitly equating the casting out of the snakes with the expulsion of paganism by Christian missionary zeal. No snake has worn this diadem: it is the relic of an older faith, now superseded.

Likewise is the more recent past superseded by Severn's brave new world of industrious modernity. It is, in a sense, a return to a golden-age past that has been till recently overwritten by legend, by bog and by anachronistic administration. Sutherland finds within the revealed floor of the Shleenanaher evidence that the limestone of the Snake's Pass was worked by human hands before the stagnation of the bog obscured human industry (1990, 241). With obstructions both natural and cultural now removed, the region may power itself with modern hydroelectricity (178) and look outward to the sea, and to the world, through a proposed 'harbour on the south side...as safe as Portsmouth and of fathomless depth' (178). Though still a border, the hinterland of the Shleenanaher has now become outward looking, a place from which to depart, and one through which to bring home industry and wealth in a modern world in which nationalistic dissonance has been replaced by an implicitly sensible submission to paternalistic rule and the bounty of wealth brought through change. To view the sunset at this later stage of the region's development is to look outward through the piers of a harbour, seeing that which lies beyond the sunset rather than being contained by a land which refuses to exceed its own boundaries.

BIBLIOGRAPHY

Daly, Nicholas. 1995. 'Irish Roots: The Romance of History in Bram Stoker's *The Snake's Pass.*' *Literature and History*, 4 (2): 42–70.

Grant, C. J. 1835–1836. 'The Modern Saint Patrick; Or, the Irish Titular Saint Driving the Vermin Out of Ireland.' *The Political Drama*, print no. 118. London: George Drake: unpaginated. Accessed 9 March 2016. http://theprintshopwindow.com/2013/06/13/the-modern-saint-patrick-driving-the-vermin-out-of-ireland.

McCarthy, Michael, J. F. 1901. *Five Years in Ireland, 1895–1900.* London: Simpkin, Marshall, Hamilton, Kent.

McCormack, W. J. 1991. 'Irish Gothic and After, 1820–1945.' *The Field Day Anthology of Irish Writing.* Vol. 2. Ed. Seamus Deane. Derry: Field Day. 831–949.

Stoker, Bram. 1906. *Personal Reminiscences of Henry Irving*, 2 vols. London: William Heinemann.

Stoker, Bram.. 1978. *Under the Sunset.* North Hollywood: Newcastle.

_____. 1980. *The Snake's Pass.* Dingle: Brandon.

Afterword

Affective Gothic Landscapes

Ruth Heholt

It is with the movement, the passage and dissolution of impressions, images, sensations, that analysis leaves off, that continual vanishing away, that strange perpetual weaving and unweaving of ourselves. (Walter Pater 1868, 311)

Throughout this volume the Gothic has reared its head; or perhaps more accurately, hydra-like, its multiple and shifting heads. Each of the chapters has touched on the darkness of the Gothic landscape. Haunted landscapes are not safe landscapes and although Joanne Parker states that 'landscape is first and foremost a way of creating belongingness and tying us together' (Cited in Richardson 2015, 242), it is apparent in the essays collected here that landscape is just as likely to be a site of fracture, violence, dislocation and trauma. Robert Mighall states that 'the "Gothic" by definition is about history and geography' (1999, xiv), and the Gothic landscape is perhaps the epitome of the haunted landscape. This volume demonstrates that the 'history', the past, will inevitably return to haunt the present. Dark, brooding, mysterious, threatening and layered with history, identity and memory, the Gothic landscape looms over us both in fiction and in cultural and touristic perceptions of nature. All Gothic sensibilities are tied up with varying conceptions of nature: from the dark Alpine forests, ruined castles and abbeys of traditional Gothic fiction to the menacing landscapes of modern writers like Richard Matheson or Helen Oyeyemi that 'bite back', the Gothic is *located*.

From the earliest forays into Gothic fiction, landscape and nature have been of central concern, as felt-reality, as metaphor, as warning, as material threat or sanctuary. As Anne Williams puts it, 'most important to Gothic romance, as to Romanticism, was the idea that nature is *significant*' (1995, 83, original emphasis). In the Romantic tradition, it is argued, nature is seen as unified, purely 'natural' (rather than in any sense 'cultural'), healing and as conveying a moral sensibility. Nature is perfect and should be surveyed as such. Yet in the Romantic view of landscape, critics propose that there is a *distancing*, a detachment from the landscape itself, for the subject who surveys. There is a 'looking at' landscape rather than an immersion in it or a full bodily experience in relation to it. Anne Mellor notes this in relation to Wordsworth who she says 'takes a stance of the spectator *ab extra*' (1993, 95), surveying from outside. The ultimate Romantic landscape is the sublime one which inspires awe and wonder. Yet, so the argument goes, the contemplation of the lofty heights of the Alps or the majestic scenery of Snowdonia is more a mental connection than a physical one, the ideal being of lofty contemplation that raises the mind to higher planes and which can commune with the transcendental spirit of place, to expand and elevate human understanding and thought. As Mellor argues, 'for Wordsworth, the experience of the sublime entails isolation, a struggle for domination, exaltation, and the absorption of the other into the transcendental self' (1993, 101). In this Romantic schema there is a negation of the bodily experience of landscape in an exaltation of the capacities of the mind to contemplate the sublime: *using* the landscape to expand the spiritual and perceptual powers of the personal, individual psyche. In much criticism about the Romantic view of landscape it is Kant's dichotomy of mind/body that is cited whereby the mind is by far the loftier and more important of the two. Mellor continues: 'Wordsworth attempted to represent a unitary self that is maintained over time by the activity of memory, and to show that this self or "soul" is defined, not by the body and its sensory experience, but by the human mind, by the growth of consciousness' (145). The body and the senses are over-passed and the material experience of being, in this schema, is negated and seen as some-how less 'true' (or at the least, less valuable), than the life of the mind and the expansion of consciousness within the psyche.

Yet things are not necessarily so clear. Mellor cites Paul de Man who she says has 'rightly argued that Wordsworth's project was undercut by his own recognition that language can never be more than an alienating "garment", can never be "the air we breathe"' (1993, 145). Here it is the language that is the distancing factor; the moment, the experience, the 'air we breathe' is the *immanent*; the experienced. And if, as Nicola Watson's chapter title in *Romantics and Victorians* suggests, Wordsworth is a 'poet in a landscape' (2012, 9), then just as any landscape can only ever be apprehended, at least initially, via the senses, so Wordsworth's landscapes must be haunted by the (im)possibility of the body. The body itself must be the ghostly, spectral pres-ence the often negated but ever present materiality of *being* in the landscape. Watson describes what she terms the 'Wordsworthian' saying: 'this may be summed up as the concentration upon the poet's solitary, imaginatively intense experience within a natural landscape which results in profound and permanent, if unquantifiable, spiritual benefit to the poet's inner life' (22). For the purposes of this essay and this volume, it is the concept of an 'intense experience' that resonates. Any sort of 'intense experience' will be *felt* and even for Wordsworth, to contemplate and communicate with a landscape is, in some respect, to *feel* it. Acknowledging that I am being selective in my quotation, Wordsworth, in the final book of 'The Prelude', when talking about the transcendental sublime, asserts: 'That Man least sensitive see, hear, perceive, / And cannot chuse but feel' ([1798] 2000, 379, lines 85–6). The mind might strive to overcome the body, but, whether acknowledged or not, whether chosen or not, there will be a bodily and emotive reaction. Wordsworth continues:

> The power which all
> Acknowledge when thus moved, which Nature thus
> To bodily sense exhibits, is the express
> Resemblance of that glorious faculty
> That higher minds bear with them as their own. (379, lines 86–90)

The note to this passage asserts that 'the "glorious faculty" is the imagination', which exhibits 'mastery over sense' (n.7). Yet nature is exhibiting 'her' power to 'bodily sense' and the 'glorious faculty' is merely the 'resemblance' of that power: it is body first and imagination afterwards. The power the imagination can conjure up is only *similar* to; can only *imitate* the power of nature that was apprehended by the body.

Recently Tim Ingold has denied the definitional boundaries of the mind/ imagination and that which is presently and physically experienced and perceived. He argues:

> perception and imagination are one: not however because percepts are images, or hypothetical representations of a reality 'out there', but because to perceive, as to imagine, is to participate from within in the perpetual self-making of the world. It is to join with a world in which things do not so much *exist* as *occur.* (2012, 14, original emphasis)

Here he collapses the inner and the outer, the imagined and the perceived, bringing both together in a contemporaneous moment in time. He continues, 'if imagination is the work of the mind, then it is a mind that far from remaining disengaged, wrapped up in its own auto-generative deliberations, mingles freely with the world along multiple lines of sensory participation', finally arriving at the conclusion that 'perceiving landscape is, in short, tantamount to imagining the landscape, in so far as we do not just live *in* the world but are simultaneously alive *to* it' (16–17, original emphasis). In this way it is possible to argue that, even for Wordsworth, to perceive and imagine the sublime *is* to sense it, to feel it and to be 'alive to it'.

Stephen Ahern associates this sensory, emotive response with the eighteenth-century 'cult of sensibility'. Although in *Affected Sensibilities* (perhaps oddly for a book with such a title) Stephen Ahern does not cite affect theory, his discussion of the concept of eighteenth-century 'sensibility' resonates clearly with contemporary notions of affect. Ahern cites G. S. Rousseau (1976) who argues that many in the eighteenth century defined sensibility as 'a term to connote self-consciousness and self-awareness' (cited in Ahern 2007, 16). However, Ahern asserts that 'its etymological root indicates [that] *sensibility* denotes a physiological capacity of sensation or sense perception' (16, original emphasis). Wordsworth is, from this point of view, born into an age of 'sensation or sense perception'—an age of feeling. Ahern asserts that 'in the broadest sense sensibility can be defined as a capacity for living intensely that is demonstrated in a heightened sensitivity to one's environment' (12). Here we have the juxtaposition apparent in Wordsworth's work of intensity and sensitivity to the environment. If there is no 'real' distance, the sublime landscape cannot be 'over there'; it can only be felt and lived. There is an affective collapse whereby to feel is to be *within* the landscape. Quoting Seigworth and Gregg, Berberich et al state that 'in its most basic meaning, "affect" refers to something that moves, that triggers reactions, forces or intensities "that pass body to body (human, non-human, part-body and otherwise)", simultaneously engaging the mind and body, reason and emotions' (2013, 314). The dichotomy between mind and body is not possible in this immersive paradigm of affect. Here, there is no inside or outside; there is only the worldly, material, bodily experience of affect, force and encounter.

Nicola Trott suggests that although the Romantic writers and commentators did not always agree about the significance of the sublime, one thing that they did accede was 'that the sublime escapes the limits of representation. ... As a result, the sublime presumes an aesthetic of excess or non-representability' (1999, 79). For the Romantic writers this 'non-representability' was a prerequisite for the transcendence sublime nature could supply to the (male) mind: the imaginative leap that could elevate the human spirit. In *The Gothic Sublime*, Vijay Mishra identifies the anomalies and contradictions already present in the concept of the non-representable sublime. Acknowledging the work of Elizabeth Napier he states that

> Failure ... is part of the design of the sublime insofar as the sublime threatens our very capacities of cognitive judgment. The nonrepresentability of the idea is a consequence of an acute disjunction between the signifier and the signified that puts into doubt the meaning-making capacity of linguistic signs themselves. (1994, 16)

The Romantic project that relied on the sublime *as* making and generating meaning is one that cannot succeed as the non-representable inevitably goes beyond meaning, judgment and reason. In relation to that which cannot be represented there is an inevitable slippage and failure of connection between the signifier and the signified—landscape and its 'meaning'.

Further, in the context of this book, within the theoretical framework of cultural geography that *Haunted Landscapes* is concerned with, the 'non-representational' as a term is used in a specific manner and signifies something different: something that is even more anomalous to the Romantic view of landscape. Nigel Thrift in his book *Non-Representational Theory* posits 'a *material schematism* in which the world is made up of all kinds of things brought in to relation with one another by many and various spaces, through a continuous and largely involuntary process of encounter' (2008, 8, original emphasis). This schema does not imbue the landscape with meaning; rather there is a continuous moment, an immanence, of 'encounter'. The non-representational is a material schema that has no space for the transcendent. 'Representational theory', it is argued, was 'overly pre-occupied with the interpretation of meaning and the key role of the intellect in such a process' (Dixon & Straughan 2013, 37). In a sense this reflects the criticism of the Romantic, 'Wordsworthian' view of the landscape and nature whereby it is the intellect (the mind) whose interpretation of the sublime is predominant. The landscape means something other than, and perhaps more important than, itself. There is something 'other' to be gained from surveying a landscape. The mind can gain spiritual expansion and transcendence from the landscape both in the sense of *taking* from the landscape, and also in the sense of *distancing* from the landscape. In this way too, it was argued, 'representational theory' took from the landscape to make something that was somehow *more*. The 'non-representational' however, moves away from giving landscape 'meaning' that is outside, or transcendent to its own materiality and/or the self that is within it and which sees and experiences it. Thus if, as Trott asserts, the Romantic view of the sublime landscape 'presumes an aesthetic of excess or non-representability' (1999, 79), then this deserves attention. From this point of view, the supposedly distanced, isolated, dominant (to echo Mellor) transcendental experience of the sublime is not, even under Wordsworth's deft pen, either possible or representable.

Mishra contends that 'the Gothic sublime brought a dangerous, negative principle of nontranscendental subjectivity' (1994, 4). This collapse between 'inside' and 'outside' whereby there can be no transcendence of subjectivity is a key feature in Gothic narratives. In the recent book *Eco-Gothic*, Andrew Smith and William Hughes contend that 'the problem with the Gothic is that, at one level, "nature" is a more contested term as it is one which [...] appears to participate in a language of estrangement rather than

belonging' (2013, 2). These ideas of 'estrangement' or 'belonging' reverberate between the Romantic and the Gothic landscapes depicted in fiction and
art. Trott looks at Edmund Burke's work in which she says 'the Burkean
sublime is defined by its ability to pre-empt the efforts of rational analysis'
and which 'stems from a rejection of (Enlightenment) clarity for a darkness
that is "more productive of sublime ideas than light"' (79–80).[1] Romantic
landscapes in both literature and art are full of darkness. Yet it is in the
simultaneous (and not separate) movement of the Gothic that the darkness becomes celebrated and the blackest of fantasies indulged. Romantic
landscapes comprise light and darkness, of belonging as well as distance.
Gothic landscapes arise concurrently with the Romantic, yet they belong
to the dark. Emma McEvoy claims that 'for most twentieth-century critics who choose to theorise Gothic and its relation to literary Romanticism,
Gothic was to be distinguished from Romanticism, and the opposition set
up between the terms was a tool in the definition of the transcendence of
Romanticism' (2007, 19). However, in *The Art of Darkness* Anne Williams
proposes that the ' "Gothic" and "Romantic" are not two but one' (1995,
1), and as McEvoy points out 'in terms of periodisation "High Gothic" is
very nearly synchronic with the Romantic period' (2007, 19). This conflation of the Romantic and the Gothic has become of central concern recently
and it proves fruitful for this discussion.[2] Coral Ann Howells contends
that 'Gothic fiction represents the extreme development of the eighteenth-
century cult of Sensibility' (1995, 8). The refusal to absolutely separate the
Romantic and the Gothic is of interest in the discussion around the ideas of
sensibility, the transcendental sublime, feeling and, finally, for our purposes
in this volume, haunted landscapes.

Lisa Kröger notes a similar reactive stance to that of sensibility in Ann
Radcliffe's Gothic texts. She states:

> The environment, at least for the characters of Radliffe, acts as a kind of con-
> duit of emotions, a way to experience feelings and sometimes to purge them.
> Whether it is a feeling of creativity and renewal or even an indication of the
> potential evil in someone, the environment is alive as it responds to these char-
> acters who reside within its boundaries. (2013, 19)

Here the landscape is 'alive', conducting emotions, responding to characters. In the criticism of Gothic forms, the natural Gothic landscape is often
foregrounded as important and in art we have the recognizable mountains of
Caspar David Friedrich, the fiery pits and chasms in John Martin's monu-
mental paintings and the relatively ubiquitous (although also gorgeous) paintings showing rushing torrents, dark and threatening landscapes filled with
bandits and peril. In his critical discussion of the Gothic landscapes penned

by Ann Radcliffe, Ben Brabon cites what he calls her 'Gothic cartography' whereby she combines 'the effects of detailed panoramic surveys of space with imaginative sublime Gothic vistas' (2006, 840). Brabon associates this 'Gothic cartography' with art and says that her 'literary geographies [have] both an accurate representation of space and an artistic impression' (843). Radcliffe draws her landscapes accurately and with care, whilst allowing the artistic imagination free rein. Radcliffe's work is most often associated with the 'female Gothic' (Moers 1995, 90), and here the natural landscapes are sometimes seen as being of secondary importance to the buildings which offer either sanctuary or entrapment for the female protagonist in some sort of warped domestic sphere. Brabon says 'the broad outline of the "female Gothic" plot relies upon a heroine trapped between a picturesque retreat and a menacing castle' (2006, 843). These are the spaces that house people and which are therefore (at least ostensibly) human in scale. Yet the sublime landscapes that they sit within go beyond the human and haunt the imagination, and even when the emphasis is on the terrifying ruins and desolate castles, where so much of the action takes place, the natural landscape that surrounds them is never far away.

In *The Mysteries of Udolpho*, as Emily St Aubert first approaches the castle, Radliffe paints the following scene:

> The sun had just sunk below the top of the mountains she was descending, whose long shadow stretched athwart the valley, but his sloping rays, shooting through an opening of the cliffs touched with a yellow gleam the summits of the forest, that hung upon the opposite steeps, and streamed in full splendour upon the towers and battlements of a castle, that spread its extensive ramparts along the brow of a precipice above. (2005, 240)

As the light fails, the castle remains visible, 'silent, lonely and sublime, it seemed to stand the sovereign of the scene' (240); the focus is on the Gothic castle. Angela Wright who glosses the above passage in Terror and Wonder states that 'what is of importance here is what Emily the beholder, sees in the castle. This is no objective description of it but one that characterises it as the "sovereign of the scene"' (2007, 82). However, in Radcliffe's own words it only 'seemed' to be so. The castle does not encompass the whole scene; Emily sees far more than just the castle. There is the forest, the sun setting, the precipice and the valley below, without which the castle would not have the same visual or affective impact. In Gothic fiction the entire landscape—man-made *and* natural—penetrates the being of those who travel through the landscapes or reside within them.

In Gothic fiction unlike (so it might be argued) Romantic fiction, the distances between inside and outside, self and place are collapsed. Coral Ann Howells says:

Gothic fiction with its castles and abbeys, persecuted heroines, ghosts and night-mares, projects a peculiarly fraught fantasy world of neurosis and morbidity, and if we take a close look at the kinds of feeling in which these novelists were especially interested we begin to perceive how anti-Enlightenment anxieties were actually 'felt on the pulses' of a whole generation. (1995, 5)

This is a world of sensibility, of feeling, albeit of feeling that is often unbear-able. As Howells contends, the Gothic's 'main areas of feeling treat of mel-ancholy, anxiety-ridden sentimental love and horror; it is a shadowy world of ruins and twilit scenery lit up from time to time by lurid flashes of passion and violence' (5). The landscape and the dark feelings of those travelling through them are not separate. These landscapes haunt particularly the heroines of Gothic fictions, and Howells contends that for these heroines, 'there is an extraordinary heightened sense of the inter-relatedness between physical and emotional response. To be "aware" of something meant to "feel" it through the whole organism, so that "feeling" was truly a matter of sensation as much as of emotional or imaginative perception' (8–9). This is an affective response that deconstructs the distance between landscape or the material world 'out there' and the self that feels *with* it.

One of the most important crossover texts that bridge the gap between the Romantic and the Gothic, *Frankenstein*, conflates the two types of landscape as well as the two traditions. Hogle calls *Frankenstein* a 'supremely Gothic-Romantic novel' (2016, 125) and in this text the sublime *is* the Gothic as well as vice versa. The monster himself is a creature of the earth, dug up, stitched together and re-born. His spark of life does not come from the deep mystery of nature, rather it is through the material, the man-made (although not identi-fied) 'instruments of life' (2003, 58) that the creature comes alive. Nilanjana Gupta claims that 'the landscapes of *Frankenstein* have a sense of Gothic grandeur. The mountains of Switzerland, the barren hillsides of Scotland and, of course, the icy desolation of the Northern Hemisphere serve to accentu-ate the terrors of the plot' (2007, xx). Gupta (who interestingly, and against almost all other critics, denies *Frankenstein* as a Gothic novel), claims:

The landscapes of the Gothic mode were sublime and capable of inspiring ter-ror. They were landscapes that reflected the extreme emotional states of human existence where fear became terror, loneliness became isolation and action became violence. The physical settings of such stories were seen to be imagi-native correlatives of the landscapes of horror within the human mind. Mary Shelley's use of such desolate, forbidding and extreme landscapes reflects the movement of the monster's mental state. (xx–xxi)

Again we have the disintegration of the inner and the outer, the dis-tanced and the felt. Thrift in *Non-Representational Theory* starts with the statement: 'it would be possible to argue that human life is based on and in movement' (2008, 5). In *Frankenstein* movement encompasses the emotional, the mental *and* the physical. The creature is a creature of his environment: as it shifts and changes so does he. The creature is not separate from his environment; he is alive to it and within it; he haunts it and is haunted by it.

Mary Poovey asserts that 'Mary Shelley distrusts both the imagination *and* the natural world. The imagination, as it is depicted in Frankenstein's original transgression, is incapable of projecting an irradiating virtue'. She continues:

> By the same token, Mary Shelley also distrusts nature, for, far from curbing the imagination, nature simply encourages imaginative projection. [...] Mary Shelley's anxiety about the imagination bleeds into the world it invades. In the inhospitable world most graphically depicted in the final setting of *Frankenstein*, nature is 'terrifically desolate', frigid, and fatal to human beings and human relationships. These fields of ice provide a fit home only for the monster, that incarnation of the imagination's ugly and deadly essence. (1985, n.p.)

Yet if we return to Ingold and the idea that 'perceiving landscape is, in short, tantamount to imagining the landscape' then what Shelley is writing is an affective landscape where there is no separation, as 'the imagination bleeds into the world it invades' (2012, 16–17). This may be a negative 'fatal' landscape that produces no virtue and is only fit to house the monster, but it is still a setting and a landscape of affect. The Gothic landscape itself through affect, intensity, heightened emotion, darkness and desire conflates and collapses any differentiation between self and place. Lisa Kröger differentiates between male writers of the Gothic and the female. In relation to Ann Radcliffe's work she contends that 'the environment ... acts as a kind of conduit of emotions, a way to experience feelings and sometimes to purge them. Whether it is a feeling of creativity and renewal or even an indication of the potential evil in someone, the environment is alive as it responds to these characters who reside within its boundaries' (2013, 19). Kröger speaks about an environment that is 'responsive', not a distanced, remote, awe-inspiring landscape, but a more humanized space that is reactive to the human. This is a feminized landscape, and Kröger positions it against Matthew Lewis's view of nature and the landscape whereby, she argues, he 'viewed nature as a force entirely separate from humanity' (20). Writing earlier, Anne Mellor argued that the first female authors of the Gothic accepted 'the identification of the sublime with the experience of masculine empowerment. But they explicitly equate this masculine sublime with patriarchal tyranny' (1993, 91). In both these arguments gender is dominant in polarized and opposite extremes. The female equated with a more humanized view of nature and landscape, but persecuted and threatened; the male equated with the sublime, the domineering and the tyrannical. Mellor cites Kant as the extreme of this polarization. She argues that Kant tries to 'establish a triumphant transcendental ego [which] entails the detachment of this ego from the body, from the emotions, from physical nature—all realms traditionally associated with the feminine' (88). However, a Gothic landscape of whatever sort will deconstruct these binaries at least in part through a refusal to delineate clear boundaries.

If, in all schemas, the transcendental equates with the masculine and nature with the feminine, the aim for the (male) Romantic is for the mastery of the masculine over the feminine. Mary Shelley, however, views it differently and Andrew Smith argues that in *Frankenstein* she 'takes a sceptical approach to Romantic idealism. Her interrogation of sublimity in *Frankenstein* provides us with a clear example of how a Gothic narrative mounts this kind of challenge' (2007, 42). Here we have a double questioning: a critical enquiry into the claims of Romanticism and at the same time, the Gothic nature of the narrative, where there will be a negation of notions of unity, safety or certainty. Smith examines Victor's supreme self-centredness and argues that 'Victor imaginatively recasts nature so that he lies at its centre (indeed his creation of the creature suggests his "mastery" over nature)' (43). Smith examines the passage when Victor turns to nature for solace after the deaths of William and Justine. On his travels he surveys the landscape:

> Nature was broken only by the brawling waves or the fall of some vast fragment, the thunder sound of the avalanche or the cracking, which, through the silent workings of immutable laws, was ever and anon rent and torn, as if it had been but a plaything in their hands. These sublime and magnificent scenes afforded me the greatest consolation that I was capable of receiving. They elevated me from all littleness of feeling; and although they did not remove my grief, they subdued and tranquillised it. (Shelley 2003, 99)

Victor is able to transcend his 'littleness of feeling' and elevate his mind in step with the magnificent surroundings. The suggestion though is that his feelings of guilt and grief should not be seen as 'little' and that they are necessary for a realization and acknowledgement of the truth and should entail a humbling of the ego rather than acting as a 'tranquilliser' that dulls and negates feeling. Smith suggests that Shelley 'implies a relationship between egotism and the sublime, and dwells on the misconstruction of nature as a form of transcendence' (2007, 44). Yet the Gothic text teaches us that transcendence is never possible and that this separation of self and feeling, the striving for the transcendence of the ego, will finally lead to disaster. The Gothic narrative will break down this supposed distance, most often through what we can now term 'affect'. The Gothic will not erase the female and where there is male arrogance in relation to surveying a landscape or an attempt at distancing the self from it, the Gothic narrative will deconstruct this as an artificial and impossible ideal that finally harms rather than heals.

Victor's view of the landscape, however, remains unremittingly Romantic. As he journeys, ostensibly away from his feelings, his emotion, his grief, he remembers:

> The weight upon my spirit was sensibly lightened as I plunged yet deeper in the ravine of Arve. The immense mountains and precipices that overhung me on every side—the sound of the river raging among the rocks, and the dashing of the waterfalls around, spoke of a power mighty as Omnipotence—and I ceased to fear, or to bend before any being less almighty than that which had created and ruled the elements, were displayed in their most terrific guise. (Shelley 2003, 97)

The sublime landscape enables a negation of emotion for Victor, an escape from his legitimate feelings of guilt and grief. Victor speaks of the sublime landscape in terms of an expansion of the heart and mind, of something larger than his 'little' cares and woes. Victor begins to feel an affiliation with something vast and powerful, on a scale beyond the human. He ceases to 'bend' to anything less, although in the narrative of the novel, this is incorrect and a refusal of responsibility. It is an attempt at an escape from the self through the landscape. Yet as much as *Frankenstein* is a Romantic novel, it is also a Gothic novel, and there will be a critique of this schema. George E. Haggerty argues that 'space is always threatening and never comfortable in the Gothic novel; castles loom with superhuman capacity for entrapment; cloisters induce claustrophobia; rooms become too small, vistas too grand' (1989, 20). Indeed, far from affording Victor transcendence from the body and the emotions, the landscapes that he is contemplating should perhaps induce a sense of humility, a return to the body and recognition that there is no escape from its fleshly/flawed boundaries. In such a novel, the effect/affect of place should erase masculine arrogance and assumption and substitute transcendence with a more subaltern experience of humility and groundedness. Victor has created an-other (monstrous) body and therefore cannot/should not transcend his own.

All landscapes are haunted for Victor, and his very body, through its monstrous doubling, is haunted too. Victor is grounded by the materiality of his being and tethered to the earth by the creature he has created from it. His effort to transcend his body, through the contemplation of sublime landscapes, ultimately fails, and there is no resolution as he lies dying. The Romantic, Gothic landscape has, in the end, only served to show him his limitations. Berberich et al state that 'affect theory ... sees a turn away from overarching and, potentially, prescriptive or predefined concepts and theories toward the senses, the body and the mind in their varied relations with the world' (2014, 316). Victor's world and that of his creature are intimately bound up with the bodily relations of both to their environments—both social and natural. The 'senses, the body and the mind' of each are confused in a tangle of inextricable ties, obligations, bodily and emotive threads. Frankenstein is a Gothic novel of affect, and the Gothic genre is itself affective, concerned with breakdown, terror, fear, claustrophobia and extremity. Xavier Aldana Reyes in a chapter titled 'Gothic Affect' claims that 'the purpose of the gothic—to scare, disturb, or disgust—has often been neglected', and says that 'this is detrimental to areas such as … horror fiction, which commonly rely on corporeality or non-cognitive (somatic) or instinctive human reactions' (2015, 12). This echoes Shelley's own stated intentions for *Frankenstein*. In her 1831 preface she retrospectively examines her objectives in writing the story. She says she wanted 'one which would speak to the mysterious fears of our nature, and awaken thrilling horror—one to make the reader dread to look round, to curdle the blood, and quicken the beatings of the heart'. Shelley is talking about an *affective* response to her Gothic fiction. This is in part a bodily response, that pre-dates but echoes that sought by Sensation fiction writers in the 1860s, but it is also intended to have an affect on the environment, the immediate surroundings of the reader, changing the atmosphere of place for those who are reading *Frankenstein* who may 'dread to look around' (2003, 8).

The Gothic narrative is not inclined towards unity: rather collapse, deconstruction and entropy sway the movement of the texts. If we return to Oakes and Price's idea, quoted in the Introduction of this book, we can see how the landscapes of *Frankenstein* might adhere to an affective dimension. Oakes and Price discuss contemporary cultural geographers who 'suggest that landscapes may be understood as quite fluid constructs that are continually in the process of cohering and collapsing as we move through space' (2008, 151). As the creature pursues Victor, and as Victor in turn hunts down the creature, spaces, situations and landscapes disintegrate behind them; *Frankenstein* is a book of relentless movement. And, although of course deeply implicated in memory and the past, it is also a narrative that foregrounds the immanence of the *encounter*: with the monster, with Victor's ill-fated family, with the landscape. As Seigworth and Gregg proclaim, 'affect is persistent proof of a body's never less than ongoing immersion in and among the world's obstinacies and rhythms, its refusals as much as its invitations. Affect is in many ways synonymous with *force* or *forces of encounter*' (2010, 1–2). These ideas of the body's immersion, of movement, of rhythm and encounter resonate deeply with the narratives and fictions of the Gothic. These are haunted landscapes, but perhaps they are haunted as much by the *now*, by the immanence of the encounter, as they are by the past.

This volume is entitled *Haunted Landscapes*, and the Gothic landscape is always haunted. In *Haunted Landscapes* both the term landscape and the concept of haunting encompass and expand definitions of the natural and in the Gothic genre, the return, the haunting, is inevitable and natural. Throughout the essays in this collection there is an understanding that the super-natural is not separate from nature but an integral part of experienced and imagined landscapes. Timothy Morton has termed this aspect of nature the 'super natural [or] extra Nature' (2010). This idea is useful as not all the hauntings discussed in this collection are traditionally 'supernatural'. Haunting can be just as much about memory, nostalgia or individual and collective trauma as actual, embodied ghosts. And yet haunting is always an embodied experience—one of affect. The chapters in this volume have covered a wide variety of haunted spaces, from sites of trauma and violence, to disturbed domestic spaces and the liminal landscapes of varying locations. Yet throughout it has been the interaction between the landscape and the human that has been central. As we have seen, in haunted landscapes there will be an-other, the extra or super natural but as I argued in the Introduction there needs to be an encounter, some sort of human interaction for the haunting to manifest. The encounters explored in this volume are perhaps unsurprisingly dark. Horror, terror and wonder are here: the Gothic and the sublime. As each haunted space transcends the material there is an expansion of affect and imaginative recreation of place. The discussion generated by the essays collected here show a continuation of both the Gothic and sublime traditions in relation to place. Ranging from the Victorian to the present, neither association (Gothic or sublime) is ever lost in the dialectic relation between haunting and place.

Haunted Landscapes presents the concept of haunting as multiple, flexible and sometimes fleeting and ephemeral. In all the essays the possibility of transformation is suggested. If a haunted landscape is not a stable landscape then it can *shift*, and meaning and affect can slip and change. And if we look back over the contents of this volume we can see that each chapter points to a change of some kind. The darkness of trauma, violence or memory may not have been erased, but in each essay there is space for moving forward. Haunted landscapes are created by the past, but that past also enables a future that isn't fixed: haunted spaces are not static. This book treats the idea of the haunted landscape not as a curiosity or aberration but rather as an almost ubiquitous part of the sense of place; the haunting of a place *is* its 'genius loci'. In 2014 when conceiving of this project I began with this question in mind: 'Are all landscapes always-already haunted?' It is a question that has been considered throughout the essays in this volume and perhaps Michel de Certeau answers when he asserts, 'there is no place that is not haunted by many different spirits hidden there in silence.... Haunted places are the only ones people can live in' (1984, 108).

NOTES

1. Alison Milbank associates the *Philosophical Enquiry* with the body claiming it 'is "sensationalist" in the manner of much Gothic fiction where bodily affect is the main theatre of meaning' (2009, 236).

2. See, for example, the recent volumes, Angela Wright and Dale Townshend's texts: *Ann Radcliffe, Romanticism and the Gothic*, Cambridge University Press, 2014 and *Romantic Gothic: An Edinburgh Companion*.

BIBLIOGRAPHY

Ahern, Stephen. 2007. *Affected Sensibilities: Romantic Excess and the Genealogy of the Novel 1680–1810*. New York: AMS Press.

Berberich, Christine, Neil Campbell and Robert Hudson. 2013. *'Affective Landscapes: An Introduction.' Cultural Politics*, 9 (3): 313–21.

Brabon, Benjamin. 2006. 'Surveying Ann Radcliffe's Gothic Landscapes.' *Literature Compass* 3 (4): 840–5.

de Certeau, Michel. 1984. *The Practice of Everyday Life*. Trans. Steven Rendall. Los Angeles: University of California Press.

Dixon, Deborah and Elizabeth R. Straughan. 2013. 'Affect.' *Wiley Blackwell Companion to Cultural Geography*. Ed. Nuala C. Johnson, Richard H. Schein and Jamie Winders. Chichester, West Sussex: Wiley-Blackwell. 36–8.

Gregg, Melissa and Gregory J. Seigworth. eds. 2010. *The Affect Theory Reader*. Durham, NC: Duke University Press.

Gupta, Nilanjana. 2007. 'Introduction.' In *Frankenstein: Or the Modern Prometheus*. Ed. Mary Shelley. Delhi: Dorling Kindersley. ix–xxxviii.

Haggerty, George E. 1989. *Gothic Fiction/Gothic Form*. University Park: Pennsylvania State University Press.

Hogle, Jerrold, E. 2016. 'Gothic and Second-Generation Romanticism.' *Romantic Gothic: An Edinburgh Companion*. Ed. Angela Wright and Dale Townshend. Edinburgh: Edinburgh University Press. 112–28.

Howells, Coral Ann. 1995. *Love, Mystery and Misery: Feeling in Gothic Fiction*. London: Athlone Press.

Ingold, Tim. 2012. 'Introduction'. In *Imagining Landscapes: Past, Present and Future*. Ed. Monica Janowski and Tim Ingold. Farnham: Ashgate Publishing. 1–19.

McEvoy, Emma. 2007. 'Gothic and the Romantics.' *The Routledge Companion to Gothic*. Ed. Catherine Spooner and Emma McEvoy. London: Routledge. 19–28.

Mellor, Anne K. 1993. *Romanticism and Gender*. New York: Routledge.

Mighall, Robert. 1999. *A Geography of Victorian Gothic Fiction: Mapping History's Nightmares*. Oxford: Oxford University Press.

Milbank, Alison. 2009. 'The Sublime.' *The Handbook of the Gothic*. Ed. Marie Mulvey-Roberts. Basingstoke: Palgrave Macmillan. 235–40.

Mishra, Vijay. 1994. *The Gothic Sublime*. Albany: State University of New York Press.

Morton, Timothy. 2010. *The Ecological Thought*. Cambridge, MA: Harvard University Press.

Oakes, Timothy and Patricia Price. 2008. *The Cultural Geography Reader*. London: Routledge.

Pater, Walter. 1868. *Poems by William Morris*. *Westminster Review*, 34 (2): 300–12.

Poovey, Mary. 1985. 'My Hideous Progeny: The Lady and the Monster.' Accessed 20 March 2016. http://knarf.english.upenn.edu/Articles/poovey.html.

Radcliffe, Ann. (1794) 2005. The Mysteries of Udolpho. New York: Barnes and Noble Books

Richardson, Tina. 2015. *Walking Inside Out: Contemporary British Psychogeography*. Lanham, MD: Rowman and Littlefield.

Rousseau, G. S. 1976. 'Nerves, Spirits, and Fibres: Towards Defining the Origins of Sensibility.' *Studies in Eighteenth Century Culture*, 3: 137–57.

Shelley, Mary. *Frankenstein: Or the Modern Prometheus*. London: Dorling Kindersley.

Smith, Andrew. (2007) 2013. *Gothic Literature*. 2nd edn. Edinburgh: Edinburgh University Press.

Smith, Andrew and William Hughes. 2013. *Eco-Gothic*. Manchester: Manchester University Press.

Trott, Nicola. 1999. 'The Picturesque, the Beautiful and the Sublime.' *A Companion to Romanticism*. Ed. Duncan Wu. Oxford: Blackwell. 72–90.

Watson, Nicola J. 2012. 'William Wordsworth: Poet in a Landscape.' *Romantics and Victorians*. Ed. Nicola J. Watson and Shafquat Towheed. London: Bloomsbury Academic. 9–36.

Williams, Anne. 1995. *Art of Darkness: A Poetics of Gothic*. Chicago: University of Chicago Press.

Author Biographies

Dr Rosario Arias is Senior Lecturer in English Literature at the University of Málaga (Spain). She has published a number of articles and book chapters on neo-Victorian fiction, haunting and spectrality, the trace, and memory and revisions of the past, and co-edited (with Dr Patricia Pulham, University of Portsmouth) *Haunting and Spectrality in Neo-Victorian Fiction: Possessing the Past* (Palgrave, 2010). She has also published *Science, Spiritualism and Technology*, a facsimile edition of Spiritualist texts, which belongs to the collection *Spiritualism, 1840–1930* (Routledge, 2014), with Patricia Pulham, Christine Ferguson and Tatiana Kontou. She is the Research Leader of 'VINS: Victorian and Neo-Victorian Studies in Spain' Network and several projects on the notion of the 'trace'. Her next project is a monograph on neo-Victorianism and the senses from the perspective of phenomenology.

Dr Karl Bell is Senior Lecturer in History at the University of Portsmouth (United Kingdom). He is the author of *The Magical Imagination: Magic and Modernity in Urban England*, 1780–1914 (2012) and *The Legend of Spring-Heeled Jack: Victorian Urban Folklore and Popular Cultures* (2012). He is also the director of the Supernatural Cities project, a multidisciplinary research initiative exploring supernatural folklore, 'superstition' and imagined geographies in historical and contemporary urban environments.

Dr Kevin Corstorphine is Lecturer in English at the University of Hull, UK, where he teaches on American Literature and the Gothic. His research interests are in horror, Gothic and fantasy fiction, with a focus on the representation of space and place. He has published on authors including Bram Stoker, Ambrose Bierce, H. P. Lovecraft, Robert Bloch and Stephen King. He is currently working on haunted house stories and the intersections between fiction, 'real-life' narratives and myth.

Dr Niamh Downing is Head of English & Writing at Falmouth University, UK. Her research is in twentieth- and twenty-first-century literature and its relationship to landscape and ecology. She has published on gardens in literature, folklore in beekeeping and is currently working on a monograph on archaeologies of contemporary British and Northern Irish poetry. She is an award holder on two current AHRC-funded projects in the area of environmental humanities—'Telling the Bees' as co-investigator and 'Orkney: Beside the Ocean of Time' as principal investigator.

Dr Ruth Heholt is Senior Lecturer in English at Falmouth University, UK. Her research interests lie with the supernatural, the Gothic and crime fiction. She has published on ghosts, haunting and the Gothic in Victorian and contemporary literature, film and television. She has edited a critical edition of Catherine Crowe's 1847 novel *The Story of Lilly Dawson* and is currently working on a book on Gothic localities and regions with Professor William Hughes. She is the founding editor of *Revenant: Critical and Creative Studies of the Supernatural* which can be found at www.revenantjournal.com.

William Hughes is Professor of Gothic Studies at Bath Spa University and an immediate Past President of the International Gothic Association. He is the author, editor or co-editor of 17 books, including *That Devil's Trick: Hypnotism and the Victorian Popular Imagination* (2015), *The Historical Dictionary of Gothic Literature* (2013), *Ecogothic* (with Andrew Smith, 2013), *The Encyclopedia of the Gothic* (with David Punter and Andrew Smith, 2013) and *The Victorian Gothic* (with Andrew Smith, 2012). He is currently writing a monograph on phrenology in Victorian popular culture and conducting research into the medical humanities.

Rebecca Lloyd is Senior Lecturer in English at Falmouth University. She completed an MA in the History of Modern Art and Design at Falmouth in 1997, having a BA (Hons) in Medieval and Modern History from Liverpool University in (1982). She also has just graduated from the MA in Professional Writing at Falmouth University. Rebecca's particular interests are in all forms of comedy and humour; nineteenth-century history, culture and performance; the Gothic and the supernatural and the politics of language. Recent publications include co-author of entry on Anne Rice for *The Encyclopedia of the Gothic* (Wiley-Blackwell, 2013), and a short fiction for *Casting Shadow: Extraordinary Tales from New Writers* (SilverWood Books, 2013).

Dr HollyGale Millette is a Senior Teaching Fellow at the University of Southampton in the United Kingdom. Her research pertains to her interest 'deep mapping' that regularly interbreeds with memorial cartography, gendered spatial practices, haunted archaeology, psychogeography, theatre and human geography. HollyGale's current writing and research is centred on Gothic and Neo-Victorian cultures, television and resistant communities.

Dr Matilda Mroz is Lecturer in Film Studies at the University of Sussex. She held a British Academy Postdoctoral Research Fellowship at the University of Cambridge (2008–2011), where her research focused on Polish cinema, and where she also completed her PhD in film theory (2004–2007). She is the author of *Temporality and Film Analysis* (Edinburgh University Press, 2012), which explores duration through the films of Antonioni, Tarkovsky and Kieslowski. She is the co-author of *Remembering Katyn* (Polity Press, 2012) and co-editor of *The Cinematic Bodies of Eastern Europe and Russia: Between Pain and Pleasure* (Edinburgh University Press, 2016).

Dr Alison O'Malley-Younger is Senior Lecturer in English at the University of Sunderland. Her primary research interests lie in Irish and Scottish Literatures, (particularly Celtic Gothic), Consumer Culture, Advertising and Literature and Monster Theory. She has published in the fields of contemporary critical theory, Irish cultural history, advertising and commodity culture, Blackwood's magazine and Gothic literatures. She has co-edited a number of scholarly collections, and is currently researching the role and behaviours of the gothic gentleman in the nineteenth century.

Dr Mark Riley is Senior Lecturer in Photography at the University of Roehampton London, UK. He graduated from Central School of Art and Design in 1985, completed an MA in Fine Art at Central St Martins College of Art and Design in 1997 and a PhD in Philosophy at Goldsmiths College in 2005.

Ryan Trimm is Associate Professor of English and Film & Media at the University of Rhode Island (USA). He has published on Hanif Kureishi, Zadie Smith, Kazuo Ishiguro, Peter Ackroyd, Peter Greenaway and Jonathan Coe; his work has appeared in *Poetics Today, Contemporary Literature, Critique, Cinema Journal,* and *LIT: Literature Interpretation Theory,* as well as collections published by SUNY Press, Bloomsbury and Palgrave Macmillan. He has recently completed a book project: *An Entailed Heritage: Culture and the Legacy of the Past in Contemporary Britain.*

Dr Daniel Weston is Lecturer in English Literature at the University of Greenwich, UK. His monograph, *Contemporary Literary Landscapes: The Poetics of Experience*, was published with Ashgate in January 2016. He has published work on contemporary poetry, prose fiction and non-fiction, with particular emphasis on literary geographies and place writing.

Colin Younger is Senior Lecturer and Programme Leader of English and Creative Writing at the University of Sunderland. He is founder and director of Spectral Visions Press, a publishing house hosted by the University of Sunderland. A reputed poet, song writer and scholar of Borders Theory, his works include *Border Crossings: Narration, Nation and Imagination in Scots and Irish Literature and Culture*, (2013), *Spectral Visions: The Collection* (2014) and *Spectral Visions: Grim Fairy Tales* (2015).

Index

Lightning Source UK Ltd.
Milton Keynes UK
UKHW03f1156180418
321261UK00001B/87/P

9 781783 4888